Blues Music and Gospel Proclamation

Blues Music and Gospel Proclamation

The Extraordinary Life of a Courageous East German Pastor

THEO LEHMANN

Edited by
RICHARD V. PIERARD

Translated by
EDWIN P. ARNOLD

WIPF & STOCK · Eugene, Oregon

BLUES MUSIC AND GOSPEL PROCLAMATION
The Extraordinary Life of a Courageous East German Pastor

English translation Copyright © 2008 Edwin P. Arnold and Richard V. Pierard. All rights reserved. Except for brief quotations in critical publications or reviews, no part of this book may be reproduced in any manner without prior written permission from the publisher. Write: Permission, Wipf and Stock Publishers, 199 W. 8th Ave., Suite 3, Eugene, OR 97401.

Translated by Edwin P. Arnold and edited by Richard V. Pierard from the 3rd German edition: *Freiheit wird dann sein: Aus meinem Leben*, published by Aussaat Verlag, Neukirchen-Vluyn, Germany, 2005, Copyright © Theo Lehmann.

ISBN 13: 978-1-55635-544-8

Publication date: October 1, 2008

Cataloging-in-Publication data:

Lehmann, Theo, 1934–
   [Freiheit wird dann sein. English]

   Blues music and gospel proclamation : the extraordinary life of a courageous East German pastor / Theo Lehmann ; translated by Edwin P. Arnold ; edited by Richard V. Pierard.

   xxiv + 240 p. ; 23 cm.

   ISBN 13: 978-1-55635-544-8

   1. Autobiography—Germany. 2. Germany—Religion—20th century. 3. Blues (Music). I. Arnold, Edwin P., 1936–. II. Pierard, Richard V., 1934–. III. Title.

CT105 L4 2008

Manufactured in the U.S.A.

Contents

Editor's Foreword vii

Translator's Foreword xiii

Biographical Notes on the Translator and Editor xxi

Translator's Acknowledgments xxiii

1 The Answer, My Friend 1

2 Precious Lord, Take My Hand 24

3 When Christ Returns 31

4 Yet We Are Standing Again! 44

5 Blues & Trouble 57

6 No, We're Not Any Better 71

7 Only One Way 89

8 With You Alone 96

9 That's When Freedom Will Really Be Ours 116

10 A God for All Situations 147

11 There Is a Word 182

12 God Wants Everyone 194

13 Thank You, Jesus, Thank You 209

14 Dr. Blues 221

Addendum for German-Speaking Readers 233

Editor's Foreword

Richard V. Pierard

THE TWO FOREWORDS PROVIDE background information on Dr. Theo Lehmann's life and experiences. They also explain the genesis of the project and why two American evangelical academics became so interested in his life and convinced that his story needed to be told to Christians in our country. They will help you to understand his historical situation and why he is such an important person in contemporary evangelicalism.

Communist East Germany is now just a historical relic, a fading memory of the Cold War. No German today under the age of 20 even remembers this dismal political entity that existed in the eastern half of his or her country. Yet for those of us who lived through the tension-filled four decades known as the Cold War, it was a harsh reality. The 800-mile fence and the ugly Berlin Wall are forever etched into the minds of us who passed through these barriers. They insured that the citizens of what euphemistically was called the German Democratic Republic would not have normal relations with people outside of the Soviet bloc states. They symbolized the abject failure of Marxist-Leninist communism and its vision of the future.

For people in the West, the Soviet Union was distant, mysterious, and not easy to visit. East Germany was much closer. West Berlin was a vibrant, democratic island in the midst of the Red sea, and visitors there were encouraged to cross through the Wall and see for themselves what "real existing socialism" (the East German term) was like. They could experience the "first workers' and peasants' state on German soil" as the regime trumpeted itself. The bright lights and new buildings in East Berlin made it the showpiece of communism, but it was still a dingy city and the scars of the World War II siege of the city were everywhere. It masked the fact that the reality elsewhere in the GDR was much more depressing.

Yet, there was life there. Individuals went about their daily routines like people all over the world, and they made the best of their situation. Theo Lehmann's memoir communicates what life was like and how people adjusted to the situation. In some ways conditions in the GDR gradually improved over the years, and living standards were higher there than any other Soviet bloc country, including the Soviet Union itself. But people were always aware of what went on elsewhere in spite of the rigid censorship, because West German television could be received everywhere except in the most distant corners of the country. Their West German relatives and friends from abroad came to visit and brought all sorts of goodies from the outside world. When the East German regime embarked on a campaign to gain international respectability and diplomatic recognition, more and more visitors flocked to the country and new ideas came with them. It was only a matter of time before this house of cards would come tumbling down.

For those unfamiliar with the historical situation, let me point out that during World War II the Allies worked out agreements for the treatment of Germany. They included the division of the defeated country into four occupation zones (British, French, American, and Soviet) with the ultimate intention of rehabilitating it and preparing it for eventual self-government and readmission to the family of nations. The capital, Berlin, lay inside the Soviet Zone in the East, but it was divided into four sectors, an inter-Allied body was to oversee the city administration, and air and surface access would be guaranteed to the other three occupying powers. In actuality, the military commander in each zone was virtually a dictator, and efforts to coordinate occupation policies and reconstruction quickly came to naught in the emerging Cold War.

Frustrated by Soviet intransigence, the other three Allies proceeded with reconstruction and restoring self-government in their zones and eventually merged their administrations. This prepared the way for the establishment of the Federal Republic of Germany in 1949 and it was granted diplomatic recognition by most countries. The Soviet plan had been to reunite Germany under a communist government, but Western actions thwarted it. The Soviets reluctantly allowed the communist functionaries in their zonal government to form a separate state, and the German Democratic Republic came into being a few weeks later. German

Editor's Foreword

division was now a fact and the two states reflected the political values and constitutional structures of their patrons. In Berlin the Soviets tried to force the Western powers out of the city by cutting off ground transportation, but the Berlin Airlift of 1948–49 thwarted this. The city now was divided into two parts just as the country was, but until the infamous Wall the entire city was open to people from the East.

East Germany had a constitution and parliament, but the real power lay with the governing party, known as the Socialist Unity Party or *SED*. It was a merger of the prewar Communist Party and Social Democratic Party carried out under Soviet auspices. Its first secretary, Walter Ulbricht, and from 1971, Erich Honecker, exercised the real power in the GDR. The Soviets theoretically ended their occupation, but they stationed at least 300,000 troops in a country the size of Tennessee and everyone knew where the real power lay. This was demonstrated in the failed workers' uprising in June 1953, and the building of the fence on the border with West Germany. The erection of the Berlin Wall in 1961 insured that the communist system would continue in spite of widespread dissatisfaction at home. Sealing off the country and preventing the emigration of skilled workers did, however, lead to significant economic development and a gradual rise in living standards. Also people had more freedom to express themselves, particularly in the realm of religion, than most observers in the West recognized, but still they always had to contend with the all-seeing secret police.

As long as the regime had strong Soviet support, it was secure. But a slowing economy throughout the Soviet bloc and the realization by Mikhail Gorbachev in Moscow that the Cold War was leading to an economic meltdown and better relations had to be forged with the West placed the GDR regime in peril. The secret police and military were having increasing difficulty handling the peaceful protests, many of which were closely linked with the churches. Gorbachev's unwillingness to permit armed action like that which the Chinese government carried out against opponents in June 1989 resulted in a rapid crumbling of the GDR regime and finally the unification of Germany in 1990.

The church was the one institution in the GDR over which the regime was never able to gain full control. The numerically small Roman Catholic Church was largely ignored. The Protestant or "Evangelical" church was a different matter. Over the centuries since Martin Luther it had evolved into a number of "regional" or "territorial" churches (*Landeskirchen*) that corresponded to the internal political boundaries and was subject to oversight by the rulers. After World War I the monarchies were eliminated but the churches still functioned autonomously on a territorial or "regional" basis, a situation that continued in post-World War II Germany. To coordinate their efforts, the regional churches in 1948 created the Evangelical Church in Germany (*EKD*). After intense pressure from the regime, the eastern churches in 1969 withdrew from the *EKD* and formed a separate Federation of Evangelical Churches in the GDR (*BEK*). A "free church" was any Protestant group in Germany that did not affiliate with one of the regional churches.

The Saxon Regional Church was one of eight such bodies in the GDR, and each church had its own distinct administrative hierarchy. A bishop presided over the Saxon church and superintendents oversaw local districts. The central administrative office (*Landeskirchenamt* or *LKA*) was in Dresden; various "church councilors" carried out its work. The Saxon church was a "Lutheran confessionalist" body, in that its doctrinal basis was the three Ecumenical Creeds (Apostles, Nicene, and Athanasian), six documents from Luther's time (the Small and Large Catechism, Augsburg Confession and Apology to it, Schmalkald Articles, and Treatise on the Power and Primacy of the Pope), and the Formula of Concord (1577). Rejected was any confessional compromise with Calvinism. Confessionalists are regarded today as theological conservatives.

Theo Lehmann's life took place against this historical backdrop. Realizing that much of this would be unfamiliar to readers in the Anglo-American world, I have taken the liberty of including explanatory material in the text from time to provide contextual clarity. Moreover, we asked Dr. Lehmann to review our translation and he was able to catch a number of errors and clarify vague points. This insured greater accuracy and that the message of his life could come through loud and clear.

On a personal note, I began coming to the GDR in 1963 and became intrigued by this political entity that had so many contradictions. I developed a number of contacts over the years, one of whom was Dr. E. Arno Lehmann. We had begun an exchange of correspondence, and he had just retired as professor of missiology at the University of Halle when I first was able to visit with him in his home. He encouraged my growing interest in the study of German Protestant missions and especially that in India where he had served. I treasure my autographed copy of *It Began at Tranquebar* (1956), his seminal account of German missionary work

Editor's Foreword

in South India in the eighteenth century. In fact, one of the highpoints of my life was to be present in Tranquebar in 2006 for the 300th anniversary celebration of the founding of the mission.

During a subsequent trip to Halle in 1971 he suggested that, given my evangelical orientation, I would appreciate meeting his son who was a pastor in Karl-Karx-Stadt (Chemnitz). He arranged for me to visit Theo at his apartment at the Schlosskirche, and the result was a friendship that has lasted to this day. Afterwards, I saw him every so often and even obtained phonograph records from his "want list" which I brought with me or mailed to his father, who had permission to receive materials from abroad.

We had pleasant encounters at the Manila Congress on Evangelism in 1989, in the GDR during the height of the revolution, and in the United States in 1994. I arranged for him to appear with me at the Baptist World Alliance meeting in Dresden in 1999 in a session where he and a young Baptist minister spoke from their hearts about their experiences in the revolution. I structured it as a question and answer format, and I had never seen an audience so spellbound. On a warm August day in 2005 we spent the afternoon together in Halle where we took a boat ride on the Saale, reminisced about his youth there, and even had a cool drink at the restaurant he mentions in the book.

I can honestly say that I know of no other Christian leader I admire as much as Theo Lehmann. When Ed Arnold asked me if I would help out in this project to make him known in the English-speaking world, there was no way in the world that I could refuse. The book is really Ed's labor of love. I hope you are as moved by his life story as I am.

Translator's Foreword

Edwin P. Arnold

I STAND IN AWE of Dr. Theo Lehmann. In my estimation he is a modern-day Joseph. This translation makes his story available to English-speaking readers.

There is much truth in the statement that one is known by the company he/she keeps. This book is about a man, who has been a pastor and youth evangelist in the former East Germany. His life was greatly influenced, either directly or indirectly, by such a widely diverse number of people as Martin Luther, Billy Graham, Pete Seeger, Helmut Thielicke, Martin Luther King, Jr., Charles Spurgeon, Louis Armstrong, Bessie Smith, Dietrich Bonhoeffer, and Mahalia Jackson. Each of these contributed in some way to Theo's development as a preacher, musician, evangelist, lover of the blues, and one who has long appreciated the African-American experience, especially the struggles under slavery.

In the late winter of 1994 I got an unexpected telephone request from Jörg Swoboda in Buckow outside Berlin. I had just finished translating a book into English that he had compiled concerning the events of the 1980s that led up to the fall of the Berlin Wall in 1989. I had arranged for him and his good friend, Theo Lehmann, to come to Clemson University that spring for a speaking engagement. He wanted to know if I would mind getting tickets for the New Orleans Jazz Festival later that spring. He would repay me, but it would be easier for them if I would take care of the matter from here in the US. I thought it was an unusual request: two former East German evangelists interested in a type of music not normally associated with Germans. Later, I learned the reason for their interest in the Jazz Festival. More importantly, I would learn volumes about the man who is the subject of this translation, Dr. Theo Lehmann.

Blues Music and Gospel Proclamation

In 1990 Swoboda, a pastor and composer/performer of Christian music in the former German Democratic Republic, had edited the above-mentioned book *Die Revolution der Kerzen* (*The Revolution of the Candles*). As a Christian, and as a professor of German at Clemson University, I had been particularly fascinated with this closed society since the early 1970s. In 1972, I and all the students in an honors class decided to get pen pals in a German-speaking country. Amazingly, all but one of the addresses that Letters Abroad sent me were in East Germany. I contacted a local FBI office to make sure we wouldn't run afoul of the authorities. We proceeded with their approval. This decision completely changed my life and greatly affected the lives of scores of students and families on both sides of the Iron Curtain.

Fast-forward twenty-one years, which included eight Clemson German Study Abroad trips, and personal trips into both Germanys. In 1993, having been granted a sabbatical leave, I went to the former East Germany and interviewed a number of people who had made the "peaceful revolution" happen. In the course of that trip, Swoboda's book was recommended to me. When I read it back in the United States, I was overwhelmed by the gripping stories that lay behind the headlines that most of us knew when the unthinkable happened in November 1989: The Berlin Wall fell!

In 1994, when Swoboda and Lehmann came to the US, I had my first face to face encounter with the two. I can never forget the moments after I met them at a motel in Clemson. I was jolted somewhat when I learned the first thing they wanted: They were parched and it was Sunday. Could I find a place where they could get a beer? Having been to Germany numerous times, the request wouldn't have bothered me if we had been in Germany. However, for the sake of credibility among my largely conservative Christian friends, I secretly hoped that they would only ask *me* when they wanted another "cold one." After all, I soon learned that this friend of Jörg had been called "the Billy Graham of East Germany." In all fairness, I should add that virtually every one of my Christian friends in Germany, likewise of a conservative bent, drinks beer as well as other alcoholic beverages. It is largely a non-issue among most Christians there.

When Theo sat down in the back seat of my car, I asked him to open the folder on the seat. It contained an article from a 1976 issue of *Die Bunte Illustrierte*, a popular weekly illustrated magazine from West Germany. I have to admit that I was an inveterate pack rat, especially re-

Translator's Foreword

garding articles and pictures dealing with people and events in the GDR. In preparing for their arrival, I had remembered that somewhere I had come across Theo Lehmann's name. In leafing through the hundreds of articles I had collected, I found this particular one. In one picture there were hundreds of students packing his church in Karl-Marx-Stadt. He had never seen this picture. In fact he never even knew it had been made. After all, it was a publication from the West. This book is largely about just such worship services involving young people in the grip of a communist regime. Theo Lehmann was the catalyst.

In 1976 after my application to attend a month-long Herder Institute for German teachers at Karl Marx University in Leipzig was approved, I began to look for names of individuals with whom I could feel "safe," that is, in whom I could confide while in the country. One of the individuals I learned of was Dr. Christoph Haufe at the Protestant Seminary in Leipzig, an independent Protestant institution. He had written an article about an amazing phenomenon: Students at East German universities were meeting informally to give expression to their Christian faith. What I, of course, could not have known at that time was that many of these were being influenced by Theo Lehmann. I was delighted to learn that the Protestant seminary played an important role in Theo's life.

At this point I would like to interject an account of a meeting I had during that most meaningful summer. One name I had gotten from an American professor who had taken numerous groups into East Germany, was that of Dr. Jürgen G. My source, a well-known Christian apologist, assured me that Dr. G's family was Christian and I could, therefore, speak freely with them. I located the family in the center of Leipzig during our first week. As I sat down we started with small talk. Then I asked some pointed questions about life as a Christian family in this state. I was jolted when, instead of answering my question, Dr. G. put his finger to his lips indicating I mustn't say anything more, at least, not for the moment. He pointed to his wife and directed her to the telephone on the other side of the room. She got down on her hands and knees and crawled across the floor, reached under the telephone table and pulled the plug out of the wall. His only comment was, "You never know!" This told me volumes. *Or so I thought!*

Unfortunately, this story had some bizarre, and bitter, twists and turns I was to learn about 25 years later. My current belief now is that I most likely was duped to gain my confidence. [I am awaiting one more secret police file to either prove or disprove this belief.]

This was the GDR that Theo Lehmann lived in. When given the opportunity to emigrate, he refused because he felt that, without question, God had called him to this place at this time to preach to young people.

What Made Me Decide I Had to Translate This Book?

When I read the very first pages of his memoir I realized this man had had an incredibly difficult and perilous childhood. He and his family lived out their lives under the Nazi dictatorship. It was a childhood that reduced the time of one's youth to a fraction of the actual years lived. At age 10 he survived the horrendous bombing of Dresden on February 13-14, 1945. Within weeks Hitler was dead and the nation's leaders surrendered to the Allied forces. A reason for hope? Hardly. The country was in ruins, with food supplies, utilities, water, and functioning civil authorities in very short supply. On top of these daunting challenges came another one. Being one of the victorious Allied forces, the Soviet Union received as its occupation zone the eastern part of Germany. It was, of course, not about to pass up the opportunity to nurture the establishment of socialistic rule in all the areas under its control. So, this eastern portion of a defeated Germany came under the heavy thumb of the Soviets. This meant more life under a dictatorship: this time red instead of brown.

How did a solidly Christian family come to grips with these ghastly circumstances? This, too, is a major reason for making this story available to English-speaking people. How could a family that desired to be ambassadors for Christ in two repressive societies, do so? The story of the faithfulness of the Lehmann family in serving Christ is a testimony to God's grace.

As a young boy Theo was deeply moved by one scripture verse from a sermon that the family's pastor preached. It remains with him to this day as he relates in the third chapter: "The mountains may depart and the hills be removed; but my steadfast love [In the German Bible the word can be translated 'grace'] shall not depart from you, and my covenant of peace shall not be removed, says the LORD who has compassion on you" (Isa 54:10). He goes on to tell how this particular text impacted his life as a boy and continued to do so throughout his life. The promise of God's grace was the one certainty that remained through the dark years of the

Second World War and the German Democratic Republic and found its fulfillment with the fall of the Berlin Wall

Try to imagine this scenario: A young pastor sees that the congregation is dwindling and most of those who do attend are older people. He feels too many aspects of the worship services work against attracting young people—the liturgy of the church; the particular Bible translation used; the hymns, a large number of which are over 400 years old; the organ music; even the clothing worn by the pastors—being some of them. He decides to assemble a team of like-minded individuals who put together a worship experience they call "Worship Service-Somewhat Different." The result: The first service had a lead singer, a "band" consisting of a guitar, a banjo and a *wash board*. He served as the preacher. The music consisted of melodies known to the audience by the Beatles, Bob Dylan, and others, or ones based on Negro spirituals, all retrofitted with texts written by the pastor.

Then consider this: The regular morning service earlier that same day in the same church, attracted perhaps 60 of the faithful; the very first youth service held that evening drew between 500 and 600 young people. The year was 1971. It continued and grew fourfold through the years during the entire rule of the communist government in East Germany.

Determined to reach them with music and sermons that spoke to them more directly than the Lutheran liturgy, hymns, and outdated language, he made use of elements found in the music he had come to love. These meetings were precursors of our present-day "contemporary worship services." It was the start of an incredible career. In fact, conversions and commitments made at one of his services in the St. Nicholas Church in Leipzig led to the prayer vigils that began in 1983 in this very same church. The congregation was the epicenter of the "revolution of the candles" during the fall of 1989. This is how the grace of God worked itself out because of the faithfulness of Theo Lehmann and his team.

Because of his stance against the government's repression of freedoms, he was on the radar of the State Security, the hated *Stasi*. It was several years after the fall of the Wall before he had the courage to look at the files that had been kept on him. The result was devastating: In several thousand pages of reports he learned of church workers, acquaintances, and "friends" who had spied on him, some for as long as 30 years. His *Stasi* code name: "Spider." It was no wonder he suffered severe depression after reading through these pages in his State Security files. Most of the efforts of the *Stasi* had to do with creating dissension and divisions in his family and within his circle of colleagues and friends. It was their efforts that eventually "broke" Theo's wife, Elke, and led to her premature death. Vindication is better than revenge. In his later years he was presented a prestigious award in his beloved Saxony and was recognize as Germany's foremost evangelist.

Concerning the Translation Itself

My trips to Germany, especially those into the GDR, were of inestimable help in translating the book. Although there are vast differences between a democracy and a totalitarian society, many of the same words and political terms are used in both societies. However, in real life, that is, "life as it appears over the top of the newspaper page," a communist society bears little resemblance to a true democracy or republic. I had no direct contact with the State Security, as far as I knew. But then again they didn't wear special uniforms announcing their affiliation. I learned volumes from my pen pals, Gudrun and Reimar Zerm from Lommatzsch, a town near Meissen, and, of course, from many others.

In some letters, but mostly in person, I would get to hear the jokes making fun of the current situation or a particular leader. For example: Customer in a retail store to clerk: "Could you tell me where I can find tennis shoes?" Clerk: "Certainly. But you are in the wrong place at this counter. Here we don't have running shoes. Over there we don't have tennis shoes." As Theo points out, political humor was a game, a means of releasing pent-up emotions to make fun of their situation because so many things were no laughing matter.

A word regarding the chapter headings and subheadings is in order. All, or most, of these somewhat curious titles were conceived by Ralf Marschner, Theo's son-in-law, who also is affiliated with Aussaat Verlag, the original publisher of this book. Most of them are plays on words, rhymes, puns. They are very clever; some, I would have to say, almost too clever. Although I had taught German my entire professional life, the intent of some of these titles eluded me. I had to seek clarification from Marschner and Theo himself. For example, the specific problem with the subhead *Sowieso mit Rumpelstolz und Co.* (Let's Go with Rumpelstolz and Co.) is discussed at length in the addendum for German-speaking readers at the end.

Translator's Foreword

Frankly, I enjoyed playing with these titles, but I'm still not sure I got them all just right. For this reason I have included the original German for each of them in the addendum. Some, particularly those well-versed in life in the GDR, may feel they can supply a more appropriate translation, or one that rhymes better. I would be delighted to hear from any reader who would like to make a suggestion. My e-mail address is miriamed5@aol.com. To keep the story flowing we decided not to touch on these issues in the body of the text but deal with them in an appendix that contains the original German and my translation. I try to do justice to the German titles by recreating a similar type of syntactical expression in English. You will perhaps note that a number of these differ considerably from the titles and subtitles that appear in the text itself.

A distinctive feature of the original, and one that we retained in the translation, are the lyrics of a song written by Lehmann that concludes each chapter. His songs are widely used in German evangelical circles today, and the texts provide a flavor of his work.

I recommend two sources for the interested reader who wants to know more about how the GDR came to an end. First, I would suggest that you contact Mercer Press in Macon, Georgia to obtain a copy of *The Revolution of the Candles*. [I can send you a copy at a 20% discount, plus postage] Second, be sure and see the 2006 motion picture, *The Lives of Others*. It won an Academy Award as the best foreign language film that year. It is a chilling tale about a dedicated *Stasi* officer who is spying on a playwright and his girlfriend suspected of subversive activities. In the course of his banal life solely devoted to reporting on their lives, he is strangely changed. The film gives the viewer a real feel of the GDR during the 1980s. It will also help you to get an idea of what Theo Lehmann went through. A DVD of it with English subtitles is available. Recently, I was jarred to read the obituary for Ulrich Mühe, the one who took home an Oscar for his masterful portrayal of this agent.

An American who was of great importance in Theo's life is Pastor Ralph Hamburger from California. In the book he refers to various American Christians who were shepherded into the GDR by pastors like Hamburger. The one name he actually mentions is Walter James. Theo has the highest praise for him and the group he and Hamburger founded: the Berlin Fellowship. It started in the early 1950s in the Hollywood Presbyterian Church, sometimes known as the "church of the movie stars." In his book *Tumbling Walls* Walter James tells of their trips to Germany to work with churches in rebuilding the country and promoting reconciliation. It is the story of an incredible group of "ordinary Christians" who were completely sold out to Christ and who felt called to take upon themselves great hardship in order to "light a candle" in the midst of terrible darkness. Older readers may recognize the name of Colleen (Townsend) Evans, a successful movie star who was a part of this group. To obtain the book contact the Diaspora Foundation, 20455 Elfin Forest Rd., Escondido, CA 92029, (760) 744-1447. Lehmann's name appears several times in it.

Biographical Notes

Richard V. Pierard

Richard V. Pierard, editor, was born in 1934 in Chicago, Illinois, and was raised in Richland, Washington. He served in the U.S. Army, graduated from California State University, Los Angeles with a B.A. in 1958 and M.A. in 1959, and received a Ph.D. in German history from the University of Iowa in 1964. In 1962–63 he studied at the University of Hamburg in Germany. While there, he spent three weeks working at an archive in Potsdam, East Germany, the first of what would be many trips to the GDR.

He joined the faculty of Indiana State University at Terre Haute in 1964 and served as professor of history. After retiring in 2000, Gordon College in Wenham, Massachusetts, invited him to be a scholar-in-residence and Stephen Phillips Professor of History. Retiring again in 2006, he now lives in Hendersonville, North Carolina, and writes and lectures on a regular basis. He has frequently taught abroad, and was twice a Fulbright Professor in Germany—at the Universities of Frankfurt/Main and Halle-Wittenberg. During the latter appointment, he personally experienced the East German revolution and the opening of the Berlin Wall.

He is the author or co-author of numerous books, articles, and encyclopedia entries, including the centenary history of the Baptist World Alliance, *Baptists Together in Christ* (2005). He contributed to the German edition of *The Revolution of the Candles* and edited its American translation. His research interests include religion and politics in Europe and America, civil religion, and the history of world Christianity. Married for over 50 years, he has two children and one grandchild.

Edwin P. Arnold

Edwin P. Arnold, translator, was born in 1936, on Staten Island, New York. He attended the University of South Carolina where he completed his Bachelor's degree in education. He taught German in high schools in the

State of South Carolina for ten years. In 1968 he completed his Master's degree in German at Kent State University. In the same year, he accepted a position at Clemson University (SC) where he taught as professor of German until his retirement in 2000. During the academic year 1973–74 he taught at the Gymnasium Nabburg in Nabburg, Bavaria.

A pen-pal relationship with a couple from the former GDR, begun in the fall of 1972, led to a friendship still very much alive. This close relationship was also the impetus for twelve ten-day trips into the GDR between 1980 and 2000 and scores of student pen-pal relationships in both the GDR and the Federal Republic. He has been an active member of several professional societies and became an officer in most of them at various times during his career.

Certified by the National Translator Certification Service in 1978, he has translated some 80 articles, brochures, and pamphlets including Swoboda's *The Revolution of the Candles* and a 2001 promotional brochure for the city of Berlin. Since his retirement in 2000 he continues to translate for individuals and companies. He is involved as a member and co-worker in the local Habitat for Humanity organization. He has been married since 1959 and has four children and five grandchildren.

Translator's Acknowledgments

Soli deo gloria! At the outset I would like to give glory to the God and Father of our Lord Jesus Christ. From the very beginning as I read this book in German, I had the strong compulsion to translate it into English. The story of Theo Lehmann's life had to reach a wider audience. I felt it would glorify the God whom we both serve. Although the process took much longer than I had hoped, nevertheless, it is now complete. It gives me great satisfaction as I reflect on a number of circumstances which confirmed to me the rightness of this project.

To Miriam, my wife of 49 years, I have the highest praise. She has "stuck it out" with me during the numerous student groups I led, plus a number of other trips that took me to both German states. In addition, she has served as a copy editor. She has taught writing at the college level and her assistance has been invaluable in preparing the book for the printer. My daughter-in-law, Lora Arnold, provided help in the final formatting.

I would be remiss if I didn't mention the ones responsible for my continuing interest in the GDR over the years: my pen-pal family since 1972, Reimar and Gudrun Zerm in Lommatzsch; Klaus(†) and Gisela Grabner, Leipzig; Hans Seidel, Markkleeberg; Frau Marga Humbert, Eisleben; Peter and Uta Finke, Borna; and many more.

I express my special thanks to God for His provision of Dr. Richard Pierard. Having written a chapter in *The Revolution of the Candles,* he agreed to serve as the editor for the American edition, and he graciously consented to assume the editing task of the present book. He is a "stickler" for precise writing, and due to his efforts the text reads more smoothly and with greater clarity. For both of us, this book is not about money or professional reputation but doing something we couldn't avoid doing.

I want to thank Theo and Jörg Swoboda for their continuing friendship and especially for their infectious enthusiasm and zeal in reaching others for Christ.

Too, I must express my appreciation to the 140 plus students who went on Clemson's study abroad trips between 1980 and 2000. Their interest spurred me on. We had much joy, as well as our share of sadness during the 12 trips, including one near fatality. Needless to say, we got much closer to one another than was possible in any class situation back here in the States. I owe a great debt of gratitude to Dieter and Sibylle Pfisterer, Herr and Frau Goedel and many other friends in the town of Nabburg, Germany, which served as my base of operations during each of my trips to Germany. I am greatly indebted to Anna Faye and Larry La Plue for their friendship and encouragement. It was they who aided a student pen-pal, Andrea Pätz, to escape from Dresden only weeks before the end of the system came in the fall of 1989.

Since my formal retirement my life has taken on a totally new direction. I am now one of the local Habitat for Humanity regulars. I would like to dedicate this book in part to them. We have come to really appreciate one another's skills while serving our Lord together in the "gospel of the hammer" as well as sharing the incredible joy of completing homes for families that otherwise might not be able to afford housing.

1

The Answer, My Friend

"IN NO WAY WOULD I be a pastor." This was my standard boyhood answer to all those who asked me about my eventual career goal. It was not that I had anything particular against pastors. The roly-poly man with the double chin, who, in his black robe, bulged over the altar rail during the children's worship service, enjoyed my highest respect. My father too was a pastor, and I had even greater regard for him. That is just my point: I had too much respect for this profession. Somehow I had gotten the idea as a little kid that one doesn't become a pastor as one might become a barber. Just as I regarded it as stupid that someone should become a barber just because his father operated a barbershop, so I found it even more incomprehensible that one would enter the Christian ministry because of family tradition. And yet, what did I become? A pastor, no less.

On our birthdays we children always inquired as to whether something noteworthy had happened on that day, such as whether a fire had occurred in the neighborhood or were the first cherries of the year picked that day? On the day I was born, May 29, 1934, Adolf Hitler made an official visit to Dresden. In fact, that could have been disastrous. Because the jubilant crowds jammed the streets, my father had great difficult in taking my mother to the Deaconess Hospital. Although I was already past my due date, I delayed until the demon had

1934—With my mother and Johannes, left

left the city and made my appearance in the world a half hour before midnight. Mother noted in her diary that, when the nurse handed me to her, she said, "Now, the little missionary has arrived." That was not intended as a prophetic prediction; it simply reflected the existing situation—the profession of my parents.

Although at the time they were on home leave, they were serving in South India under the confessionalist Lutheran Leipzig Mission in the town of Shiali. It was located near Tranquebar, the place where the first German Protestant mission in India was initiated in 1706. My father, Erich Arno Lehmann (1901–1984), grew up in the town of Kaitz near Dresden. He hailed from a rather humble family background. His father was a bank clerk with socialist leanings, unusual for that time, but he died at an early age. After that, my grandmother and her six children moved into the city where she worked for several well-to-do families as a washer woman, cook, and domestic servant. Every child had to contribute to the support of the family. My father himself chased balls on a tennis court, the very same one on which I would later learn to play.

My mother, Gertrud Lehmann, nee Harstall (1901–1964), came from an old family in Poppenbüttel (a suburb of Hamburg). A distant ancestor was named Pippin from Herestall, and I always was impressed with that name. It would have not hurt my feelings if I had been named Harstall instead of Lehmann. Even my parents considered using this as the family name at the time of their marriage, but out of consideration for the self-esteem of the Lehmann clan ("So our honorable name isn't good enough for you any more?") they gave up the idea. In any event, such a decision would not have guaranteed the continuance of the Harstall name. In the Lehmann family there has been only one male descendant.

On my mother's side of the family were the Grundigs. Perhaps from my great-grandfather Hermann Grundig, a master brass caster, I got my passion for brass artifacts. In my living room today are more than 25 brass candlesticks and similar objects. I spent my childhood under his oversized portrait that occupied most of the wall of our little living room in Dresden-Leubnitz. Painted by the Dresden artist, Franz Siebert, it was a life-size painting of a patriarch dressed in black, with a gold watch chain across his vest. With one hand he was supporting his cranium: "head" really isn't the appropriate word here. Above his magically blue eyes, his large, spacious forehead made an arch over his nose where the steep "Grundig fold" was obvious. I inherited this facial feature. After the death of my parents we had a family dispute as to who would inherit the portrait. Sadly I lost out, but I do have a photograph of it hanging on the wall beside my desk.

Near it, on top of my desk, stands a copy of the sculpture made by his son Clemens Grundig (my great uncle) who was a professional sculptor. It depicts my great-grandfather in a long work apron with rolled-up sleeves and a large hammer in his hand. Clemens had worked on the famous sculpture ensemble by Johannes Schilling (1828–1910) entitled "Four Times of Day." They stand at the four corners of the stairs leading to the Brühl Terrace beside the Elbe River in Dresden. The sandstone originals, which are now beside the palace moat in Chemnitz, were cast in bronze and placed on the terrace. Whenever I am in Dresden, I like to walk up the wide stairs of the Brühl Terrace and gaze at this. I never cease to be amazed and grateful at how much beauty is concentrated in this one spot. With a single glance one can see the Hofkirche (Court Church), the Semper Opera House, and the baroque stone bridge over the Elbe. For me it is the most beautiful place in the world. And the very thought that one of my forebears contributed to this majestic work of art fills me with an eerie but deep sense of pride.

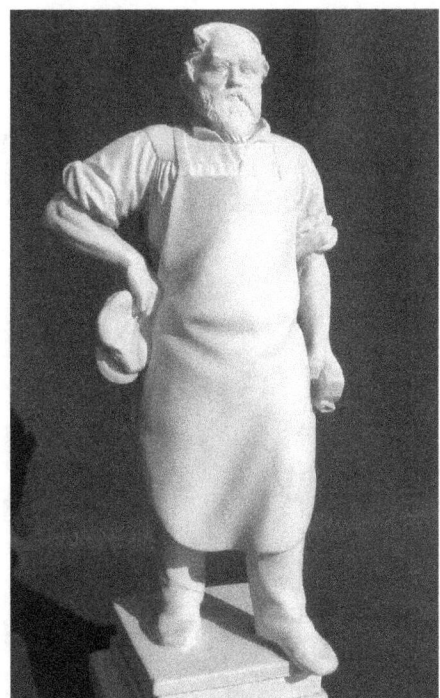
My great-grandfather

When my grandfather Carl Harstall married my grandmother Alma Grundig, he hoped that the family connection would be financially beneficial to him. Instead, because the life of an artist is usually one of poverty, he gained nothing and died broke in 1923. I know about as little about him as I do of my paternal grandparents. The only recollection I have is that of my grandmother Alma, who died in 1940. I have a fond memory of the velvet ribbon she wore around her neck which, to my young mind, gave her a very elegant look.

Because of their chronic economic difficulties, the Harstalls repeatedly moved in search of cheaper lodgings. While they were living on the Holzhofgasse in Dresden, my father met my mother. On the same street is located the Dresden Deaconess Hospital, where both I and my first grandchild were born. My daughter, Mirjam, worked there as a nurse for many years. My daughter Constantia still works as a preschool teacher in the kindergarten housed in Building 13, the very place where my parents announced their engagement on March 22, 1925.

THE CALL TO INDIA

My father's goal in life was to be a missionary, particularly in Africa, and he enrolled at the Leipzig Mission's seminary. There were six candidates. Upon completion of their studies, they were all commissioned in a worship service that took place at the Leipzig University Church of St. Paul. The service opened with the hymn, "As God leads me so I will follow, setting my own will aside ... As he leads me, I will go, step by step, in childlike trust." Already my father began to feel uneasy. The noted Professor Paul Althaus stepped to the pulpit and delivered a sermon on the text, "My thoughts are not your thoughts, and my ways are not your ways, says the Lord" (Isa 55:8). That really stimulated the future missionary to think about what was to come.

After it ended, Professor Ernst Sommerlath, the seminary's director, summoned the six to his office, and they seated themselves on a large sofa. Now the decision about placement would be announced. "Gentlemen, you are sitting just where you should be—you three on this side will be going to Africa and you three on the other side to India." My father was sitting on the "wrong" side—with those destined for India. As he had set his heart on Africa, his whole world seemed to fall apart, and it would take him a couple years to come to terms with this decision. Then, India would become his great love! In his later life he became a leading scholar of Dravidian language and culture, and his doctoral work in translating Tamil texts eventually resulted in his becoming a professor at Halle University.

My father

But at that time such thoughts were out of the question. From the beginning he devoted himself solely to the task of being a missionary and carrying the saving message of God's love to another continent. Today, we hear a lot about "charismatics," and I suspect that such individuals see the Holy Spirit primarily as a power to help them get ahead and to enhance their own spiritual lives. However, I am convinced that the Holy Spirit was expressly given for "foreign service," that is, missionary work in other lands. "You shall receive the power when the Holy Spirit has come upon you; and you will be my witnesses ... to the ends of the earth" (Acts 1:8). For me, the many missionaries and their wives who have literally gone to the ends of the earth—into the farthest corner and most distant isle—are the true charismatics and spiritual heroes of humanity. They were filled with the power of the Holy Spirit and wanted to do only one thing—to make the name of Jesus known throughout the entire world.

My mother

My parents, who served under the Leipzig Mission in India, belong to these heroes. My mother paid a heavy price in the murderous heat of the tropical climate. She experienced unimaginable discomforts, culminating in the loss of her health as well as a son. Only on the Day of Judgment will the extent of the sorrow, tears, sacrifices, and struggles that all of these missionaries experienced as they lived as witnesses of Jesus be fully known. These people, who went unnoticed by the world, were despised by many, and even today are ridiculed by some in the church as lackeys of colonialists, are—I repeat again—are the great saints of the Christian church. I am filled with pride and thankfulness that I can number my parents among these saints.

The practice of the time was that, after serving seven years in India, a missionary family would be granted a period of home leave. So it was in 1934 my parents and their eldest son Johannes, born in India, returned to Germany. Unlike him, I was born in Germany, in Dresden and not Madras, and I have always envied him for this.

Blues Music and Gospel Proclamation
A YOUNG BOY'S DREAMS

I spent my first sixteen years in Dresden. Because mother had developed a heart condition in India, she could not go back to the tropics. (Perhaps I inherited my own cardiac deficiency from her.) Father faced the prospect of returning to his beloved India alone or remaining in Germany with his family. He opted for the latter but continued to serve the Leipzig Mission as its home secretary (*Missionsinspektor*). With the outbreak of war all mission work ceased, and he accepted a pastorate at Christ Church in Dresden-Strehlen. We lived in Leubnitz-Neuostra on the southern edge of the city, and our hillside location provided a splendid view of the city. A few years later, after we had moved to Halle and I was now in my last year of high school, I revisited Leubnitz. I could not believe how narrow the streets and tiny the gardens were, and how small the world was where I had spent my youth. But as a child this had not bothered me at all; for me our tiny yard was a paradise.

Snowdrops grew underneath the currant bushes along the fence. Every year on February 12, my mother's birthday, I would brush away the snow and pick the first bouquet of these harbingers of spring. On the nearby meadow was a giant cherry tree whose glorious blossoms so fascinated me that it made me want to become a painter. In the summer we would pick chives in our garden plot for supper. In the fall I was drawn to our apple tree. Plucking grapes from the tall, creeping vine growing on our house was, however, the sole responsibility of my father. There was also a sandbox, a swing, a shady spot to enjoy our afternoon coffee, and most importantly a larch tree.

This majestic tree stood in front of our house at the edge of the street. It had several "stories" in which we children had created some nice "dwelling places." From these we would observe the whole area and toss fir cones at neighbors whom we disliked. We pulled up the necessary utensils for our "meals" with a rope. The larch, with its resiny-spicy odor emanating from the branches, gave us a feeling of freedom and security. It was one of the most important and beautiful places of my childhood.

Years later, after I had assumed a pastorate in Karl-Marx-Stadt (the absurd name the East German authorities had given to Chemnitz even though he had never even visited there), I discovered a few meters of open space in front of the house where the church had assigned us an apartment. In fact, I still live here today. One of the first things I did

The Answer, My Friend

was to plant a larch in that spot. Today it has grown as high as the house itself and its needles lie everywhere in the vicinity. They fall in the autumn and establish themselves in every crack with unbelievable tenacity. Nevertheless, the effort expended in the constant struggle against these needles is completely offset by the sight of this magnificent tree. The larch tree is an essential part of my life! When I return home from a business trip, I must first open the driveway gate to gain access to the garage. The larch stands right beside the gate, and when I get out of the car to open it, I pause for a moment, take a deep breath, and savor the aroma of my favorite tree. Only then can I say that I have finally arrived back home.

I was not as adept at choosing the clothes I would wear as was my younger brother, born a year after me. I had my own ideas about which clothes looked best on me. My mother's reaction was my first experience with the "theory of relativity." If I insisted on wearing a certain item of clothing that she did not feel was in keeping with the proper norm for Sunday dress, she would shout at me theatrically: "What shame you are bringing upon me!" When I grumbled about another piece of Sunday attire that I would not want to be caught dead in, she snapped back with: "Who will be looking at you anyway, you little snot!"

Father assigned each of us three boys a small garden plot to care for. Undoubtedly he intended this as means to teach us the virtue of responsibility. I doubt if I was seen nearly as much in this area of my paradise as in the larch tree or on the swing. One time, I believe before I had even started school, I was swinging back and forth and I began singing a song that I probably had heard in the church. I had no idea of the meaning of the text, but I was belting it out at the top of my voice:

1936, left to right, Jochen, myself, Johannes

"So you're not a monarch who rules (*führt*) over all,
God's in control and does (*führt*) all things well."

When mother heard these sounds through the open kitchen window, she bounded out the door and into the yard as if she had been bitten by a tarantula. Breathlessly shouting at the top of her voice, she told me to shut my mouth and stop singing this song. I could not understand what it was about the piece that upset her so much. All I could hear was: "What if the neighbors hear you singing this?" Some of them were Nazis. How could a little guy like me understand that they might think I was hinting at Hitler just because I was using a form of the verb *führen*, and Hitler had chosen the title *Führer*, obviously derived from it? Or that a ditty warbled by such a pip-squeak as I was really an attack on the state?

In any event, the climate of fear in Germany at the time was such that the pastor's wife had to forbid her little boy from trilling such songs. Even though I did not understand the political relationships of this period, it was the first time that I sensed the frightening power of the dictatorship and anxiety that people had about its representatives. This power had now intruded into the idyllic life of my childhood. Otherwise, like every other young boy, I grew up in my little world with its games, tussles, special occasions, and "catastrophes," such as the death of our beloved kitty cat.

Even the fateful day of September 1, 1939 passed by me virtually unnoticed. I do, however, remember quite clearly the moment as we were seated at the breakfast table enjoying homemade jam on our bread rolls when father uttered the words: "War has begun." I also recall that mother fell silent. Both of them knew what war meant because they had experienced it once before. But my innocent five-year-old mind had no idea what war meant. This lesson remained to be learned.

I do remember bidding farewell to the soldiers marching off to war. I stood along the roadside watching as men and young women tossed bouquets of flowers to the "boys" in uniform. In fact, our neighbors' housekeeper, a boy-crazy young thing, really put on a show of enthusiasm. I stood in silent amazement watching the uniforms, horses, drums, swords, and flags. For me the soldiers marching to the east along the Dohna highway near our house were nothing more than a colorful, thrilling spectacle. I have no idea whether any of them came back alive. I only know that six years later on the very same Dohna highway the Russian forces moving into Dresden came by in their armored vehicles. This time the snappy sounds of marching band music that set our feet to moving were missing. Instead, the frightening howling of these drunken, raping hordes paralyzed us with fear.

TRAUMATIC SCHOOL EXPERIENCES

While the war itself was for me a kind of stage play, school was a genuine threat. I never liked school. I dreaded it most of time; seldom was it enjoyable. During the many years I spent in the schools where people sought to educate and shape me I suffered from anxiety and feelings of inadequacy.

My twelve-year march through these institutions began in the Leubnitz elementary school, an imposing building erected in 1907. Teachers were still allowed to engage in the painful practice of rapping the knuckles of students with a cane. The principal, a Nazi, would hit us on other parts of the body as well as our hands. One day a boy was caught running through a grain field and tromping down the stalks. While the principal whacked the unfortunate offender on the backside, all the classroom doors were open and instruction came to a halt. We shuddered as the wailing and screaming of the delinquent reverberated through the hallways and it froze our souls.

Although I would never condone such a barbaric method of discipline, I must admit that none of those students forced to listen to this torture would ever trample on these valuable stalks of grain. Nowadays, whenever I see school children traipsing through the field behind my apartment and treading down the grain with their bikes and mopeds, I recall this horrific scene. But what I feared most about school was not corporal punishment but failure itself, of being unable to do something demanded of me. I despised the whole "business of school" and the "herd mentality" that was integral to it.

Of course, there were some more pleasant and carefree moments in the school calendar. I always enjoyed the music periods, taught by the choir director of the local church, class field trips, and the visits to the zoo. I enthusiastically committed to memory poems like:

> "At the place of a gentle innkeeper
> I was recently a guest.
> Hanging from a long branch,
> A golden apple was his sign..."

An extremely unpleasant experience was the time when my teacher Herr Meinel gave me the title of "acting classroom leader." I was supposed to write on the blackboard the names of pupils who misbehaved, but I found this repulsive. I cannot remember ever actually having done it. On the other hand, I was quite pleased when Herr Schwerdtner actually visited our home. He had been the teacher of both Johannes and me. The Schwerdtner family were hard-line Nazis, so much so that they even greeted one another at home with "*Heil* Hitler!" His nickname among the students was "Strawberry." Somehow he heard that Johannes had given him this name, and he came to complain to my father. The climax of the conversation was when he indignantly growled: "Pastor, I am not a strawberry." To this, father wisely and truthfully replied: "No, Herr Schwerdtner, you aren't a strawberry."

CLEVER TRICKS

The first winter of the war (1939–40) was bitterly cold. For us children it was an unforgettable experience to run across the solidly frozen ice on the Elbe River. The bad part, though, was that we shivered inside our inadequately heated homes. The only item on my Christmas wish list was a warm living room on that joyous day. My parents were always able to give us presents, even in the hardest of times. We boys as well managed to come up with something that would bring them a little bit of joy. One time we learned this song by heart: "I will go with the shepherds to gaze upon my Savior." We all sang it without our songbooks as we entered the gaily decorated Christmas room. Another time we memorized the Christmas story. When father began to read it, as was his custom, we chimed in as a chorus and recited the whole story with him.

We had a family tradition on Christmas Eve. After attending the vesper service (first in the chapel at the Deaconesses' House and later in the fellowship hall at Christ Church in Strehlen), we returned home. Father disappeared into the living room where he piled up the presents and lit the candles on the Christmas tree while we waited patiently in front of the door in the darkness. Finally, the elephant bell we had brought from India sounded—once, twice, three times. It was the sign the door was about to open. We entered singing the song mentioned above and took up our positions in front of the Christmas tree, sneaking a peek at the presents as father read the Nativity story. Then it was the "official" time for us to turn to the presents. We spent the rest of the evening opening packages, expressing surprise, examining the various gifts, and, of course, eating and drinking.

The Answer, My Friend

The year 1941 held two special events for me. The first was the visit to Bärenstein Castle near Glashütte, about 20 miles south of Dresden. Johannes was spending his summer holidays there, and I was allowed to go meet him and come back home with him. It was a real castle with a tower and a donkey on which people could ride. I really envied the young fellow who took care of this animal. The second noteworthy thing was that our parents had engaged an artist to paint our portraits. Several days in the month of September we climbed up the stairs to the attic studio of the artist, Kurt Scheibe, to sit for the paintings. He got 100 marks for each portrait plus 42.50 for the frame. I wasn't too keen on this whole project because we had to sit still for so long at a time. But now I am grateful that I possess this childhood portrait. What I remember as fascinating about the place was the strong odor

With my brothers

of the oil colors and the whole atmosphere of the studio, with its large skylight windows and pictures standing everywhere.

After this contact with the world of art, I decided the following year to turn to another branch of art—to become a writer. Even earlier I had expressed myself as a songwriter and storyteller while lying in bed at night, but, of course, I never wrote down any of these spontaneous effusions of verse. That changed when father published a book entitled *The Transition to Older Years*. The day after this book appeared, I sat down and spent an entire day writing my first work which I called, *Fictitious and True Stories from My Life*. I introduced it one evening at a family gathering by reading aloud. When Jochen dared to interrupt during this process of creative expression, I summarily silenced him with the remark, "One doesn't disturb a writer when he is writing."

The next year, 1943, I extended my artistic ambitions to the realm of music by taking piano lessons. I won't tell all the things that disturbed my teacher, Herr Paulig, about my piano abilities. He came to our home and used the piano in the living room for the lessons. What annoyed me in particular was that he never stopped at the appointed time. So I decided to place an alarm clock on the large ceramic stove (I really wanted to put it on the piano) and set it to go off at 11:30. When it rang exactly at the appointed time, I stood up, said "My time is up," politely bowed, and disappeared. Needless to say, that was the end of my career as a pianist. Some years later, I made another attempt at learning how to play, but it went nowhere.

That summer Crown Prince Pater George of Saxony died in a drowning accident. Father very much wanted us to view the remains of this member of the former royal house of Wettin, since it was an important link with the past. He took us to the Catholic Hofkirche, where the casket rested splendidly covered with banners and flowers. As I stood silent, I was deeply moved by the significance of the moment. Since the magnificent pulpit of the Hofkirche was bricked up as a protection against bombs, it was a strange contrast to the splendor where the prince was lying in state.

THROUGH THE STENCH TO THE SCHOOL BENCH

The route to the schoolhouse led through "Stinky Alley." It was a narrow path that ran between the properties of two farmers. To the right and left were lattice fences, tall stinging nettle bushes, and behind them vegetable gardens, horse paddocks, stables, and a pig pen. The pungent odor of the pigs that wafted through the openings in the barrier gave the path its name. The most interesting thing about this route was when we walked past the sty when the pigs were being fed. We could hear the swearing of the farmhands and the squealing of the pigs as if they were being slaughtered. One this wall we would use chalk or stones to inscribe graffiti—thus we were forerunners of the "paint spray-can generation." Being a fiendish little rascal, I, too, left wicked little sayings as my own "handwriting on the wall" directed against people who I felt didn't like me. Some years later, I strolled along the "Stinky Alley" and discovered some remnants of my childhood wall painting. I was deeply moved.

At the end of Stinky Alley were some worn steps that led downwards into the center of the village. To the right was the church, to the left, the Moses' family farm and our beloved restaurant, the *Leubnitzer Höhe*. Straight ahead, down a steep embankment, was the city hall and a square with an oak dedicated to Hitler, an obligatory action in small towns, and the studio of the portrait painter. Going further, one passed a tiny house with the sign "Small but it's mine." It was occupied by the shoemaker who had his shop at street level and we saw him sitting at his workbench as we walked by.

At the end of the street before it entered into the meadow called *Heiliger Born* (the Sacred Fountain) was a hill where the schoolhouse was located. We kids referred to it as the "Fortress" (*Zwingburg*) because it seemed more like a prison to us. I especially recall the dreary schoolyard and wretched gym beside it. Here is where I would soon come to understand what Nazi ideology was.

FAMILY TIES

Fortunately, my life didn't consist solely of going to going to school. There were holidays, festivals, and birthdays. On such occasions the participants were primarily family members, except when special friends were invited. The family consisted of Grandma Harstall, Aunt Elsbeth (my father's sister), Aunt Dorschanni (my mother's cousin) and her family, Uncle Erich (father's brother) with his wife and daughter (they were called the Stetzschers because they lived in a western part of the city called Stetzsch), and finally Aunt Olga (father's sister). Unfortunately, after Olga converted to the Jehovah's Witnesses faith, we never saw her very much and most of the family was just as happy. Of all those I saw at these occasions, the ones I most appreciated were my mother's brother, Uncle Paulus and his family. The procession of the relatives always seemed to occur like a phenomenon of nature, like thunder following lightning, and our tongues started wagging about this or that member of the family.

I greatly admired Uncle Paulus, who was also my godfather, because he fulfilled a dream that most boys of my age had at the time, namely, to have a saber. I never got upset with him except once when I observed him giving my mother a kiss upon arrival and then at departure. What irritated me even more was that my mother went right along with him. My moral standards have always been rather high, and this kissy-kissy action of her with a man other than my father really rubbed me the wrong way. Eventually I realized that the two were siblings, just as Jochen, Johannes, and I were. To be sure, I didn't go around kissing them either. In any event, Paulus and mother had a particularly close relationship, but it was clouded from time to time because of a dispute over a memorial stone in the cemetery for their two brothers, Hugo and Rudolf, who had fallen in the First World War.

Nevertheless, everyone visited one another, and when Uncle Paulus came to our house after the war, I had to take him to the station in our handcart since he had difficulty walking. He took the train to Heidenau, just south of Dresden, where he lived after the attack on the city in which he lost a daughter. He told us once about a dream he had had where he died but was turned away at the gates of heaven because "it was not his time yet." Ironically, he died on the same day as my mother.

IN BRIEF—SCHOOL DAYS AT VITZTHUM

At one of my earlier birthdays, before my taste in gifts had degenerated to that of military swords, I was in an "Indian-trapper" phase and very much wanted a trapper hat. Before the presents were due to be passed out, I was playing outside in the yard. I happened to glance in the window and noticed that the long desired hat was lying on the gift table. Of course, I was as happy as could be and it was very difficult to feign surprise after I had seen the hat there. Still, I believe I would rather have had my innocence than this knowledge I gained by chance.

I was quite proud at a later time about another head covering, the dark-brown school cap of the Vitzthum *Gymnasium*. It was an academic high school, and in the final year the students had to pass a rigorous examination known as the *Abitur* which qualified them for admission to a university. I was admitted to this school after completing four years in the elementary school. Each of the various Dresden *Gymnasien* traditionally had connections with various social circles. An all-boys school, this one was populated by the sons of pastors and the aristocracy. The school, founded in 1828, was located in the city center near the main railroad station. Therefore I had to get up quite early each school day to catch the streetcar into town. I was already familiar with most of the teachers, as Johannes had been a student at this prestigious institution for several years. His custom was to tell us the latest stories from school while the family was gathered for the noon meal. My father just "ate them up," as the saying goes.

While I already knew about the principal, Dr. Kleinstück, as well as Etienne and Rollo, it was not correct to say that they knew me. So it was that Etienne, who happened to be a hall monitor one day, fished me out of a large group of boys and asked: "What kind of a cheeky new face do we have here?" The person must have had a special kind of eyes, because I don't know what would have seemed cheeky about this little guy with the plain head of hair. Since the students were drawn from various parts of the city and even farther (the so-called external students came by train each day), contacts that extended beyond the boundaries of the school day were difficult to maintain.

The one exception was Vyacheslav von Zarembski. I had never visited in such a fine, richly-furnished home, but unfortunately I never learned what high post his father, a Russian émigré aristocrat, occupied. He was certainly an awe-inspiring person. The family lived near the Russian Orthodox Church, and one time they took me to a service there. The atmosphere of the church with its many candles, incense, priestly vestments, and singing completely overwhelmed me. My attendance at this worship service marked the beginning of my great love of icons, which has grown increasingly deeper over the course of my life. For the first time, I saw the mysterious, earnest faces of the Madonna and Christ shimmering in gold. These now surround me in every room of my apartment.

I don't believe any real Nazis belonged to the school's faculty. Here the old spirit prevailed, while patriotic speeches with meaningless, hackneyed Nazi phrases seemed to be insincere exercises we were compelled to endure. Two students in my class who came from a distance on the train appeared on Wednesdays and Saturdays in their Hitler Youth uniform. Those days we had compulsory service (*Dienst*), and they had no opportunity to go home and change out of civilian clothes. So they sat in class in their uniforms, but they seemed to us like two aliens. They simply didn't fit into the culture of the Vitzthum *Gymnasium*.

A PRISONER IN A MASS SOCIETY

By now I had reached the age where I would have to don a uniform. Boys aged ten to fourteen were required to belong to the junior version of the Hitler Youth (*Hitlerjugend*), known as the German Youth (*Deutsches Jungvolk*). They were called *Pimpfe*, colloquially "young squirts." Like the older boys they wore a special uniform, and I could hardly wait until I could have my own. For this reason I could not understand the behavior of my older brother who already had enjoyed this good fortune for a few years. Whenever he returned home from his time of "service," he slammed the front door and often, howling with rage, tore off the hated clothes while he was still in the foyer and threw them on the floor. At that time I stupidly yearned for the belt buckle, brown shirt, and all the rest of the repulsive trappings. Thus I trotted off on Wednesday and Saturday afternoons to the after school "service" activities, feeling important because I now "belonged" and participated in the routines and shouting with the others.

But this all ended the day I saw my classmate Dudek marching in the schoolyard. To be sure, I had no close connection with him. He was older and far beyond me socially, and I regarded him as a person of higher quality. He and his brother boarded the same streetcar at the Wasaplatz stop that I took to school. There was something special and noble about the two, perhaps even a hint of arrogance as well. They also caught my attention because even in summer they wore leather gloves. Not only did they have a cultured appearance but also a distinctively shaped head that came to a point at the rear of the skull which I labeled in my youthful lingo, "anvil turnip." In any event, they were special people, traveling in higher circles and were, for me, the embodiment of that which is noble and intellectual.

One day, as we were carrying out our monotonous marching drills on the Leubnitz school playground, I spotted my classmate Dudek. This higher being, a person who in my eyes was made of "better stuff," was standing in a formation doing his military exercises with arms bent and legs kicking up. The mere sameness of these idiotic movements conveyed the entire humiliation of the situation. It was bad enough that we other middle class sons and country yokels were compelled to take part in this circus, but what happened here was in my eyes a catastrophe. The entire scene played itself out in a few seconds. I saw Dudek for only a fleeting moment as my column marched past his, but this scene was embedded in my mind as a symbol of the degradation of the noble by the vulgar, the suppression and rape of the spirit through brute force.

From that second on, I hated not only the uniform, the Hitler Youth, the Nazis, and everything military, but absolutely all things that even hinted at uniformity and bringing individuals into conformity. This is the origin of my ongoing refusal to engage in marches, to clap in rhythm, or even to take part in *Schunkeln* at a festival or a restaurant, when everyone sways from side to side with arms linked. For me the latter is particularly horrific. Even reading a text aloud in unison at a worship service is an abomination to me. I can only do this when reciting the Lord's Prayer and the Confession of Faith. When the congregation responsively reads Bible verses and Psalms, I simply tune out. When the applause in a concert or theatrical production becomes rhythmic clapping, I explode in anger. My hair stands on end the moment that the concert applause machine takes off. This dreary clapping in unison of the masses is frequently even in the wrong rhythm.

The only exception to my policy is with jazz music. The allure of this music is that the listeners clap not with "one-and-three" as it the case with march music, but "two-and-four," that is, "off-beat." Generations of music lovers have not grasped this reality because they have been polluted by march tempos. Therefore, even at jazz concerts the so-called jazz fans many times clap along in the wrong rhythm even as they grin blissfully. When this happens, what pleasure I get from the music is dissipated and in disappointment my hands drop to my side. I always remember the time when Mahalia Jackson was holding a concert in Hamburg and she asked her "dear German friends" to cease clapping because it destroyed the swing of the gospel music. Perhaps my love of gospel music and jazz arises from the fact that this music embodies freedom, not the stupid rhythms of the industrial age that degrades humans to the level of machines.

In any event, this key experience set the theme for my life during the forty years of communist dictatorship, and it is epitomized in the song "Then There Will Be Freedom." The required marching in the schoolyard was my first lesson about the suppression of the spirit and freedom through might and force.

NIGHT

The next lesson I had to learn was much more unpleasant. This had to do, not with the annihilation of the spirit but rather the annihilation of life. This lesson I learned on the night of February 13, 1945.

It was Mardi Gras—Carnival Tuesday. For some years people were not celebrating this occasion as they customarily had. Too many had been killed in the war, too many families were grieving, too many were suffering from anxieties. During the last year of the war it was seen as inappropriate even for children to dress up in odd clothing and engage in the revelry of Mardi Gras. No longer was there a large parade in which all the youth in Leubnitz took part, nor the throwing of confetti, exploding of caps, and fluttering of brightly-colored streamers. Everyone behaved in a calm manner. One year we kids did slip into our costumes but we ended up crawling under the dining room table and found it idiotic to be in such a cramped position. It was no fun and we put the wretched costumes back in the box where they were kept. There was nothing to celebrate. By 1945 no one even tried to work him- or herself into a Carnival mood.

In the morning I had to go into the city with Jochen to take some things to Aunt Elsbeth and pick up some other stuff from her. Although technically it was a holiday, I saw no hint of any Carnival atmosphere. I do remember a little girl with a small dog running along behind her. The animal got away from her and raced off with the leash dragging on the ground. The girl enthusiastically shouted: "He's flying! He's flying." I do not know why such insignificant details leave impressions on our minds while really important things escape from our memory as though they had never happened. A few hours later, as the city was engulfed in flames, this child came to mind and I wondered if she had been incinerated along with her little dog.

According to my father's diary, this was the 158th air raid alarm. The first had occurred on August 29, 1940. Then we sat huddled together in blankets in a cold living room. Later on we gathered in our cellar where a small electric heater had been installed. At that time few really took these alerts seriously. In fact, a number of children of relatives and friends from Oldenburg and Hamburg who had actually experienced air raids and who were evacuated to our area imagined (wrongly, it would prove) they were safe here. Since no attacks followed the alarms, always made by howling sirens, we became accustomed to the nightly disruptions of our sleep. We even began Christmas Eve 1943 by spending the hours from three to five in the morning inside an air raid shelter.

Then in the summer of 1944 the first bombs fell. Some struck the Wettin *Gymnasium* where Johannes and I were now attending school since the Vitzthum *Gymnasium* had been converted into an infirmary for wounded soldiers. Horrified, I looked down the badly damaged Palmstrasse and for the first time I saw dwellings destroyed by bombs. One could look into rooms where people had been living but now some of the walls were missing. Wires were hanging everywhere and a stove lay at an odd angle in an upper floor. The apartments seemed to have been pried open and torn apart. It was as painful as it was frightening to gawk

The Answer, My Friend

into the living space of strangers. I could not get rid of this depressing image for a long time.

As a result, our classes were moved to the Kreuzschule, the school at Holy Cross Church, a splendid, venerable, dark-stone building behind the Theodor Körner statue next to the city hall. Whenever the sirens sounded during daytime, we were dismissed from school. One time I ran to catch the tram that left the downtown area but I could not get on any of the packed cars. Suddenly I spotted my mother in the crowd; it was a remarkable stroke of good fortune not to have to be alone in that dreadful hour. From December 1944 the air raid sirens sounded virtually every day and this continued even after the fateful day of February 13. Only on April 20 was the last alarm heard in Dresden—the 208th.

When the sirens began howling at 9:40 in the evening, father was away from the house. Since he was in charge of the nearby Strehlen church, he had gone there for some kind of a congregational function. Mother, being home alone, hustled us three boys into the cellar. We had hardly reached it when an indescribable racket broke loose above us. I really can't describe it; there are no words for this madness. There was neither light nor heat. We lay stretched out on the ice-cold stone floor, shivering from the cold and fear of death, screaming, and praying. I called out all the names of Jesus that I could recall—God, Deliverer, Helper, Savior, the Resurrected One, etc. Often the shrill whistles of falling bombs and subsequent explosions drowned out our cries. We didn't know whether the floor beneath us was heaving or the house above us was collapsing. We only heard crashing, splintering, thundering, and we breathed white wash, dust—it was truly the end of the world!

Sometime later—after an eternity—it seemed to be over. We went upstairs and the house was still standing, but roof tiles had been torn off, all the windows were shattered, and glass shards lay everywhere. Then we saw the burning city. As far as the eye could see were flames and thick clouds of smoke. Inconceivable, indescribable, unnerving! In any event, we were still there. But where was our father? Finally, he appeared—we were all alive.

Now that the all clear had sounded, father, the conscientious shepherd that he was, understood that he belonged to his congregation, the church, and returned to be with his flock. He took my older brother with him and actually was able to save Christ Church, the house of God, from total destruction by removing the fire bombs from one of its two towers. Built in 1903–5, the Art Nouveau Strehlen church, just a couple miles from downtown Dresden, was the first one of this type in the city.

When he left mother and the two younger sons in the chaos of our damaged house which was without water, electricity, and gas, he had no idea that a second attack was imminent. It began at 1:15 a.m. Now the brightly illuminated, burning city received the death blow with additional waves of saturation bombing. Added to the fear of death that gripped us was concern about our father and brother. What fears my poor mother must have suffered during that night! Of course, at the time this did not cross my mind; she was for us the only rock to whom we could cling. But later, I often asked myself what must she have thought and done as she huddled alone in this inferno with her two youngest sons while her husband and eldest son were outside in the hail of bombs. She undoubtedly prayed just as we did. Praying, praying, praying—that was everything. Sometime later, father and brother showed up. They had run past bomb craters, corpses, and burning buildings to save their lives.

I don't recall where and how we slept that night. The beds were full of glass splinters, the windows were empty open holes. Everything was destroyed and life was uncertain. Then at midday came a third aerial assault. For weeks afterward the sirens sounded almost daily. We went to bed each night in our clothing.

What terrified me the most in the weeks after February 13 was the sound of approaching bomber squadrons. I no longer saw any flak in the sky that defended against the airplanes. Unchallenged and unhindered, the bombers flew over all of Germany. It always started when we heard off in the distance a deep, rumbling sound, one that became louder and louder until we could see the planes. Now it was only minutes until they were directly over us. The question then was: would they fly on past us or would they drop their payloads on us? Helpless and powerless, we could only watch as they slowly approached. This sense of impotence, inevitability, and foreboding as the droning of the motors grew increasingly louder produced my greatest anxiety. The louder this sound grew, the greater was my panic. Then we would run into the cellar.

During one of the assaults on February 13–14 Jochen wanted to escape from the shelter where we had sought refuge. He simply could not stand the dark room any longer. Fortunately we were able to restrain him, since the intense pressure waves from the exploding bombs would surely have meant his death. For the first time in my life I saw corpses.

Also I saw body parts that belonged to a girl who had left the public air raid shelter out of panic and was torn to pieces outside. Someone had half-way covered the body with packing paper, but I saw in horror that it was a human being, a corpse. And then I saw the stream of refugees who, except for their own lives, had lost everything. They were fleeing to the higher elevations south of the burning city and in the direction of the Erzgebirge uplands. They were silent, ghostly, and many naked or scarcely clothed and badly burned.

NO MORE PHOENIX

Appearing at the door of our relatively intact house were families from the congregation and our circle of friends who had been bombed out. They had lost everything in the conflagration and sought a roof over their heads. As a result, a family was "camping out" in every room of our small house, while more and more came, hoping to receive some help from my father. He then went to a Nazi bigwig who lived on our street with just his wife in a single family dwelling and asked him if he would take in a few needy "comrades" [*Volksgenossen*—the distinctively Nazi term for the German people]. His reply: "Not possible." He claimed he was expecting a number of his own relatives. None ever came and they remained in the house alone.

Father had the key to the house across the street that belonged to two well-to-do ladies who were away on a trip. In this house he placed yet another family that had come to him for help. A young man with torn clothing and a sooty face had knocked on the door and pointed to a horse-drawn wagon standing in front of the house. On it under some junk was a basket containing a newborn child. Next to him sat an older man with an expressionless face (he had lost his wife in the attack), while seated next to the driver was a silent young woman. Neither of them could walk. The woman had been buried in the debris and her legs were virtually paralyzed while the old man had not been able to walk anyway. They had crawled on hands and feet out from under the rubble and left all their belongings behind. The woman had given birth in an air raid shelter (they were called "bunkers") and the people there named him "Little Bunker Hans." Someone had used the small pieces of cord from incendiary bombs that were lying everywhere to stitch together a pillow from an emergency bed in the bunker as a blanket for the new-born infant.

Father took this heap of human misery that had landed in front of our overfilled house to the neighbors' dwelling. I noticed two things about the father of Little Bunker Hans. His pants were shredded with the largest hole being at the knee, and I could see that he had an artificial leg. This sight fascinated me as much as how he exhaled the smoke from a cigarette out of his mouth in a thick cloud and then inhaled it, a deep drag—and he did this with very thin, self-rolled cigarettes.

Mother gave away all the clothing and fabric items that we did not absolutely need for ourselves. Every day she cooked a meal for all these people, but I have no idea where she got all the necessary foodstuffs, let alone the strength to do so. It is astonishing what people are capable of achieving in times such as these when it is a matter of life and death. It took nearly twenty years for her to work through these experiences of this "glowing Carnival time" and relate them in a collection of novellas. During all of this she not only experienced serious personal tragedies, such as the death of her niece (the daughter of her brother Paulus) on February 13, but also the loss of Dresden, the jewel of beauty and art treasures. No one could have imagined that even in this murderous war there existed people who would stoop to the barbarism of destroying the "Florence on the Elbe," especially since it was then populated primarily by women, children, and wounded soldiers and it lacked either military or economic significance.

I cannot really say that I, as an eleven-year-old, had the faintest idea of what the loss of the beauty and cultural treasures of Dresden meant and what pain the inhabitants and admirers of the city felt. Reflection on this would only come much later. It seems to me that that I lived the next few months in a sort of never-never land. I remember very little about the time, other than it was a matter of survival and caring for our day to day needs. One of these was obtaining water. For example, a farmer in Leubnitz had a functioning well and I would trudge there regularly with two buckets to get water. Also, as in the old days, people exchanged information at the well. Someone had connected a radio to an auto battery and heard where the battlefront was, where the Russians were located, and other news reports and rumors that were making the rounds.

We children busily carried out tasks that would enable our survival. One day I salvaged some pieces of wood from the ruins of a burned-out villa and loaded it onto our handcart. The odor of the fire was still strong even though it was now weeks later. Because I had been told that as a

The Answer, My Friend

Pimpf I was expected to report to the Hitler Youth, on my way home I parked my cart in front of the office and went in to register. The Hitler Youth punk who was on the desk did not know what to do with me and couldn't think of anything better, so he ordered me to go sweep the street outside the office door. This, however, was the first time I actually refused to obey an order. I told him that I had no time to do so because right now I needed to push my wagon full of wood up the hill as I was responsible for providing heating material for several families.

And that was the absolute truth. In the months after the attack there was no time for fun and games. Childhood had simply ceased to exist. This situation only changed when life began to run in a more or less orderly fashion once again. This is not to say that life soon become what it once was before. Nothing was "normal" from then on. And then everything was turned upside down when Hitler's Germany completely collapsed and the Russians arrived. "The Russians are coming" was the next threat with which we had to deal.

> What is life and what is death?
> What is this time in between?
> Why do we love, and what is harm?
> Why do I experience desire and pain?
>
> The answer, my friend,
> only Jesus can give.
> The answer gives Jesus alone.
>
> What is good fortune and how do I find it?
> Which is the road to attain it?
> Who is the hope for me and the world?
> Who brings peace to us all?
>
> Where did I come from?
> And where am I going?
> What is the sense of it all?
> When do I arrive, when do I reach the goal?
> When do I finally come home?

2

Precious Lord, Take My Hand

As I mentioned earlier, some Russian emigres lived in Dresden before the war and an Orthodox congregation worshipped in a splendid church near the main railroad station. There were also the unfortunate men the Nazis brought in as forced laborers for the factories and young girls as domestics in German homes. On Sunday afternoons they gathered by the hundreds in the square in front of the main post office, which the locals snidely called "East Square," a play on the words *Post* and *Ost* (east). Strange-smelling persons who talked a seemingly unintelligible language flooded the precinct.

For a time, we employed a girl named Nadja to help with our family of five, and she cooked borscht, her national food, for us. One day she took mother and us boys to visit her Russian friends. Situated along the Elbe near the Ballhaus Watzke, a popular brewery restaurant and dance hall, was what appeared to be an old factory building that served as a hostel for hundreds of young Russian women of all ages. The narrow barracks-style sleeping rooms crammed with double bunk beds, the strong odors, and chaotic sounds of the jabbering women caused me considerable anxiety. Since the Russians so love children, we were quite a sensation. Everyone wanted to touch us and all were enthusiastic and happy for the chance to cuddle a couple of children. For my part, I felt much more at ease when we got away from these demonstrations of affection and found our way back into the fresh air. Following the air raid, I often asked myself what had become of these women. Surely few of them survived the war.

In May 1945 the question everyone faced was: shall we stay or flee to the West? Even as late as May 7 many chose the option of flight, but our family decided to remain. Horrible rumors circulated about the Russians. For example, we heard that they would take all jewelry for themselves. If they could not pull a ring from someone's finger, they would simply hack it off. A young woman with two children who had taken refuge with us after the attack was in that situation. Since she was unable to remove her gold wedding band, my older brother Johannes took a file and sawed it open without the assistance of or even informing us younger ones. Also, we were unaware that our parents had buried an assortment of valuables in the yard.

Not only material things were hidden but also people. A girl whom my father was preparing for confirmation along with her mother and sister hid in our attic because they were fearful of being raped. Their stay in that tiny room, the heat, and the constant fear must have been torture in itself. And then the Russians came.

The first ones I saw rode down our street on motorcycles. They had on different uniforms than German soldiers and only after they had passed did I realize they were Russians. Immediately we hung a small bed sheet out the window, and everywhere white flags appeared, even at the house of the Nazi bigwig. Then the foot soldiers appeared, went into the houses, and confiscated whatever they wanted. The first of our things to pass into the hands of the Soviet Occupation Power was our camera and bicycle.

This plundering went on for several days, but we came out relatively unscathed whereas others suffered much more. For instance, a man who was a member of father's congregation and owner of a large nursery came to us weeping bitterly. He reported that soldiers had raped his daughter Hanna, whom father recently had confirmed. It was the first time I had ever seen a grown man cry.

RUINATION BY ALCOHOL

Before long, our relationship with the Russians began to take on more of an economic character, that is, bartering. For one thing, father exchanged a pair of black pants for a loaf of bread. Then we boys got one of the occupiers to agree to let us have a horse belonging to the large herd that grazed in the *Grosser Garten,* a nearby city park, for a few bottles of schnaps (a distilled alcoholic drink). The problem was that we didn't have any schnaps to trade, and even if we did get the horse the next Russian who came around the corner might seize it for himself. So perished my dream to possess a horse of my own.

Rather friendly relations developed between us and the adjutant (valet or servant) of a Russian officer who had taken up lodging in the most beautiful house on our street. The villa belonged to a factory owner we kids called "Cheese-Man Friedel." A kind man, he had heard the crying of our infant refugee from the February bombing, Little Bunker Hans, and provided us with powdered milk that essentially saved the child's life. Later, after he had regained possession of his house from the Soviet occupiers, Herr Friedel deeply impressed me in another way. I was asked to do something for him one Sunday, and I found him there with an open Bible and hymnbook.

The aforementioned adjutant sat in the sun on the villa's entrance steps working on a pair of handcrafted boots for his boss. The work seemed to go best when he drank *Pivo* (the Russian word for beer). He often gave us boys some money and sent us off to fetch this life-giving fluid at the Leubnitzer Höhencafé only a few steps away. I had gotten my first part-time job at the village shoemaker's shop assisting with shoe repairs at the same time I entered the Vitzthum *Gymnasium*, and one might say that because of my expertise as an apprentice shoemaker I was able to appraise the *Tovarishch's* (the Russian word for comrade) handiwork.

Unfortunately, I must acknowledge that I have the comrades from the Red Army to thank for introducing me to smoking. During the war my friends Pit and Atze Zöffel employed a Russian woman as a domestic. Since things had gone well and she had a good relationship with the family, she served as a kind of guardian angel when the plundering Russian army came through. Then the "captain," an officer with several aides, appeared at his home. He became "interested" in this female from his homeland and carried on some wild orgies with her, assisted by generous quaffs of vodka from water glasses they found there. Herr Zöffel took advantage of the situation. He had become an alcoholic as the result of the death of his wife, a beautiful and imposing woman who had been a competent business person. Her agonizing and losing struggle with cancer so affected him that he began drowning his sorrows in alcohol. He drank away his factory and possessions and came to the point where he was taking his beloved phonograph records to the bar to trade for schnaps. He also shared in the vodka flow with the "captain."

One day the entire bunch had gotten so drunk that none of them realized that some passing members of the victorious Red Army had opened Zöffel's garage door. An auto enthusiast, he had a bright-red, open cockpit sports car. The vehicle was a Wanderer, a prestigious German automobile made in Chemnitz and possibly an early forerunner of the Ferrari make. Well-known in Leubnitz, it must have been a very special car, maybe even one of a kind. Actually, the vehicle had not been driven in years and was up on blocks, as the tires had been removed so they could help win the world war just ended. The band of soldiers requisitioned the red sports car, pulled it into the street, and towed it away with a Russian auto—on its rims!

We boys assumed that such mishandling would render the car worthless. To no avail, we tried repeatedly to get the attention of someone in the drinking troop to what was going on. To save the auto, all the "captain" needed to do was stick his head out the window. But he was either unable or unwilling to do so. Herr Zöffel staggered down the stairs and stood speechless with glazed eyes and in utter unbelief as his jewel was destroyed before his nose and hauled away. Perhaps he never really grasped what was going on. My compassion for the man was as great as my dismay at the power of alcohol, whose destructive force exceeded even the destructive capability of the Red Army.

EVERYTHING COULD BE USED FOR SMOKING

The Russians also smoked during their carousing and this brings me to my main topic. Nearly all of the ordinary soldiers smoked hand-rolled Machorka cigarettes [a type of Russian tobacco popular among the Soviet troops], as this was typical of the lower classes. I didn't learn about the production of Machorka cigarettes until a few years later when I was a high school student in Halle/Saale and helped out at the train-station mission. At that time, Soviet soldiers were on patrol at every station. In the intervals between trains we got into conversations with some of them, and I watched how *Tovarishch* Patrullovich made his weed. He tore a sheet from the Soviet newspaper *Pravda*, fished a handful of Machorka from his pants pocket, spread it on the paper, rolled it, "glued" it with saliva, and the fag was ready. The comrades good-naturedly laughed at my first failed attempts to duplicate this feat. It took a long while before I mastered the art of *Papyrossi Produktion* (rolling my own) as ordinary Soviets did it.

On the other hand, the "captain" had real cigarettes. How some of these along with a few cigars came into my friend Pit's possession, I have no idea. I believe I am on the right track when I assume that it was the "booty of war," that is, "pinched" goods. Still, this meant absolutely nothing to me. The Zöffels had a small garden house but only we boys ever used it. Then one day we were in there and on top of an old suitcase we spotted a nicely sorted row of cigars and cigarettes. Immediately we went to work on them and so began my "career" as a smoker which I did not end until three decades later. But by then it was already too late; in 1979 I suffered a heart attack. When the "captain" soon disappeared and with him went Pit's source of tobacco, we passionate smokers faced hard times. We had to make do with dried rose petals and chestnut leaves. It was a lot of effort until the cultivation of tobacco finally took hold here. But even then we found that the harvesting and production of this was a really sticky, messy business.

Nicotine addiction also made me into a thief. Occasionally, someone gave my father cigarettes, but from his standpoint these things were only suitable for those about to be confirmed. He only smoked cigars and a pipe, especially a long one whose gigantic bowl rested on the floor. It went on up between the knees to the mouthpiece through which the smoke was drawn. We boys were often given the task of opening up the gift cigarettes and putting the tobacco into a can from which he would fill the pipe bowl. You can imagine how I felt as I was told to tear open real Camels or Chesterfields, like cutting green beans. At the time these brands were legendary, and everyone knew the jingle: "Imagine we had something to smoke—a Camel or a Chesterfield."

My pangs of conscience regarding ripping open a cigarette were apparently greater than the qualms I had regarding theft. In any event, at the conclusion of these "pull and slit" sessions a few undamaged "Amis" [American cigarettes] found their way into one of my pockets. Whether the snitched things tasted good, I don't remember any more. However, I was ashamed about this theft from my father.

PLATES FOR THE TRASH, WORDS OF DELIGHT

Sometime before the end of the war, the meeting and fellowship rooms of the Strehlen Christ Church that father pastored were requisitioned by the SS, the Nazi elite military and police corps. They fled as the Russians came and occupied the space. Once they had left, a squadron of women from the congregation came to put things back in order. I don't know if the Russians were simply venting their rage at the hated SS, but in any event they acted like the Vandals. The condition of the toilets was indescribable. At the end they simply relieved themselves in the drawers of the desks.

We children were given the task of getting rid of the SS dinner service. They had their own plates, saucers, and cups on which the SS rune symbol, the swastika, and Nazi slogans were imprinted. We dragged the stuff behind the church and had great fun throwing the porcelain against the church wall, so that each piece shattered and fell into the pile of shards on the ground. As we were cheering each broken plate, a refugee family came by. Everything that they possessed was loaded on the small wagon they were pulling. When the man saw how we were maliciously destroying the dinnerware, he shouted at us: "Are you crazy?" They pounced on the unbroken SS porcelain and took as much as they could fit on their cart. They didn't care if Nazi symbols were on them. A plate was a plate, and they had none at all.

The church hall, located in the building next to the church, was the only one, or one of the very few, in Dresden which had a large stage, curtain, and public cloakrooms and still was in a usable state. So it was that the beginnings of theater life after the war took place in this hall. Father asked Erich Ponto, a noted actor, to do an evening performance. Ponto, who is still remembered today for his role in *Der Feuerzangenbowle* (*The Flaming Red Wine Punch Bowl*) and his famous line "Sit down, you're stupid," lived in a villa by the *Grosser Garten* just a few minutes from Christ Church. In fact, on February 13 he had escaped from his burning house by sliding down the downspout.

This unique and famous Dresden actor came one evening and read texts from the Bible. The most unforgettable was when he read the concluding verse of Psalm 23: ". . . and I will dwell in the house of the Lord forever." One could even hear that the word "forever" (*immerdar*) had two "m"s. I understood for the first time what significance the beauty of language has when combined with the art of oratory. Even today, I shrink when pastors or lectors ruin a biblical text because they did not rehearse it ahead of time and thus read it poorly. "*Immerdar*" à la Ponto—that's music, that's melody, and eternity resonates with it.

Blues Music and Gospel Proclamation

Take me, Lord, by the hand,
lead me to the Promised Land.
Alone I can't do it, I'm too weak.
Through death, through judgment,
lead me, Lord, to your light.
Take me, Lord, by the hand and lead me home.

Let me, Lord, go with you,
let me understand your Word,
so that I really do what you desire.
Through the sorrow, through this trial.
Lead me, Lord, into endless time.
Take me, Lord, by the hand and lead me home.

Take my guilt, Lord, far from me,
and have patience with me, too,
there is so much in me to change.
Through the ridicule and scorn,
lead me, Lord, on to your throne.
Take me, Lord, by the hand and lead me home.

3

When Christ Returns

It seems like an eternity has passed since the hunger days: the years before the end of the war. Even worse were the ones immediately thereafter. My last food ration card from the Nazis ("For Children") for the period from May 20–31, 1945, was as follows:

> Ration:
> Meat 20 gr., fats 20 gr.,
> Peas, beans, pearl barley etc. 20 gr.,
> Sugar 25 gr., potatoes 500 gr.
>
> Monthly Ration:
> Salt 400 gr., coffee substitute, 100 gr.

That was it! But it really wasn't, since many of these items simply weren't available in any quantities. For weeks, we didn't have any fat or anything containing fat and, of course, no butter. The first butter after the war, 50 grams per person, was only available in August 1945. Water, electricity, and gas were restored after May 17. Since a number of people were living in our house, we got several pieces of butter. They lay like bars of gold on the kitchen table. We looked at them as if it were a miracle of world proportions. For Christmas of 1945 there was an allocation of pork and 100 gr. of flour plus a half pound of sugar. My brother Jochen had become skin and bones. Father called him "the scrawny ghost." We owed our very survival to church members, friends, Christians, and later, to American Christians who sent packages. I am still astonished how mother was able to feed us all. Everything was parceled out equally, but yet we avoided envy and fighting. Still, the hunger pangs were so great that we often engaged in stealing, and one day I was caught when I stole a slice of bread.

Our house at Eigenheimweg 3 belonged to the Leipzig Mission, and it was a stopping point for many transient mission personnel, from Mission Director Ihmels on down to ordinary workers. They were all fed here. Years later, as a young pastor, I went to a ministers' conference in Karl-Marx-Stadt. The speaker, a professor whose name I have forgotten, talked to me before the meeting began and told me that once, during the hunger times, he was in Dresden, where he had visited our home and ate a meal with us. That said, he then gave a theological lecture regarding the New Testament accounts about the miracle of the multiplication of the loaves. He maintained that this was not a miracle, since miracles don't happen. Yet this poor man had told me about a miracle that had occurred at our table. As he ate from our pot of food, which really didn't have very much in it, his hunger was satisfied—he had become full. The *Herr Professor* had learned nothing that day.

For me it is a miracle that we did survive the hunger years. Many of our friends had things to exchange for food—material possessions or their own labor. But a pastor like my father wasn't able to do this. Who would exchange a sausage for a sermon? But God sent people who helped us. It was exactly the way my father described it in his diary entry: "Before they call, I will hear them" (Isa 65:24). We even got help from Indian prisoners of war who were being held in a camp in Königsbrück, near Dresden. My father was often used as a translator because of his knowledge of Indian languages, and as a result he came into contact with some prisoners who were receiving assistance from the Red Cross. Whenever he took us there for a visit, we were treated to cookies, chocolate, and similar delights.

I enjoyed a particularly close relationship with two of them. They were honored guests at my tenth birthday party: Santanam, a handsome young man from Pallallatti, Ammayanayakanur (so he wrote in the diary), and the smaller, Sri Ramulu, who had pockmarked skin. I still have photos of them which I greatly cherish. There is a long story about Santanam. One day, a letter came from him that father read aloud to us children because he found his manner of expression so extraordinary. But mother was outraged by the letter, precisely because of this particular passage, and she didn't want us to hear what Santanam was saying. He said he had become acquainted with a German woman and that "we have born a child together."

I got to know this child after the war. His mother had asked if she could come for a visit. As she was talking with my father, I sat in the yard next to this handsome little fellow with beautiful dark-brown skin named Veit, and rolled a ball carefully back and forth with him. I visited him often through the years, and one time after I was married he looked me up. He became a scholar and learned Indian languages from my father. Following father's death, he gave a fascinating oration in his honor at an academic memorial ceremony at the University of Halle/Saale. But, sadly, he never found his way to the Christian faith. He told me that he simply could not accept the concept of the grace of God. Unfortunately, he couldn't come to terms with life either. After his marriage failed he took his own life. Although she did not live long enough to experience this sad end, my mother did write a novella about a tragic love story between an Indian prisoner and a well-educated young German woman.

In March 1946 we didn't have a single potato in the house. Then we received two *Zentner*, that is, around 220 pounds, of potatoes "out of the blue." They came from two unknown people. Father wrote in his diary, "God *can* help."

Along with the hunger was the cold. Winter temperatures prevailed from December to March, at times reaching minus 20 degrees Celsius. People froze to death in their beds. There was no coal and schools were closed. Our house was an ice palace. Normally we would heat only one room, the living room. It was very small as it was, but, in addition, father's secretary had to work at a table by the window. The office at the mission had been destroyed in the air raid. Everything took place in this room. Father wrote his doctoral thesis here. It is astonishing what people can achieve during times and situations that are anything but normal. Later I heard several theology professors talking about the hardships they had suffered in the hunger years. Then Gerhard Delling, the New Testament scholar at Halle, quite proudly declared: "But we *did* work."

MOSES' POTS OF MEAT

I had also worked, on a small farm. In 1944 while we were sledding I met a boy who not only pulled *his* sled up the hill but mine and those of others as well. What struck me, besides the strength this well-fed guy demonstrated, was the list of animals he told me they had at home—dogs, chickens, cats, geese, pigs, cows, and horses. That was too much. To dispel our doubts, he invited Jochen and me to visit Farmer Moses at Altleubnitz 35.

As I walked through the large barnyard gate, paradise opened before my eyes. It was not only the way he had described it, it was even more beautiful. A real farm! As I walked through the gate, I saw a gigantic chestnut tree on the right, and on the left a dog house. The courtyard, paved with cobblestones, led directly to the barn. On the left side were the horse stall, a work area, and servants' rooms. To the right was the house.

Several generations of animals and people were living on this farm. My friend Siegmar had a grandfather who was a picture-book *Opa*. Although he wore eyeglasses, he could not see very well. He always wore long, blue overalls and was constantly involved in some kind of project, even as he reached a ripe old age. His little room was in the left wing of the house where Hilma also resided. In one of her rooms she had various kinds of animals, rabbits, for example. She was one determined old lady who, with her loud voice, made her wishes known about the house. For a number of weeks I thought she was the mistress of the house, but then I learned that she was actually only the sister of Siegmar's father. He was a strong man with a deep voice and was the absolute authority there. Whenever I stood behind him on the horse-drawn wagon, I marveled at his bull neck and his broad head that was always covered by a sweaty cap. Equally demanding respect was his somewhat pudgy wife, who was gracious, resolute, and just. Last but not least was their daughter Christine, the same age as I, but a distant and unattainable creature. However, it was for her I felt the first tender feelings of admiration rising up in my little boy's heart.

At a later time I was permitted to enter the holy place, the "*gute Stube,*" normally off limits to us. It was a quiet room reserved for special occasions with friends and relatives. There I saw a picture on the wall of Siegmar's mother when she was young. She looked very much like her daughter, Christine, but not at all like the person I had met wearing her kitchen smock. This caused me to devise a plan: In the future when I am drawn to a young lady, as had happened here with Christine, I will take a close look at her mother. By so doing, I will be able to imagine how she will look as a grown woman. But later, in "real life," I did not act at all according to my original plan.

One entered the farmhouse through a cool, tiled hallway. Large milk cans stood along the walls and exuded a fabulous aroma of freshness. From here one entered into the kitchen, separated from the cow stall by a simple, wooden door. The wall behind the stove was dark black, not from soot, but rather from the thousands of flies that floated back and forth. That's simply the way it was. It didn't bother me, and the food always tasted great.

We ate at the table in the kitchen. The living room next to it was reserved for the family. Only the chief farm hand, Kurt Eichhorn, and the maid were allowed to sit at that table. Lesser workers such as Jochen and I sat with the others at the kitchen table. I had my place next to Walter Beger, called "Waldi." He was in charge of the cow stall. He never washed before he came to eat. His finger nails were black and his big "paws" were covered with mud and cow manure. Mucous was always dripping from his nose and saliva drooled from his mouth into his beard. He was a hygienic catastrophe. I wonder even today how I—with my aesthetic standards—not only put up with sitting next to this reeking cow-stall boss but also downed my food with gusto at his side. Nevertheless we loved "Waldi" and respected him.

Of course, people said he wasn't mentally all there; yet, on the other hand, it was said that the farmer, Father Moses, copied from him when they were school children together. Thus, he must have had something "upstairs." Be that as it may, "Waldi" poked around in the linseed oil provided for the hot potatoes with a knife worn down from long use. This dripping oil mixed with the other "stuff" in his beard as he delivered comments on matters of the moment in his crow-like voice. For us pastors' kids, hungry and emaciated, these meal times were probably what saved us. In any event they helped us get over this hunger period.

For supper one evening we each received an egg. I had never seen such a thing in my entire ten years of life. I somehow cracked it open and began eating it with my spoon until the boss, Siegmar's father, came past the kitchen table and suggested that I try some salt on it. "That would really make it taste good," he said. And so, I had gone another step forward in my gastronomical education.

SHEAVES OF GRAIN ARE BETTER THAN STARVING

Under normal circumstances, we earned our food through hard work. Of course, there were times when we only fooled around, but these were the exception rather than the rule. For the most part we were an integral part of the day's work schedule. There were certainly things we preferred to avoid, but there also were things we loved to do. One unpleasant task was sweeping the farm yard on Saturdays. We used a birch broom to remove the straw, chicken droppings, and clover leaves lying around. The boss always examined the result of our work. This ritual always gave me a feeling of cleanliness and completion of a week of work.

Behind the house, between the kitchen and the large market garden with its rows of beets and fruit trees, stood a long wooden bench beside the wall where metal ladles were hanging. Here the farmhands washed up. They stood with their legs apart and rinsed the dust and sweat from their bare, muscular chests. This sight not only stirred me, but also I noticed that the young servant girl, who normally worked inside the kitchen, conveniently seemed to have a number of things to do outside then.

I experienced the tilling of the soil in the spring, the harvest in the summer, the threshing of the grain in the winter, the birth of a calf, and the slaughter of a pig. This latter was actually illegal at the time and it had to be carried out in the winter. I was given the honor of going with Siegmar's father to take the pig to the butcher in Goppeln, about two miles away. After we were done, we celebrated it with a glass of schnaps. The butcher looked at me, "What will we give him?" Father Moses replied, "Give 'im one, too." That was my first glass of schnaps.

The high point of our strenuous activity was the grain harvest. For this purpose, a whole squadron of women from the village was mobilized, as well as every other available hand, including us children. What I enjoyed most were the times when I could sit on the reaper. I was allowed to pull a certain lever, an action that was always accompanied by a lot of noise and a breathtaking dust cloud that stretched from one end of the field to the other, and the stalks of grain fell to the ground. We then gathered up the sheaves and bundled them in stacks. This task was done in a rhythm by people working in pairs. We labored for hours during the heat of an August afternoon until we could no longer move our weary, insect-bitten arms. This was for us little guys a real achievement.

Our reward for this slave-like labor wasn't just the evening meal of bread smeared with a coating of animal fat (heavenly!) but also the thanksgiving festival that followed. Everything moved feverishly toward this harvest festival. The horses were all nicely brushed and combed and a little bouquet hung on their necks. It was, of course, an honor to be allowed to ride in the wagon in the harvest parade. On the wooden stage erected on the village soccer field a couple of sweating men wearing white shirts and black vests played for the dancers. The brass band was kept fired up by generous libations of freshly tapped beer. During an intermission, my school classmate, Richter, grabbed the microphone and sang a capella a popular song: "When in Capri the Red Sun Sinks in the Sea", which resounded loudly over the entire area. He was the hero of the moment and, from then on, the heart throb of the girls. Now I not only knew what brass music was but also what it took to become a star: simply shout into a microphone at the right time.

A SHORT WORD ABOUT KURT

The aforementioned head farmhand, Kurt Eichhorn, was the confidante of the boss. A big, heavy, strong man, only he could work with the team of draft horses, Fritz and Migge. Fritz was really dangerous because of his tendency to bite and to throw his weight around. We children were permitted to ride only with the team of Hans and Lotte. We were as afraid of Kurt Eichhorn as we were of Fritz, although neither one of them ever touched us. But Eichhorn didn't want to have anything to do with us kids. We avoided him whenever we could.

But, one day, I of all people had to go out to the field to help him. During a break, as we were waiting for the next team of horses, we were seated on one of the large handcarts that were used for the hay and grain harvest. We sat on the cart and simply dangled our legs over the side. He didn't consider it worth his while to talk to me. Suddenly he discovered a four-leaf clover on the field in front of him. He told me to get down from the cart and get it for him. I brought it to him. He took his cap off, stuck the clover behind the cord on the cap and said to me, "Look here, Theodor, a person has to have luck."

It only lasted ten minutes. A policeman appeared in the field and arrested Eichhorn. I had to wait alone until the next horse-drawn wagon came. I told the boss what had happened and hurried into the village because I was supposed to pick up my watch from the clockmaker that afternoon. The shop was by the final stop on the street car line opposite the Edelweiss restaurant.

I still remember, as I was standing there with the watch in my hand, that I saw both Eichhorn and the policeman coming. They walked next to one another as if they were two friends. In the meantime they had been to Eichhorn's apartment. His wife and daughter were not there, however, and he was unable to say goodbye to them. He had put on his good Sunday jacket, dark blue and made of strong material. When he wore this jacket he looked like a sailor in a festive mood. I saw both of them board the trolley and go away. I was the last person to see Kurt Eichhorn. To this day, no one, not even his family, has learned what became of him and why they arrested him. He had simply disappeared into thin air. This would be a regular occurrence in the post-war period as well.

FOR ONE SEMESTER A HORSE TESTER

Most of all, I loved to be around horses. The high point came when I was allowed to ride along on the coach. I was excited when I sat in the coach bench next to the boss and he gave me the reins. After a while he said to me in his bass voice, "Thedor" (this is the way he always pronounced and spelled my name), "Thedor will someday be a good coach driver." That was the highest praise I could imagine.

I felt it was a special honor when, one day, I was sent to take the horse Hans by myself to the village blacksmith because he needed new shoes. In contrast to me, the blacksmith might have felt it was a bit much for the boss to send a little squirt like me. It isn't an easy thing to hold the bent foot of a horse—that is, while he is standing on only three legs and the smith comes holding the glowing iron shoe in the tongs. He presses it onto the foot so that it sends up smoke and the burned hoof gives off a pungent odor. Then it really takes all the strength one can muster to hold the foot tightly while the smith pounds the nails in with his heavy hammer. When I left the blacksmith's shop with "Hansi" and marched through the village, I swelled with pride and felt I was now a man. And it was also a sign of confidence on the part of the others to let a little guy like myself do this job or even to let me take the reins of the team of horses pulling a wagon.

That was especially the case in the fall when I was given the task of hauling away the manure. First, I had to drive the horse down the sloping way out of the courtyard to the street with the brake pulled tight. Then I quickly released the brake and went through the narrow pathway, driving the horses with the awful load of the heavy, black, steamy manure, all the while holding tightly onto the reins. I was happy and proud every time that I did this and then reached the top of the hill when I could relax the reins.

Besides my job as a wagon driver, one day I got to be a life-saver. A really young duckling fell through a gap in the wooden beams which covered the liquid manure pit and circled around anxiously quacking in the depths of the pit. Heroically, I lowered myself into this stinking Hades and fished the once-yellow bundle of fluff out of this smelly liquid. As a reward for saving this duck's life and bringing it back up into the light of day again, Siegmar's mother gave me three eggs. I proudly laid them on our family kitchen table that evening. In 1944 three eggs was a sensation!

It was also a sensation when Siegmar came to my birthday party. His present was a four pound loaf of bread and a jar of black sugar-beet juice. No one today can possibly imagine what good fortune this signified! Of course, I shared this with the entire family. But, for once, to be able to eat until I was full—and I mean absolutely full—that was heaven on earth.

Typically, the conclusion of my activities on the farm was associated with something edible. In the fall I looked after cows. Beyond the school, the village ended. That is where *our* fields and meadows began. A tiny brook made its way through a valley—to the right were the *Schrebergärten*, the individual family-owned garden plots, to the left, the meadows, on which the young people went sledding in the winter. The brook originated in the *Heiligen Born* (the Holy Spring), from which the meadow took its name. From the little hut that covered the spring one could hear the incessant sound of the bubbling water.

On Easter morning many villagers drew water from the spring and called it "Easter water." One day I was tending my herd at the *Heiligen Born*, but unfortunately I neglected to watch my packet of breakfast bread. Something happened that I needed to tend to. I got up from my seat. Suddenly, that wretched bovine, Lola, gobbled up my slices of bread smeared with vegetable fat. Those were the last ones that were made up for me as it was my last day on the job.

Fall had now arrived and it was brisk and cool. The cows were frisky and I was only a boy in the confirmation class—it was easy to sense that an era was coming to an end. In spite of all of the hunger we experienced, it was a wonderful time. Even today, I only need to step inside a cow stall or enter a farmstead and the odors remind me of that time of my young life. This mixture of smells of hay, cow manure, leather goods, and grain dust is incomparable—it was my childhood.

GOD'S CHURCH STANDS FIRM

What decisively stamped my life as a child was my relationship to God. Two weeks after I was born I received the sacrament of baptism in the Church of the Resurrection in Dresden-Plauen. That was the crucial date as it marked the foundation of my faith. God's grace was bestowed on me at the very beginning. God declared me to be his child and adopted me into his family. This is something that cannot be surpassed, repeated, or explained. That is grace! After that came Christian upbringing and instruction in the faith. As a child I memorized the Ten Commandments, the Lord's Prayer, the creed, and the 23rd Psalm. When we learned these portions of the catechism, we recited them at the dining room table as Father listened. All of this took place in the good old Lutheran tradition in our own home, in our "house church," so to speak.

But, the church as the House of God for me was the venerable fifteenth century village church of Leubnitz. I regarded it as the most beautiful church in the world. With its white benches and golden Flemish chandeliers, it made a splendid impression. In front, attached vertically to the inside walls, were several ancient gravestones. On many of them one could see knights in armor chiseled in the rock, kneeling, praying. At the front was the altar. At the sides of and above the altar hovered angels with long golden trumpets. At the highest point in the church was the eye of God whose rays of light shone from a gilded wreath. This sight became deeply embedded in my child's soul. It left its mark on me.

Our pastor was an elderly, short, pudgy man. When he stood above the congregation in the pulpit it was always as if he were a gigantic blackbird in a tree. All of my childish interest was devoted to his prominent double chin. The two strips of white cloth of his Geneva collar hanging beneath it bobbed up and down while he was preaching. I don't remember anything about his sermons, but there was one sentence which I have never forgotten. I can still see the awe-inspiring figure of this man of God before my eyes. Indeed, I can almost hear him now as he proclaimed with his marvelous voice and rhetorical flourish, kindly, insistently, consolingly, "The mountains may depart and the hills be removed; but my steadfast love [In my German Bible translation the word appears as 'grace'] shall not depart from you, and my covenant of peace shall not be removed, says the LORD, who has compassion on you" (Isa 54:10).

It is strange that one particular text among all of the hundreds of other Bible verses and sermons I had heard should impress itself so upon the soul of this young boy. Now I am an old preacher, even if not a pudgy one, but when I look back, I can say with a thankful heart I have lived my entire life under and by God's grace. The first time I heard this text was from that aged pastor during the difficult times of the Second World War when our houses shook and crumbled in the horrific nights of bombing. Then the Nazi Reich fell apart. Later on came the GDR. Finally, the Berlin Wall fell. In everything one certainty remained: the promise of God's grace.

There have been countless times, at least once every Sunday during the worship service, when I have received anew the promise of God's grace. I was encouraged by the assurance of forgiveness that followed the confession, at the Lord's Supper, and during the benediction at the conclusion of the service. It didn't make any difference what was happening in the world at large or in my own life—in the highs and the lows—the promise of God stood firm, unchangeable, "My grace shall not depart from you."

It remains God's secret why this one text so rooted itself in my being. Thousands of other texts went right by me as I sat, bored, in the pew and did what generations of bored children before and after me have done: play with the clothing hook attached to the back of the pew in front of me. By the way, moving this back and forth hundreds of times produced a quiet squeaking sound. Sometimes my playing around was interrupted when my mother, sitting next to me, gave me a dirty look or smacked my fingers.

As much as I loved my mother, I didn't like to sit next to her in church. Often I was ashamed as I sat there. I cringed inside from embarrassment due to her poor singing ability. She was a passionate singer, but in church she simply found it difficult to find the right notes. The louder she sang, the worse it got. What she was singing was clearly something different from what the others were singing. And, what made it worse, she was so loud. I simply had not understood that she was singing the alto line. And she could only do this in church where she had other singers around her. I can still hear her today as she led the singing of her three young boys in her firm, jubilant voice:

"I will go with the shepherds
to behold the Saviour."

Or:

"I stand at your manger here,
O, Jesu, Thou, my life."

There was a time when I played the accordion, accompanied by my mother on the piano, and we both bellowed out the old *Reichslieder*, the *Songs of the Kingdom*:

"Wonderful, wonderful it will be,
when we enter Zion's halls."

Once I sat with father in the Leubnitz church. Shortly before the beginning of the worship service, someone handed him a slip of paper. As he read it, I sensed a certain tension. Something was in the air; something wasn't right. Not until later did I learn that the pastor or bishop was going to make an official pronouncement regarding the current political situation, or that the pastor was about to say something that might lead to his immediate arrest. In the note, father was asked to conclude the service if this were to happen. Years later, when I, too, reckoned with an arrest following a service, I was able to imagine what tension must have existed at that time in the Leubnitz church.

In 1948 I was confirmed by my father there. His sermon text was, "Follow me!" Interestingly, my confirmation verse happened to be the verse of the day on which I am writing these lines in the *Moravian Daily Texts*: "And whatsoever you do, in word or deed, do everything in the name of the Lord Jesus, giving thanks to God the Father through him"(Col 3:17).

I took my confirmation promise—my "yes" to Jesus and to my baptism—and my affirmation of faithfulness to His church, very seriously. Confirmation was, so to speak, my conversion experience. I can't really talk of a "normal" conversion where one can point to a specific date and hour. There was neither a nighttime spiritual crisis under an old oak tree nor did it occur under the thundering proclamation of a fiery evangelist.

When others told how bad they had been until Jesus came into their lives, I could only listen in silence. I had always been a "good" boy. I had a normal Christian birth but was a late starter. The parsonage was my home and there I experienced a very sober, powerful Lutheranism, the best soil in which to grow a pastor. I matured, step by step, into everything that had to do with the church. Most often, I realized only later that I had taken another step.

That is really my problem. Generally I notice somewhat later that God had pushed me in a certain direction, and after I had stumbled around for a while, then I realized: This is it. This is your path. Most of my sermons come about the same way. When I begin to preach, I don't know where it is leading, and when I am through, I am astonished where I landed up.

In the same way I could say that I ended up as a worker in the church. Yet, I have been at loggerheads with the church all of my life. I even thought about titling my autobiography *I Don't Belong in the Church*. As an institution I have constantly been at odds with her, even considered applying for a kind of heresy trial against myself because I deviated so widely from the theological pluralism that prevails in the church. The reason for enduring lifelong suffering at the hands of the church is the fact that I love her as my spiritual mother. Only one who loves the church can continue in spite of the pain she creates. Only he who suffers because of the church's failures really loves her.

> When Christ returns, then all will be well.
> No more wars; we'll only know peace.
>
> When Christ returns, then all will be beautiful.
> No more sorrow, only joy will abound.
>
> When Christ returns, then everything will be free.
> No more chains, only freedom with exist.
>
> When Christ returns, then all will be clear.
> No more riddles, we'll all understand.
>
> When Christ returns, then all will be new.
> No more graves, life alone will then rule.

4

Yet We Are Standing Again!

AFTER FATHER COMPLETED HIS doctoral degree in 1948, there came a veritable hailstorm of job offers, from director of a mission society to senior pastor at the prestigious St. Michael's Church in Hamburg. If the latter had happened, I would have grown up a *Wessi,* someone from West Germany. In this case I would have learned to speak pure *Hochdeutsch* (High German), and would not have endured lifelong derision as a speaker of the Saxon dialect.

Would have! All such speculations are, of course, pointless. What would have happened if—leave that to your imagination. The reality was that we moved in August 1950 to the city of Halle-on-the-Saale [River]. Father was appointed to the Theological Faculty of the Martin-Luther-University as professor of missiology and religious studies. From a/n churchly/ ecclesiastical standpoint, Halle lay in the territory of the *Union,* the church created in Prussia in 1817 that gave equal validity to both the Lutheran and Reformed confessions. For a strongly committed Lutheran, this was the greatest logical and theological abomination.

My father was probably the only theologian at Halle who occupied a chair that allowed him to adhere to strict Lutheran confessionalism. He was as much respected as misunderstood for his stand. He accepted the professorship only on the condition that he would not be required to join the Union Church, but could remain a member of the Saxon Lutheran Church. He wanted to show his absolute faithfulness to his church, and for him as a professor (the word professor means one who professes something) it was obvious that membership in a church depended on one's profession of faith and not on where the moving van happened to stop. It is no wonder that having a father with such a viewpoint, I as his faithful son likewise held fast to my profession of faith in Jesus. This meant that from the very outset of my school days in Halle I forfeited any possible sympathy from the school administration.

MISERY FROM FRAU PERKATZ

After the war when we still lived in Dresden, I attended the Holy Cross School. It was customary there that as members of the *Junge Gemeinde*, the Protestant youth organization, we attended classes wearing its insignia patch on our jackets, the cross on top of a globe. At the August-Hermann-Francke Oberschule (high school) in Halle, which I attended after our move, a different wind was blowing. Naïve as I was, hardly had I made my first appearance wearing my jacket with this arm patch attached, when Frau Perkatz, the school principal, summoned me to her office and demanded that I remove the patch. Whereupon, I decided to join the Free German Youth (*Freie Deutsche Jugend* or *FDJ*), the communist youth organization, and attached the *FDJ* patch right next to that of the *Junge Gemeinde*. This provocation resulted in another summons to the office and I told her: "If I have to remove the cross, then I will also remove the *FDJ* patch." It is clear that I found no love from the other side with such rebellious little games.

The line in the sand was clearly drawn from the first week on, but it was an unequal struggle. That was demonstrated two years later when I stood for my *Abitur*, the final or school-ending exams. Frau Perkatz sat at the end of the longer lever, since she was a member of the testing committee. On the same day an article appeared in the newspaper attacking my father, who had refused to sign some document, and thereby was exposed as being an "enemy of peace." I can imagine that Comrade Perkatz flashed this article before the other comrades on the committee and commented that I was one of the good-for-nothing children this professor had produced. Be that as it may, the day of reckoning had come. Frau Perkatz flunked me in Current Affairs. And that was all it took. With my usual 4 (a D grade) in math (I never did well in this area), I failed the *Abitur*.

Apart from this fiasco at the end, my two years in Halle were among the most pleasant of my memories. Seeing the cross on my jacket, my classmate, Klaus-Peter Mücke, recognized me as a member of the *Junge Gemeinde* and invited me to attend the worship service that opened the school year. A relatively small group met there in a side room of the Moritzkirche (Church of St. Maurice), a beautiful structure that I loved very much. I had now found some friends. At St. George's Church, where August Hermann Francke had once been the pastor and now was in a terribly run-down condition, an even smaller group met before class for morning prayers. Each of us took turns leading them.

Our favorite song, one we bellowed out every second time we met, was: "Jesus has come, foundation of eternal joy." Just before each devotional time, I met with my friend Mücke to ring the church bells. We tugged on the ropes as though we were sounding a fire alarm. We had a trick to prevent the after-ringing from the bells. We would grab the heavy clapper with our hands to prevent it from hitting the bell again. This church tower must have been inhabited by a brigade of guardian angels since not even once did our fingers get squashed by the swinging clapper.

NO OPERAS PERFORMED IN THIS UPPER HOUSE

I belonged to a distinct group in our school class that specialized in learning classical languages, and thereby we felt we were somewhat special. To bestow even stronger emphasis on this feeling, seven of us formed our own separate group which we named, rather arrogantly I would say, *Das Oberhaus*, the Upper House. (This was also a word play on the German term for opera house.) Mücke and I belonged to it. As an outward sign of our exclusivity, we had shirts made. They had a conspicuous blue-checkered pattern, along with epaulettes and gold buttons. One fine day we appeared in our new outfits in the school yard. The unauthorized formation of a group! Uniforms! Western-style no less!

The uneasy peace was once again in danger. The faculty members were glued to the windows as we proudly showed off in the courtyard. They sent the art teacher, Herr Bewersdorf, to our parents to put a stop to such goings on, which they regarded as influenced by the West. Especially impertinent was the way we wore these shirts outside the pants and this had to be stopped. When he came to speak with my father, the professor had just returned from playing tennis. He received the messenger from the faculty with shirt pulled out over his pants! That didn't make it any easier for Herr Bewersdorf to come to the point of his mission.

When one looks at the situation nowadays with regard to clothing worn at school, one sees the craziest garments, as well as the lack of them on some parts of the body. In today's perspective our little clothing demonstration seems rather tame. But in 1950 this act took on revolutionary proportions. Along with the usual impulse at this age to show off, to provoke, and to create a distinctive image of oneself, we were setting ourselves against the *FDJ* blue shirts and their efforts to "uniformize" the human spirit.

As would be expected, the *Oberhaus* members spent their free time together. Often we wasted time simply doing nothing or engaging in nonsense. Not every afternoon's conversations attained a high philosophical niveau. But at times we engaged in hot discussions about all sorts of problems. Sometimes we would spend hours in the game of reading quotations from Büchmann's *Collection of Quotations* and then trying to determine the author of each one read. I have never observed such use of free time to further one's own education by the youth of the current generation.

The basis for our free time activities was the bicycle. I didn't have one. I trekked to the *HO* department store [*Handelsorganisation,* the mercantile collective that existed in the GDR] weekly for several months where I made friends with a saleslady whom I asked to keep her eye open for a bicycle. It paid off, and through my persistence and outrageous bit of good luck, I was able to get myself a bike. No one who has sat in his newly purchased Porsche could have been happier than I was as I rode on my bike through the streets of Halle for the very first time! Gears? Unknown then. And in comparison with the sporty little jobs one can ride today, my bike was an old heap. Sometime later, the members of the *Oberhaus,* riding such antedeluvian clunkers, made it all the way to Italy. Part of the time we were on foot, pushing the bikes high up the Alps, and then we raced downhill all the way to Milan. From there we tramped on to Rome.

I also went on my bike to the biennial church congress that met in Berlin that year. Since Mücke was a distant relation of the Bishop of Berlin, Otto Dibelius, I had the opportunity one day to be invited to have lunch with him at the bishop's residence. Personalities like this man are rare today. Nowadays, many of them are stars who try to conceal the fact that they lack a genuine personality. They do this by wearing a particular hat or cap, generally turned around to the side or to the back of the head, and then they get up on the stage or appear on talk shows. On the other hand, Dibelius even at the dining room table was a towering figure, who in spite of his small stature radiated authority and commanded respect. He embodied, however, a past era, just as the entire church congress of that time was totally different from those of today.

The church assemblies were not dominated by the godless God-is-dead theologians like Frau Dorothea Soelle or by representatives of non-Christian religions such as the always-grinning Buddhist Dalai Lama. Then, biblical lectures were given by God-fearing men who opened up the Holy Scriptures for us and enabled life-changing consequences. In spite of my previous rejection of theology my mind was now made up: "I will study theology." I don't even remember which lecture it was or under whose preaching I made this decision. I know only that it was the day on which I rode the 110 miles from Berlin to Halle I decided I wanted to join the "guild of black gowns."

Since we had to declare our future course of study before the *Abitur* exam, I gave mine as theology. This was the beginning of a string of unpleasant events. Three of us in my class chose to study theology: Mücke, Hans-Jürgen Biewend, and I. Mücke, nicknamed "Schmirijak" (the clever one), as usual, made it over all the hurdles and passed the *Abitur*. Hans-Jürgen and I flunked. Indeed, we were the only ones in our class who did. Frau Perkatz made sure of that. I stumbled on a question about the Oder-Neisse border between Poland and the GDR in the Current Events test. It was easy at that time to set up roadblocks for students by the proper choice of topics.

So, I had to stand on the sidelines and watch my classmates who had passed the *Abitur* carry on an old tradition: They were carried on the shoulders of the students in the eleventh grade through the grounds of the historic Francke Foundation to the nineteenth century statue of August Hermann Francke that portrayed him placing his hand on the orphan children and blessing them. Here, the teacher of the class gave a farewell speech that signified the conclusion of our years in school.

I rode my bicycle home and that afternoon a crisis discussion took place to which Hans-Jürgen's mother also came. It was decided that the two of us black sheep should make our way into the future through the Leipzig Mission seminary. A young man could study theology there without having passed the *Abitur,* and then be taken on as a pastor by the Saxon Regional Lutheran Church. We went together to Leipzig to the society's traditional house on Paul-List Street to enroll. But Biewends then decided to go to West Berlin, where he was able to successfully pass the *Abitur* and later become a pastor. I packed up my belongings and began my further education at the Mission House. We were allowed to call ourselves *Studenten*, the same word used by those classmates who had graduated and went on to the universities.

THE SORROWS OF THE YOUNG LEHMANN

As mentioned earlier, my father was educated at the Leipzig Mission seminary, went out to India, and after his return became a member of the mission staff. His picture was among hundreds of photographs of Leipzig missionaries that hung in the dining hall. It wasn't easy to distinguish myself in this type of situation and avoid being seen as the exact image of my famous father.

1952

Getting used to my new life at the Mission House was not at all easy. We had a four-man room for "living and learning" in the daytime and spent our nights in an ice-cold 20-man open dormitory room. Each of us took our turn during the so-called "fire week," when we had to transport the *Nasspresssteine* [compacted lignite coal-dust briquettes that were the customary heating fuel in the GDR] into the various rooms needing them and start the fires in each classroom. This had to be done long enough in advance each morning to insure they were warm by the time classes began. The food was rather Spartan and repetitious, with certain dishes, such as a kind of potato mush containing pieces of blood sausage, that we especially dreaded. We were hungry most of the time.

Added to this was the pain I suffered from the loss of my first love. It was puppy love in high school. Susanne, a Jewish girl, was one year behind me. In 1953 there were show trials against Jews in Moscow and most of the few Jews who still lived in East Germany fled to the West. The Kleinmann family was among them, and one night they suddenly left their home and belongings. I came upon a handcart filled with 78 RPM records, a treasure trove of classical music that I "liberated" under the cover of darkness. With them remained the memory of the first stirrings of love that in its tenderness and innocence probably is one of the most beautiful things a person can experience.

During evening prayers I often sat tired, hungry, and remorseful in the cold chapel staring at the altar painting in front, just as my parents had done before me. It depicted an Indian and African worshiping Jesus together as representatives of the two areas where the Leipzig Mission had sent missionaries. Although I have been consistently opposed to organized times of prayer and devotions, I must admit that during the winter months of November and December, I was especially attracted to them. Above all, the difficult, but hope-giving Advent songs made a deep impression on me. The one I loved most of all was the incomparable song written by Jochen Klepper, who himself had married a Jewish woman and later committed suicide.

> "The night is far spent,
> The day will soon dawn.
> Let us sing praise
> to the bright Morning Star.
> Even he who has wept in the night,
> Let him, too, join in the throng.
> The Morning Star shines
> on *your* fear and pain, too."

Since I already was qualified in large segments of the curriculum (Latin, Greek, German, and history), I simply tuned out during class and read other things. I had decided to get to know as much about world literature as I could. I consumed one novel after another, holding them on my knees underneath the desk. And then I met Elke, my wife-to-be. So it was that the path to the Mission House which, at first seemed like a detour, turned out to be God's way for me. At the end, after two years, I found that the malice of my enemies had turned out for me as good. This would happen over and over during the course of my life.

A GOATEE AND GLASSES ARE NOT THE WILL OF THE PEOPLE

An event that occurred during my time at the mission seminary deserves special mention. It was on the day of June 17, 1953. During a Latin class where a well-meaning lecturer tortured us with Cicero, I idly gazed out the window beside my desk. I saw a procession of protesting construction workers in their white work uniforms moving along the "Street of October 18" into the center of town. I thought to myself: I don't believe what I am seeing. Here I am struggling with Latin vocabulary words, and those people on the street are making history by risking their necks.

"Not without me!" I jumped up, ran out of the classroom, and joined in the demonstration. For hours we shouted, "We demand free elections and an end to this regime!" In the evening I was so hoarse that I could hardly talk. I crowded into the court house next to the building housing the university's Theological Faculty. Papers, typewriters, documents came flying out the windows. The *Volkspolizisten* (People's Police, the official East German name for the police force) stood, legs apart, in the corridor without hindering what was going on. As I exited the building the situation dramatically changed. Soviet tanks rolled up and shots were fired. We ran. One of my fellow students was hit in the leg. For the first time in my life I saw a person's blood shooting forth out of a wound in his body. Later, the authorities used cars at the Leuschnerplatz, less than a half-mile from the seminary, as they literally hunted down individuals they found on the street.

We quickly returned to our quarters and during the evening listened to the RIAS (Radio in the American Sector, a station in West Berlin) reports as the storm clouds began to gather. It didn't please the Russian soldier standing guard at the street crossing in front of my room that the light was still on. We put it out and saw that a Russian tank had positioned itself crosswise in the intersection.

The next day, the leaders of the Mission House didn't know what to do with me because of my hasty departure from class, and so they sent me home to my father in Halle, although neither of us knew what that would accomplish. Moreover, my father was extremely tense on the day after June 17. As the dean of the Theological Faculty at the University of Halle, he was supposed to give an address to the university senate expressing submissiveness to the government. Instead, he delivered a speech of protest. He also inserted a passage in the official university statement about the workers' uprising that was critical of the ruling communist party [officially known as the *Sozialistische Einheitspartei Deutschlands—SED* or Socialist Unity Party] and only then did he sign it. At home, both my brother and mother reproached him for even signing the document and he thereupon withdrew his signature.

This case was probably unique in the history of the German Democratic Republic, the GDR. All professors, even those who did not belong to the communist party, had formally declared their obeisance to

Walter Ulbricht, the *SED* party secretary and de facto ruler of the GDR. Only one signature was missing, and that was my father's. Of this, I am exceedingly proud, and I have preserved the newspaper article with the missing signature as a real treasure. When Bishop Johannes Jänicke in Magdeburg, who presided over the church in our region, discovered that the Lehmann signature was not there, he was so enthusiastic that he came to our place to thank him personally. Jänicke was one of those unique individuals whose bearing was truly that of a bishop. He was a great preacher and pastor and, above all, a man who never got involved with the state in an untoward manner. Such people are rare today.

I have my father's persistence to thank for the fact that two years after my failed *Abitur* I was indeed able to pass this exam. Using the legal argument "redress of a past injustice," he never relented in challenging the low grade that Frau Perkatz had given me in Current Events. Among other things, he called attention to the notes which I had made for answering the question on the "Oder-Neisse boundary," and pointed out that it was no small amount that I had said regarding the topic. Above all, he was aided by the fact that she was no longer at the school. An outraged father had demonstrated Frau Perkatz' incompetence by presenting her evaluation of his daughter's essay, where she had egregiously confused Schiller with Goethe. She was dismissed as a German teacher.

1954

As a result I was summoned one day to the Francke Schule, placed in a room, and told I was to take the entire *Abitur* again, including *all* subjects. I refused to do so and went back home, since it was only the subject of Current Affairs that was in question. Finally, I had to appear at the Ministry of Education in East Berlin, where I retook only the exam on Current Affairs before a special committee. Then I was able to send a telegram home to my parents: "Passed."

Yet We Are Standing Again!

THEO IN THEOLOGY

Having done so, I switched immediately from the mission seminary to the Theological Faculty at the Karl Marx University in Leipzig (as the East German authorities had renamed this venerable institution). Now I was off to a serious start in theology. Since I already had Latin, Greek, and Hebrew under my belt, I had time to really get into theology, while my colleagues were cramming to learn vocabulary. The only thing that I did in common with my first-year group was church history and sports. Otherwise, from the outset I attended higher level seminars, read a great deal of theological literature, and was able to delve into other areas, including psychology and church (canon) law.

Among my theology teachers in Leipzig were Professors Albrecht Alt, Hans Bartdke, Franz Lau, Albrecht Oepke, and a man I especially revered, Professor Ernst Sommerlath. I had known Professor Oepke since my childhood, as he was connected to the Leipzig Mission and was often a guest in my parents' home in Dresden. This man, small of stature but renowned as a scholar, stood up politely every time my mother addressed him. This act of respect for the wife of a pastor and missionary deeply impressed me. Even though as a child I had little idea of the greatness of this man, I felt his gesture of esteem towards a woman—towards my mother—was something very special. And that's exactly what it was, for I never experienced anything like it again.

Sommerlath, who also was connected with the Leipzig Mission, taught systematic theology, that is, dogmatics and ethics, my favorite areas of study. A man whose whole life was obviously infused with Lutheranism, he was a special role model for me. He was always dressed in black, and his white hair and glistening gold-rimmed glasses made him an awesome sight, like someone from another world. He was a good-looking man, and his niece, Sylvia, inherited his good looks. I admired her when I was a student. Later on, through a marriage she became the Queen of Sweden. From that point on, in all his letters my father addressed him as "Your Royal Highness." When this aging scholar spoke on the topic "Death and Dying" there was breathless stillness in the lecture hall. And when he sang the Lutheran liturgy for the Lord's Supper at the University Church, it was the greatest moment of combined musical beauty, devout worship, and priestly service that I have ever experienced.

In this church, a medieval structure which had withstood the ravages of war but which, in 1968, the GDR regime ordered torn down in an act of unsurpassed barbarism, I got to know some of my professors as preachers. Here, too, I stood in the same pulpit and gave my first sermon when I was enrolled in a "practical seminar." I don't know if I can describe the feelings that came over me as I slipped into a clerical gown for the first time representing a church that I would so often criticize later on.

At once, I felt myself as a part of that traditional lineup of preachers of the faith. I became aware of being set apart as a preacher of God, and that is the reason for such clerical attire—one is no longer Herr Lehmann, but rather the servant of God, commissioned by him. Then all of those taking part in the worship service recited the prayers of preparation and repentance. These things intensified even more the feeling that I was now truly in God's service. This was stronger than the normal excitement experienced when one preaches his or her first sermon. It produced in me a feeling of holiness unlike anything I have ever felt again. Holy means something more than being different from others; it is belonging to God. To serve him as a preacher had been the goal of my studies.

With my brothers

Outside of the official curriculum, I dedicated myself intensively to the study of Lutheran theology in a group that my father had established, the "*Lutherisches Einigungswerk.*" The title of the organization indicated its purpose of bringing together a variety of Lutheran theologians into a working association, "so that we may be one." In this small group consisting of students from each level of theological study, we dealt with secular world literature for a semester, followed by a semester of literature involving Lutheran studies. During this time we either read the Latin writings of Luther or the Lutheran confessions. So it was, starting with the time spent in my parents' house, I was strongly influenced to become a Lutheran theologian. Above all, the writings of Werner Elert and Hermann Sasse made a great impact on me and accompanied me along this path.

Even more influential was the theologian Helmut Thielicke. I read all of his volumes on ethics and knew them backwards and forwards. First among these were his books of sermons. He was my example, my idol. I wanted to be just like him. Once I read that he had stated that one should preach not only for those who are there, but also for those who were not yet there. This comment would later determine the way I preached. But I still had a long way until I was ready to climb up into a pulpit. First on the agenda was to finish my studies at the university and then take the First Theological Examination. I crammed a great deal for it. So it was not without a great deal of satisfaction that I learned that I had passed with a one, the highest grade.

This was not to have been expected, given my miserable grades in secondary school, but I can explain it this way: After struggling with subjects for which I had little inner motivation, such as chemistry and mathematics, I had now landed in my area of special interest, theology. Hence I was much more motivated and, accordingly able to produce real results. On the day after I took the exam, I gathered all my belongings and moved back to Halle to begin advanced studies.

There the next shock awaited me. I had applied for and expected to receive a position as an academic assistant at the University of Halle, something normally accorded to promising doctoral students. However, I was passed over without being given any reason, and as a result I was unemployed and out on the street. At the same time, however, only a few days after the exam, I had gotten married. The formal wedding ceremony was in the church. Then at the reception in the evening, a Dixieland band played for the dance and this had a special reason for me.

> They laid into me until I lost my support,
> and yet I am standing again.
> I've been shot down, thrown into the street,
> And yet I am standing again.
>
> After Death and Darkness, the victor was the Light.
> Whoever believes in the Risen One doesn't know fear.

Blues Music and Gospel Proclamation

What depresses us is our own bitterness,
And yet we are standing again.
The anxiety in this great time drives us insane.
And yet we are standing again.

We plead with the fallen and the silent ones:
Come along, stand up again!
Don't give up! We still need you here!
Come along, rise up again!

They crucify us. It goes downhill from there.
And yet we rise up again.
They lay us finally as dead in a grave.
And yet we rise up again!

5

Blues & Trouble

THE ZÖFFEL FAMILY IN Dresden lived in what one could call a "modern household." The house, a box-shaped structure with a flat roof built in the *Bauhaus* style, had the latest style furnishings in the kitchen and living areas. In the smoking room, surrounded by huge, leather easy chairs, stood a cabinet, or better yet, a "shrine," which became for me a "cult object." I would sit in front of it and increasingly offer my "devotions." It was a Telefunken record player. By opening the two doors to the cabinet one could pull out the turntable which was ready to play. Beneath it were the 78 rpm records. Not only were there a lot of wonderful hit songs and schmaltzy stuff like *"Rumba Negra"* ("Black Rumba") and *"Roter Mohn, warum welkst du denn schon"* ("Red Poppy, Why Are you Wilting Already"), but also a number of swing recordings, and best of all, a few discs with Django Reinhardt, the renowned Gypsy guitarist.

I fell in love with this kind of music, and these would eventually be the first jazz records that I ever owned. Except when I visited the Zöffels' place, I could not get to hear this music since it was forbidden by the Nazis. After the war I had a good diet of dance music. I even went so far as to make music with a few friends from school. Theo Lindemann, and "Thea" Stelzer played the piano in our living room, and I served as the drummer. I banged on a bunch of lids from assorted pots which were suspended by means of strings around a broom handle lying between two chairs. All of us sang out lustily such pieces as *"Hein Mück aus Bremerhaven"* ("Hein Mück from Bremerhaven").

Kurt Henkels of Leipzig, who directed the leading dance band in the GDR, had a weekly afternoon radio show. When I happened to be at the Mockritz swimming pool near our home and heard the first bass sounds come over the PA system, I ran to the loudspeaker and basked in the sun and the Big Band Sound that wafted over the water surface. And whenever Henkels or Günter Hörig, leader of a noted Dresden jazz orchestra, had a concert nearby, naturally I was there.

SOUNDS LIKE SWING

The most significant quality jump in my pursuit of things jazz occurred in the summer of 1949. The Lehmann family threw the "Goebbels' harp," the Nazi radio set that was tuned to only one official station, into the trash and we obtained an honest to goodness radio. This little miracle box with its characteristic lighted tube that seemed like an eye exerted a magical influence on my life. On the dial were written such mysterious names as Monte Carlo, Zagreb, Luxemburg, and Beromünster. After the family had finally gone to bed, I spent the night glued to the front of the little box and father noted in his diary the next day, "The radio once again! Theo listens to music—until three in the morning!"

As I have said, I was already a fan of Hörig and Henkels, but my musical taste hadn't really solidified although I leaned in the direction of the pop music singer from Berlin, Bully Buhlan. But now I knew what I really liked. I listened to jazz and I was hooked. The main reason was a radio program I heard in which New Orleans and Chicago-style jazz, as well as ragtime and swing, were all explained in a precise German manner. I immediately grabbed a notebook, in a no less typically German manner, and copied down the information diligently, like a good nocturnal student, and collected it in my notebook. This little piece was the first actual jazz book in the Eastern Zone. True, I didn't write it, but I did assemble it.

But the decisive change that put me on the blues track took place one year later in Halle, once again through the medium of radio. Even if I can't recall any more the names of the various stations which nourished my enthusiasm for jazz, I do remember the one that got me into blues, the AFN (American [now Armed] Forces Network). During this period, as far as the cultural scene was concerned, we in the East saw the Russians solely as those who operated jamming transmitters, whereas the Americans did something for their own people and for the advancement of their culture through the medium of AFN.

This name alone was music to my ears, and even today, I can remember precisely the voice of the announcer. The music which followed was superior to anything I had heard until then, especially that played during what I called the "holy quarter hour" on Monday. On this day I raced home from school and stayed glued to the radio when Günter Boas' program, *Blues on Monday*, aired from 1:45 to 2:00. [Boas was a prominent German interpreter of blues.] With unbelievable astonishment and deep emotion I heard the blues for the very first time and, above all, the voice of Bessie Smith, the most popular female blues singer of the 1920s and 1930s. Since then, the blues has made its home in my soul.

As important as the radio programs were for me, they had a very great disadvantage. I couldn't retain what I had heard except in the form of my notes. As a result, my desire grew to have a means of preserving the sounds for myself. I needed records! When I had enough money to purchase five 78's, I took off for Mecca, that is, West Berlin. I had to smuggle the money in and change it into Deutschmarks (DM), the West German currency The "paradise" that I discovered there was called *Sound and Wave* and was located on the Schlossstrasse in Steglitz. When I went inside and looked at all the display cases full of recordings, I thought I would lose my mind. This gigantic selection left me virtually paralyzed.

Fortunately, I had Joachim Ernst Berendt's *Jazzbuch* (published in 1953) that contained a list of records that were available in Germany. By making use of this I decided on my purchases. They laid the foundation of what would be my lifelong passion for collecting records. The first 78 that I bought was—how could it have been any other?—the "St. Louis Blues," sung by Bessie Smith. Later on, when I placed it on the record player, I forbade anyone present from conversing or making comments and demanded absolute silence. It was my conviction: "This is something sacred."

I also experienced in West Berlin my next highpoint in the realm of jazz. Louis Armstrong gave a concert in the Titania-Palast Theater. The times when I rode my bike to Berlin were now past. This time I went by car. New Testament Professor Kurt Aland, whom the communists later incarcerated for three months in a detention center, took me along on a trip to a lecturing assignment. He allowed me to sit in the front seat of the car, and I hovered in midair as if in a dream as we moved closer to my idol. And the concert truly was a dream come true. I simply couldn't grasp that this man really lived and that there he stood, incarnate in front of me, with his trumpet and characteristic white handkerchief. I took in every sound he made and had just one thought—the concert must never end. I felt as if I were in the seventh heaven, but I was rudely brought back down to the bare earth when I was subjected to a police check on the train that I rode back to Halle. The police discovered a seam in my coat that was partially open. I had opened it up and hidden a newspaper clipping in the lining. It was a report on the concert with a picture of Louis Armstrong. I wanted to save this photo, but they confiscated it with the warning that this music by "n——s" was not really culture and was unworthy of a young German's attention.

CLUELESS RUDI

Fortunately, I did not have a similar experience when I returned home from West Berlin with the fragile treasures I had bought: my first recordings. When I had doubled the number of recordings and had about a dozen 78's, I began to go on lecture tours to do "missionary work" in the area of jazz and blues. I sought out likeminded music enthusiasts and others who collected records. Meanwhile, while I was a student of theology in Leipzig, I found them in the jazz club that gathered in the apartment of Reginald Rudorf on Schwägrichstrasse 15. Rudorf had been a member of the *SED* since 1948, had studied Marxism-Leninism, and now was a lecturer in social science at the Art Institute (*Kunsthochschule*) Burg Giebichenstein and the Music Academy (*Musikhochschule*) both in Halle/Saale.

Of course, the communist authorities viewed with the greatest skepticism Rudorf's efforts to make jazz socially acceptable. His balancing act between the state, that viewed jazz as a part of the decadent *Unkultur* in America, and his enthusiasm for the music ended when he was put in jail and was forced to live a very regimented life behind bars. When he was released, he knew he had to flee to the West. I told Rudi about developments in the jazz scene in both West and East. I spirited a few of the most important records, books and manuscripts from his apartment. Then came the time for his departure. The farewell took place in the Münzgasse, one of the shortest streets in Leipzig, where, besides a milk store, there were seven bars. In one of them, we stood at the bar and drank our last schnaps together. Rudorf had me tell him about the status of the church in the West. For example, he wanted to know about the role that Martin Niemoeller was playing. When I told him, he said, "We'll criticize him from the left." That was the last sentence that I remember coming out of his mouth.

Years later, I read it once again in a book he had written, *Never Again a "Left-winger."* Never in my life had I met a person (except those who converted to faith in God) who had made such a radical turn in his or her life as this man did. The fact that someone admitted to the leftist lies he had believed and then stood up against them deserved my highest respect.

Jazz had a conspiratorial quality. It was frowned upon and the one who dabbled in it was considered "decadent." This was no laughing matter; the person had everything to fear. Most of the club meetings ended with a musical request time and we played records. One time we listened to a blues tune by King Oliver who expressed in musical terms the pressure that rested on our souls, gagged as they were by the socialist Fast Food-Conformist culture. We stomped our feet to the blues songs as if we could, in this way, cast all our anxieties underfoot and somehow kill them off. Another person requested a swing number by Benny Goodman that caused our souls to hop like little birds in the morning sun. For three minutes we floated in the realm of freedom—five minutes away from the Leipzig detention prison in which Rudorf took up lodging shortly thereafter.

And then, one evening it happened. Somebody wanted a Negro spiritual. I had heard a lot about this music which was born as an outcry of slaves who, subjugated by men had been made free by God. Now I heard this music, considered to be the very foundation of jazz, for the very first time. It was to me just as it must have been for Jacob and the ladder leading to heaven. I feared the top of my skull would split open. I know precisely which song it was, "Go Tell It on the Mountain."

What that needle evoked from that scratchy record for three whole minutes was one of the most lasting musical impressions of my life. I heard a voice like none I had ever heard before. It came to me in the heavy, melancholic marching boots of the blues, but, at the same time, it had a radiating, majestic sound, a mixture of sadness and triumph which touched the inner core of my being like a ball of unmitigated holiness. The name of the singer was Mahalia Jackson. She and her music, the spiritual sister of the blues, became my passion from that moment on. But that is another matter. For now, I must continue with my account regarding the blues. I can't tell it to its conclusion because it has no end. As the last sentence in the epilogue of my *Bluesbuch 2001* reads: "The blues live, and I live with the blues. O Lord, how long?"

Blues Music and Gospel Proclamation

BLUE FROM THE BLUES

Many of the jazz evenings ended as drinking bouts winding through the Leipzig bar scene. They often ended at the state-owned Mitropa Restaurant at the main train station where we could get, even late in the evening, a huge steak covered with horseradish, in exchange for meat vouchers. So, late in the night, a sudden, irrepressible urge grabbed hold of us. We had to hear more blues, that is, a certain kind of blues. So we hopped into a taxi and went to the room of my student friend who had a tape player. We lay down on the floor, bellies filled with beer, and almost crawled inside the machine (we must not awaken the landlady with the sound of music). We listened intently and pounded out on the carpet the beat to King Oliver's "St. James Infirmary." That was the blues that we wanted to hear, that we *had to* hear. It was an inner drive and it functioned for us like liberation. Our souls craved for these blues, almost like the craving for one final beer, although, we as mere students at the time had no idea what real life and its horrors were all about.

Later, these blues played a very important role in my life under quite different circumstances. The university jazz band under the direction of Alfons Zschockelt played it in the Magdalene Chapel at the Moritzburg in Halle for our wedding. True, the theme of the music was not appropriate, but at that time, 1959, one didn't ask so much about the content. The main thing, it was the blues. And then forty years later, when my wife died, I stole into my room on the night of her death and, crying bitterly, listened to "St. James Infirmary"

Food ration stamps—1958

"Let her go, let her go,
God bless her."

Such was my life with the blues. "Blues and trouble seem to be my best friend." *Blues and Trouble*—that was the title of my first book on the blues that appeared in the GDR. It came out in 1966. I had spent many nights typing the manuscript on an ancient *Erika* portable typewriter.

THE STAGE IN BUNA

The idea for the book was connected with the legendary jazz concerts which took place annually in Buna, a short distance from Halle. I have no idea what the festival was called officially or even how it came into being. It had been set up somewhat surreptitiously by a clever jazz fanatic who persuaded the large socialist chemical firm there to sponsor it as a cultural event. Every year the day-long festival took place. It attracted all sorts of jazz musicians from all over the GDR, and they came without any remuneration. Money wasn't even a consideration at that time. The main thing was to meet other musicians and to make music or listen to it. We were all enthusiasts, crazies, enemies of the state; in other words, jazz fanatics.

The "Emcee" at the Buna Jazz Festival

The term "moderator" (master of ceremonies) was not yet in common usage. The person who led the program was called the "announcer." That's who I was. I always loved this job and I performed my duties with great zeal. The best part of it was that it was all improvisation on my part. Shortly before each band went on stage I scribbled down some information on its name, performers, and background, even as the previous one was performing. And then it was show time, as I went on stage with an antediluvian capacitor microphone like one sees in old photos from radio studios.

It was an indescribable, tingling feeling for me to be drawn into this scene of improvised music and to become a part of all that was taking place onstage. I made good use of the opportunity as the announcer to weave together up-to-date commentaries and "color" for each performance. It was a special treat for me to be able to announce a title like

"Mama Don't Allow Jazz Playing Here." Being in a Marxist country that rejected jazz, when I spoke of a Mama who doesn't want jazz to be played, the crowd responded with laughter and this set the right mood in the hall for them to be able to listen to the loud, rumbling Dixieland sounds.

The following experience that I had demonstrates just how relaxed the jazz scene was in those days. During one of the Buna performances I had to leave before the end of the concert since one of the groups paid no attention to the time and played far too long. During my last time at the mike, I noticed my friend, Wolfgang Muth, a jazz musician who also lectured on the topic, sitting in one of the first rows. I made furtive signs to him, motioning that he should come up on the stage. He finally understood what I meant. I told him I had to leave early and asked him to please fill in for me. I said, "Bye, Bye!" and Muth was on his own.

My reason for leaving was that I had to go to Dresden, the seat of the Saxon Regional Church Administration, which was my employer and source of my income. I had been scheduled to take the Second Theological Examination. Those preparing for the ministry take the First Examination, basically academically-oriented, at the university, and then the second one at the Administrative Office [the *LKA*]. It is even more academic in character. Only after passing the second exam is one recognized as a fully-qualified minister. This was a highly significant step in my career path to the pulpit. I had to be there on time.

After arriving in Dresden, I boarded a streetcar to reach my destination. And then it happened. I was quite aware that the "American Folk Blues Festival" (AFBF) was taking place here at this time, an absolute marvel, but I was conscientiously preparing for the examination and had to forbid myself from even thinking about it. However, knowing about something and then seeing it "live" are two different animals. And I just about lost it at the last minute. I stood in the trolley with my traveling bag and stared straight ahead. Then it stopped and, looking out of the window, I saw the sign AMERICAN FOLK BLUES FESTIVAL. Just as the current German Defense Minister Rudolf Scharping's eyes bulge out of their sockets and nearly touch the eyeglass lenses when he gazes at a model of his favorite airplane, so it was with me. My google-eyes nearly touched the streetcar's window pane as I stared at the sign.

And then, it started up again, the sign disappeared from view, and all hope went with it. I *had* to go to the *LKA* instead of the AFBF. I dutifully wrote my paper on a theological topic assigned to me and passed the oral examination of the Regional Church's Central Administrative Council. All the while my blues-soul was somewhere else, on a jazz concert trip. During the entire time, I knew that a mere kilometer away, as the crow flies, my "gods dressed in black" were performing, and I would have had the first opportunity of my life to experience real blues live. My blues-soul cried. One thing is absolutely clear: No one in the GDR had more reason to want to be at the AFBF, indeed, needed to be there, than I. And it is even clearer that no one, either in the audience or on the stage at the AFBF, had the blues as badly as I did that day. Why? Because, I *wasn't* there!

PLEASE HELP ME BLUES

It was during one of these blues concerts in Buna when I was inspired to write the *Bluesbuch*. The extraordinary, euphoric atmosphere of such a wonderful day provided the opportunity for me to discuss an idea which I normally would have dismissed as pure illusion if it had surfaced while I was sitting at my desk any ordinary day. But there, in this throng of fans, the impossible was discussed as something that was possible. For some time I had been pregnant with the concept of a *Bluesbuch*. I had already gathered material, formulated some ideas, and then during the intermission, stimulated by beer and bockwurst and the revelry of the moment, my determination to produce *Blues and Trouble* was firmed up. And that was to be my third book!

Eberhard Geiler, an employee of the firm Henschel Verlag, was in on the whole thing from the beginning. He would make the connections at his publishing house and I would gather the materials. I knew the dilemma we faced from writing my dissertation on the theology of Negro spirituals. Imagine this: I now lived behind the *Wall* recently erected in Berlin, hopelessly at the mercy of the postal censors, and in spite of this, I intended to get materials dealing with music which originated in the "capitalist world," from the despised America. Moreover, in the GDR this music was still considered to be "decadent." Such an undertaking on my part should have been doomed to failure from the outset, since there was a ban on the importation of books, magazines, recordings, and any devices able to reproduce sound.

Nevertheless, the fact that I was able to succeed borders on the miraculous. Without the "special permit" that my father as an academic possessed that enabled him to receive scholarly literature from abroad, it is quite unlikely that I would have ever attained my objective. I had to come up with a lot of tricks to get the materials I needed. I always felt I deserved my doctoral title because of the brilliant "criminal coup" I had pulled off in getting responses to research inquiries and obtaining the needed materials. The actual writing of the dissertation was "a piece of cake" in comparison to securing the source material.

I now faced the same problems with the *Bluesbuch*, but with the added difficulty that I was expected to obtain photos to illustrate the book. I sent begging letters to countless people, publishing firms, magazines, etc. The difficulty, especially with photos, was that I had no way to pay for them. Henschel Verlag, my publisher, was not about to get involved in such financial matters. According to the book contract, that was my responsibility. It was a real trick paying for things with a currency that wasn't worth anything. All of value that I could offer in return were books, records, printed music, and similar things produced in the GDR. But, who was knowledgeable about such things and, over and above that, who even wanted to obtain them? Few people were interested in my proposed project.

The reactions to my pleading letters spoke volumes. The larger the institution and the more well-known the person to whom I wrote was, the smaller the amount of help that was offered, although there were exceptions. For example, I approached the German "jazz pope," whose name was found in almost every book dealing with the topic, to write a foreword to the book. He was willing to do so and allow me to have pictures from his photo archive of blues musicians, provided that his name would appear on the title page along with mine. Apart from the fact that this simply wasn't justified—he wasn't even the photographer; the photos simply came from his archive—I would have no chance of getting the book published in the GDR if it had the name of a West German on it. But it was quite a different matter when I asked Dr. Martin Luther King, Jr., to write the foreword. He was also an idol of mine. His name carried weight in the GDR, and naturally I was proud that the *Bluesbuch* could get its start with a foreword from the hand of the leader of the American civil rights movement.

When I communicated to the "jazz pope" that I simply could not agree to his suggestion for the reasons above, he sent me a letter that began with the condescending phrase, "O well, Herr Lehmann." It was followed by flowery excuses but not even a single photo. Fortunately, I was able to find enough people who would help me. They didn't have big names and many of their little blues publications, some done by typewriter, were money losers. They were people who did not expect to earn money from them but simply wanted to promote the blues. Without these "enthusiasts" in England, America, the Netherlands, and elsewhere I wouldn't have been able to write the *Bluesbuch,* or at least not in the form it appeared. It was possible through the solidarity of so many who understood what it meant to take on such a project in a country which "you people like to call 'behind the Iron Curtain,'" as I formulated it in my pleas for help.

One of these helpful people was Pete Seeger, with whom I had come into contact through the American civil rights movement. I had invited him to come to the GDR, and the result was the famous concert of 1966 held at the Berliner Volksbühne, a historic theater in the center of the GDR's capital. I withdrew my name from the actual concert preparations after making the first contacts, as I did not want to endanger the venture through my personal involvement. I actually drove to Berlin with Fred Frohberg, a Halle resident and a leading pop singer and recording artist in the GDR. I found that the concert gave an enormous boost to the grass-roots interest in group singing. It was astonishing how Pete Seeger was able to animate the crowd to sing along by simply throwing out the two words: "Try it!" And so, it took an American folk singer to show us Germans that one can sing a German folk song without having to do so in the polished manner of the Silcher-Chor, a famous choral group that specialized in performing traditional music.

MONKEY BUSINESS BY A LOT OF NE'ER-DO-WELLS

The fact that this concert took place at all was, for me, as much a miracle as the fact that the *Stasi* [acronym for the Ministry of State Security, the feared East German secret police] did not block the publication of the *Bluesbuch.* In other matters it had acted differently. For example, *Radio DDR,* the state radio network, broadcasted a series of programs called "My Favorite Song." When I was asked in 1979 to do one of the segments, I agreed immediately. But at the same time I expressed my doubts about whether it actually would work out. I was told not to worry, as the program would be recorded with many of my favorite gospel and blues songs. On the day it was to be aired, I sat in rapt attention with the family in front of the radio. I had the weekly program magazine in my hands, where I noted that everything was correctly listed, even my name. But instead of blues, Hungarian folksongs were broadcast.

I learned after the reunification of Germany when I obtained my secret police file that Major Engelhardt from the Karl-Marx-Stadt District Administration for State Security had gotten wind of the intended program and sent a letter to the Council of Ministers of the GDR in East Berlin in which he requested Major General Kienberg "to investigate to what extent the Central Office Department XX [the Stasi agency responsible for religious matters] could prevent a radio program of L. from airing on *Radio DDR II*." Reason: "Lehmann is a pastor standing fully and completely behind the reactionary forces of the Lutheran Church in Saxony." In a further letter he was insistent, "I ask you to find a way to prevent this performance from taking place."

On March 13, Major General Kienberg declared, "As I have informed you by telephone, it was possible for us, with the aid of the State Secretariat for Church Affairs, to prevent the program by LEHMANN from airing. ... A one-time contract with honorarium was agreed upon since he is the one and only (!) expert in the area of 'African music' (!) in the GDR and he maintains a very substantial archive in this specialized area involving foreign cultural matters. This program was planned in connection with an African trip of the Secretary-General of the Central Committee of the *SED* and Chairman of the State Council, Comrade Dr. HONECKER. The stated fee will be paid by *Radio DDR* to Dr. LEHMANN with the explanation that the program could not be broadcast at this time due to programming changes."

There was a mix-up here of the two words "Africa" and "America," while the intention of Erich Honecker to travel to Africa was certainly unknown to me. In any event, a pastor, especially one who "was being closely watched by our local *Stasi* service unit under the detailed operational plan bearing the code name '*Spinne*' (Spider) in accordance with Paragraph 106 of the Civil Code of the GDR," was not allowed to have his say on the radio, even though it was merely about his favorite recordings. The infamous Paragraph 106 dealt with "provocation hostile to the state." It was the *Stasi's* task to prove this to be the case.

My last letter to *Radio DDR* about the cancellation, dated May 15, 1979, went as follows:

"It strikes me that:

1. in the program magazine only my name but not my profession was mentioned, as you usually do with others,
2. two months were needed to communicate to me a reason for the cancellation of the program,
3. the reason for the cancellation is the same reason that was used to get me to come on the program (as a specialist for blues and spirituals, I was supposed to introduce something from this special area).

More about discrimination (point 1), beating around the bush for an answer (point 2), and grotesque contradiction (point 3) are really not necessary to answer my question why the program had been cancelled. Is everything clear? I hope you see this."

Later, a small piece about me was deleted from a book. Two of my friends, Gottfried Schmiedel, my former music teacher from Dresden, and my father's friend Thomas Buhé, a lecturer in music in Weimar, had published a book about the Beatles. They mentioned in one place that I had once used a Beatles song text as an introduction to a sermon. Even this harmless little item had a little too much good in it. In the second edition of the book this passage had disappeared. I had been transformed into an unperson in the Orwellian model. When I phoned the director of the publishing house and took him to task about this, he squirmed like a worm and claimed he knew nothing about it. This poor soul couldn't tell me on the phone who had told him to make my name disappear.

A similar situation occurred when I was invited to give a lecture about blues music at the Karl-Marx-Stadt University. I was unable to deliver the lecture because the intended lecture hall had to be renovated on precisely that evening! After assorted protests, a delegation from the Central Council of the Free German Youth, the official communist youth organization, actually traveled from Berlin to apologize to me for the unfortunate incident. I even received an honorarium for the event that had not taken place, but it was not rescheduled for a later date. In fact, the lecture wasn't given here or any place else later on. On the other hand and quite astonishingly, I was allowed to write the texts on the album cover of the *Amiga* label for the *Blues Collection*, released in the mid-1980s. *Amiga* was the main record producer in the GDR. My friend, Winne B. B.

Freyer, helped me a great deal on this project with his profound detailed knowledge of the songs. But, then this was taken out of my hands and put into those of citizens found to be more loyal to the communist state.

Whatever one did as a blues fan—one always came upon boundaries, or was stopped, hindered, and criticized, and, of course, got the blues. That is why I had carefully chosen these words as the dedication of my book: "For everyone who has the blues." There were more than enough of these in the GDR.

> I am often at wit's end,
> I'm beat, depressed, resigned.
> And then I realize that
> I've grasped so little about faith.
>
> People tell me, "Smile, God loves you."
> But I simply can't smile all the time.
> Too much in the world gripes me.
> Too much darkness, too little light.
>
> As a Christian, I should be a light,
> a model, a helper, protector.
> But I myself am too impure,
> full of doubt, weakness, and filth.
>
> Of course, one can't always be on top.
> Sometimes one simply has had enough.
> Then, not even prayer comes forth,
> only, "Oh, so little faith."
>
> Yes, I know I'd have to change.
> Thousands have told me so.
> As if I hadn't known for a while.
> Whether I *can* is not even asked.
>
> Oh, my God, my God, I cannot.
> My faith is far too small.
> Oh, my God, my God, I beg you
> Let my faith become greater.

6

No, We're Not Any Better

MARTHEL SYHRE, MY LANDLADY, didn't know that she had a married man in the room she had rented to me as a bachelor. This typical "student pad" was located in the attic, with the toilet in the stairwell. She provided a pitcher of cold water for washing purposes and a porcelain key, but no kitchen privileges. The fifth floor apartment was five minutes away from the university. On the ground floor was a bar—and, as difficult as it may be for you to imagine it if you are aware of the drinking habits of the modern-day student population—I didn't enter it a single time nor did I even drink a single beer from the place. But I was now married and in the final year of my time as a student.

In East Germany anyone unmarried was not considered to be a complete person and thus would not be eligible to apply for an apartment. Since I really wanted an apartment, I had to appear before the Housing Office as a married citizen. So, Elke and I marched over to the Public Registry Office on an icy-cold day in January and, without witnesses or festivities, were legally married in the customary civil ceremony. In fact, I skipped my university lecture in the morning, properly dressed for the occasion, and got the thing over with.

However, although this was only intended as a show-marriage in order to obtain an apartment and we acted in a rather perfunctory manner, we were, in fact, very much excited and touched to our innermost being. Officially husband and wife! We made a telephone call to each of the sets of parents. To add to the celebration, we splurged on a cup of coffee at Cafe Central in the Petersstrasse, no cheap treat since in the GDR a pound of good quality coffee could reach $40.00 per pound in today's money. Elke enjoyed being able to say for the very first time in her life "my husband" as she spoke to the waiter. Only some weeks later did we have the formal wedding ceremony in the church and a reception to which we invited our friends.

I said nothing to Frau Syhre about my new marital status, since I had had a number of squabbles with her during my time there. We tried to imagine how she would react if she were to catch me with a woman in my "pad" and then I would show her our marriage license to prove that she really was my wife. Actually nobody knew about the marriage—except Elke's place of employment because she had reported her name change—and our lives went on unchanged. We only officially notified the housing office, since its policy caused this whole exercise in the first place.

IN THE HALL ON THE SAALE

That we got an apartment in Halle which we could occupy immediately upon our marriage was due to my father's efforts. Without him, we would have, at best, gotten a tiny place below the Giebichenstein Bridge, but never in a villa opposite Burg Giebichenstein, an imposing stone castle. It lay directly on the Saale River, surrounded by a park containing a stand of old trees, among which was a distinctively large gingko tree. We shared the villa on Talstrasse with two other renters, and we lived in what had been the ballroom. It had a 14-foot ceiling and the two outer walls had four windows. Next to this was our bedroom, originally the anteroom to the ballroom. Its four-panel door was as big as a barn door, and only one of the panels had to be opened to pass through. The bedroom was not heated and was damp. Our shoes, which we placed on a shelf, were soon coated with a thick, white layer of mildew. At one time a door led to the neighbor's apartment, but it was nailed shut. Unfortunately it wasn't soundproof. One day we had to listen the entire day to the howling of Asro, a German shepherd. When his master came home from work, he bolted like a crazy person through the yard of the villa. We lived in constant fear of this monster.

We divided the ballroom into four sections. In the first corner were the heating stove and table on which we ate; in the second corner were the beds of our first two daughters concealed behind book shelves; the third corner was my desk and work area; and the fourth corner was the kitchen, outfitted with a cold water faucet and a two-burner electric hotplate.

In the first year, before the children were in the picture, living here was reasonably pleasurable. But then when we had to put everything into

No, We're Not Any Better

the one room, we couldn't listen to the radio in the evening, we could only speak in whispers, and the lights had to be kept low. No guests were possible. A further problem was the barely functioning toilet at the landing midway off the stairs. It was located close to the laundry room, which was by the coal cellar. Here we did our washing. We built a fire, boiled the clothes in a large tub, and then scrubbed them on a washboard. I felt unutterably sorry for Elke, while at the same time I marveled at her ability to move these large water-filled tubs around—even when she was pregnant. Today, no young couple would accept such an apartment, and justly so.

But we were overjoyed and felt as though we were in paradise. We were together and that was the main thing. Moreover, there were lots of good times. The view out of the window alone was a gift. Our gaze towards the Saale, through the overgrown park, fell upon a constant stream of barges with their share of "lazybones" of all kinds lounging on the decks. For our cat, whom we named "Napoleon"—and who later turned out to be female—we made a special access into the garden out of some long boards. She could slide down through the window into the out-of-doors.

Two of our other friends who had been present at our wedding also lived in the villa. Across the way was the artist couple Rataiczyk. He designed large tapestries which his wife weaved. Elke assisted her a lot as she worked with her loom and learned a great deal in the process. When Constantia was born, I ran to the Rataiczyks in my joyous state, and they celebrated the occasion with me with a few glasses of schnaps.

At the end of the Talstrasse in an old paper mill lived the painter, Albert Ebert. He was a genius, even though he was frequently drunk, and a most interesting and amiable human being. I bought his painting, "Flight of the Holy Family out of Egypt," as a wedding gift for Elke. Whenever the doorbell rang around four o'clock, we assumed that it would be Ebert. He knew that was our time for tea. He loved to spend this time with us in our little paradise, telling stories in his own inimitable Halle dialect. Most exciting were those that he told about the pictures he had painted on little wooden panels, and the pictures themselves seemed to come to life. I was grateful that my brother Jochen introduced us to these artists. He was beginning his own career as an artist and often took part in our little tea party. To be able to live with such people in such an atmosphere was a gift.

I should add that we lived next to the beer garden, "*Krug zum grünen Kranz*," later made famous by many TV programs. Here, direct on the

Saale, one sat under chestnut trees, whose fruits would drop into the beer glasses in the fall, as one enjoyed a fantastic view of Burg Giebichenstein. Due to our lack of money, however, we seldom went there for a beer. But when this did occur, all we needed to do was slip through an opening in our garden fence. I remember several evenings I did go there with Albert Ebert and stood in front of a well-lighted bar. It looked precisely the way he later painted it so lovingly. My father had the original. I only have a copy of it, which I hung in my house and enjoy so much.

There was only problem with this idyllic period at Talstrasse 34—I was unemployed. I had been promised a job as a scientific assistant, a low rung on the academic career ladder, but the appointment fell through. As I had received no explanation, I assumed that someone at Leipzig University had filed a negative report about me with the authorities. My suspicion was that a theologian who had always shown himself to be quite loyal to the state was responsible. For a time, I had belonged to a freely elected but, for all practical purposes, illegal student council. We demanded that this man, who was still an assistant at the university, should not be allowed to teach any seminars because of his incompetence. We presented our demands in person to his mentor, Professor Emil Fuchs. In spite of our protests he was promoted to the rank of professor. I therefore assumed he was the one who had given a negative evaluation about me. When I was rehabilitated a year later and finally got the job as a scientific assistant, I wrote him a rather malicious postal card to tell him I had become an assistant. He probably wondered about this card a good bit.

Actually, it was another person who had "reported" about me: Professor Hans Moritz. I only much later learned this when I read the scholarly volume about the failures of the church in East Germany by Gerhard Besier, *Der SED Staat und die Kirche* (The SED State and the Church), published in 1993. In the book he describes the *Stasi* strategy of trying to see that only politically reliable people among the new generation of scholars received academic positions. As an example, he quotes an "expert's evaluation" that Hans Moritz in his position both as Secretary of the local Free German Youth unit and as a member of the *FDJ*'s national Central Council had written about a theological candidate. I was that person:

> Lehmann was not a member of the *FDJ*. During his studies in Leipzig he engaged in no social or political activity. [This meant ac-

tions in support of the GDR.] In addition, the local *FDJ* unit knew of no political activity outside the framework of the university in which he was involved. In accordance with the "special standard" established for evaluating theologians, he must be considered as completely unsuitable from a political standpoint for any possible position as an assistant.

That ended my hope for attaining this position. Obviously, this internal *Stasi* memo did not show up in my university personnel file. My incessantly persistent father was only told time and again that—officially—there was nothing really standing in my way. Therefore, he led the charge to bring about "compensation for past injustice," a GDR legal principle usually reserved for Nazi victims. In this way, he obtained my rehabilitation as well as my appointment as a scientific assistant. But an entire year passed before that was achieved. At the beginning of that year, as a recently married couple, we were left with nothing, and the question for us was, "What now?"

BLACK MUSIC ON WHITE PAGES

Given this situation, it was fortunate that I already had a publisher's contract in my pocket, but I had been unable to fulfill it due to the pressures of marriage and preparing for a state examination. The story begins in 1956 when I and Reginald Rudorf, under the sponsorship of the Office of Community Service in Halle and Leipzig, organized a concert by the "Spiritual Studio Düsseldorf." It was the first concert in the GDR that featured American Negro spirituals and it made a big splash. The five very nice young people who lived in Düsseldorf, West Germany, had made a recording of Negro spirituals and Rudorf had gotten acquainted with them.

To make contact with them, I turned to the director of church music for the Protestant church in Düsseldorf, but he claimed he had never heard of the "Spiritual Studio," even though it operated in his town. I just could not imagine this. The church music "boss" had no idea about a group in his own backyard that performed concerts of church music and had even put out a recording that had found its way to the East. Of course, it was the church music of American Negroes (as they were called at that time and a term they used to identify themselves). This type of music simply lay completely outside the scope of this professional church musician. This story epitomized the narrow-mindedness and ignorance that characterized those involved with German church music in the 1950s.

A marathon of negotiations followed, requiring frequent trips to Leipzig, 25 miles away, to deal with officials at the city hall, and finally we received permission to put up posters. Then entry visas for the group were issued. The event was allowed to take place even though Rudorf was hassled by the *Stasi* right up until the last minute.

The Marktkirche in central Halle was filled to the very last seat in the upper galleries. To open the concert, a jazz group, Alfons Zschockelt's *Waschbrett-Fünf* (The Washboard Five), performed. Can you imagine—jazz in the church?! That sensational event set the stage for what would follow. First, my father gave a short talk, and then Rudorf, an atheist and lecturer on Marxist-Leninism, spoke to the crowd from the pulpit about Negro spirituals. After that, the heavens opened as the group from Düsseldorf sang "Good News."

Present at the concert was a graphic artist who worked for Koehler & Amelang, a subsidiary of Union Publishing House, which was owned by the *CDU*, the Christian Democratic Union of the GDR. [During the occupation both the Soviets and the Western powers had licensed the *CDU* as a political party, and the GDR allowed it and the other so-called "bourgeois" parties that the Soviet authorities licensed to exist. Although they were loyal to the regime, they had little power and were subservient to the *SED*. Nevertheless, their existence contributed to the image of "democracy" in East Germany.] This man had the idea of producing a book on the topic of spirituals, and the publisher asked my father whether he could write such a book. Father answered that he wasn't the expert that they were looking for. They needed to talk to his son, Theo. The contract was issued even though I was still a student and really had no time for writing a book.

Once I had been excluded from the university, I now had the time and began to work on the book. Hans Wagner, the head of Koehler & Amelang, was in charge of the project. He was a stereotypical bourgeois personality from another era, a straight-thinking optimist who suffered incessantly from the mediocrity of the cultural establishment that dominated the GDR. It was due to his efforts that licensed editions of the works of German authors living in the West, such as Thomas Mann and Franz Werfel, enriched the book market in our country. He distinguished himself positively from the other newer publishers in that he insisted on dealing with the authors personally and negotiated directly with them.

Before we began our discussions about the book, we always shared a few jokes about the *CDU* boss, Gerald Götting, and the silvery-gray lock of hair that perpetually graced his forehead. Then we got down to business. I enjoyed the conversations and correspondence with this wise man and took advantage of the relationship until he reached a ripe old age. I admired him as a father-figure and marveled, with thankfulness, at the way he worked with me, a mere newcomer to the publishing scene.

And so, I wrote my first book, one that appeared before my better-known works, *Blues and Trouble* and *Negro Spirituals*. It took the title of the old spiritual "Nobody Knows" and was the first one on this topic to be published in the GDR. Putting out a book here required several years. Getting official permission, planning the project, acquiring paper, and the waiting periods at the printers and bookbinders took large amounts of time. Finally, in 1961 it saw the light of day. By then we had moved to another apartment. When the package with the preliminary copies arrived, Elke opened it. When I got home that day, one copy of the book was fastened to the small window in our front door. The rest of them were laid out on the floor, like a long carpet, leading up to my desk.

The book contained an essay about spirituals, many photos and, best of all, a section with 50 song texts, half of them with the musical notes as well. Armies of guitar-playing young people swooped down on this first book of spirituals to be published in the country. One of them was the youthful Jörg Swoboda. *Nobody Knows* was the first book that he borrowed from someone and used to practice singing spirituals. Ten years later we met, but only after some time had passed did it dawn on Jörg that I was the author. So it was that God brought us into contact with one another even before our formal cooperation in the musical realm began.

In addition, the book led to my connection with the aforementioned Fred Frohberg. Yes, Frohberg had performed a lot of schmaltzy stuff, but he had established a high standard with his singing voice. More importantly, he was the first one to sing Negro spirituals on a GDR stage. Because he was on the lookout for certain types of texts, he asked me about them and in this way we got to know one another. One time he accompanied me to a church conference where he gave a lecture on the topic "Current Music in the Worship Service." This cooperation with me and churches earned him some "bad grades" from the *Stasi*.

Blues Music and Gospel Proclamation

SPIRITUALS AS A STROKE OF LUCK

Just as I had finished the book, father succeeded in securing my rehabilitation, and I now became a scientific assistant. The original position in theology had long since been filled, so I was given one in the area of missions and religious studies, my father's area. I worked there for four years and happily I was now able to stand on my own feet.

In the year I had lived on a freelance basis, father aided me financially and I also earned some money by traveling around giving lectures on the topic "Jazz, Blues, and Spirituals." We had an extremely Spartan existence at that time. On the weekends Elke splurged by buying two veal cutlets from the butcher shop. In our first year of marriage the only things that I got for myself were a pair of black socks and, one time, a bottle of Leipzig beer. Thus, it was gratifying, for the first time in my life, to have a steady income.

It was the customary practice, in fact, the expectation, that one would complete a doctoral degree during the term of the assistantship. I had neither thought about this nor planned to do so, but father encouraged me in this matter. We agreed that the obvious choice for a dissertation would be to go beyond the popular understanding of the origins of spirituals, blues, and gospel music portrayed in *Nobody Knows* and deal with the whole question in a genuinely scientific way. I had no desire to waste years of my life with scholarly rigamarole on some obscure problem of interest to no one but me just so I could stick the title "Doctor" in front of my name. If I were to do so, it had to be really worth the effort and would produce something of practical value, while at the same time making full use of the scientific method.

The topic "Spirituals" met this requirement. There was a real need for theologians and church musicians to pay attention to new types of music and to learn how to accommodate them and structure worship services with them. I achieved this objective with the dissertation entitled *Negro Spirituals: Geschichte und Theologie* (Negro Spirituals: History and Theology). It was published in 1965 in both East and West Germany. Noteworthy is the fact that this dissertation was re-published more than 30 years later. Very unusual! The reason for this is that it continues to be the standard text in German on the topic.

The real reason why I chose to work on this topic had little to with my musical enthusiasm, but lay much deeper and farther back. Long before I had ever heard a Negro spiritual, I learned from a radio program about jazz that these spirituals, that is, the church music of the African-Americans, were at the very heart of jazz—they were there at its beginning. I could neither believe nor even imagine it could be true. One must remember that following the war, the word "jazz" designated the worldliest kind of music imaginable. The assertion that this secular music had its roots in the church intrigued me so greatly that I decided to look into the matter myself. I had already devoted years to collecting materials in my quest to get to the roots of this music. This preparation would serve me well as I developed my dissertation.

There were three problems that I had to deal with as I embarked upon my project. First, there was no way I could work in our one-room apartment, in which two little children now played about, and where my desk sat right next to their beds. As a result, I moved my books and typewriter to my parents' place where I worked on my dissertation in a little woodshed. As the fall progressed, it became too cold outside, and I moved to the furnace room in the cellar. This was a very unhealthy situation since the flames of the constantly running gas furnace and the tiny window over my work area did not permit a sufficient amount of oxygen. Moreover, I could only use artificial light here. These weren't ideal conditions, but it was the only possibility for me at the time.

The second problem was obtaining the necessary source materials. I have already mentioned this situation. Complicating matters was that I did not receive any research grants or other funding. Whenever I did apply for financial assistance I was turned down because potential benefactors regarded my project as utter foolishness. Studying recordings of "Negro" music a scholarly effort? That had to be some kind of a joke. Only one person, my idol, Professor Helmut Thielicke in Hamburg, understood what I was trying to do and supported me by sending some records. As for going to the United States to do research in the rich treasures of primary materials on spirituals in collections there, such as the Library of Congress, that was absolutely unthinkable.

The third difficulty was finding a doctoral supervisor. There was not a single theology professor in the entire GDR who was experienced in my area of interest and whom I could approach about taking me on as a doctoral candidate. I was venturing into completely new territory, and no one except me knew enough about this area of scholarship to be able to evaluate my work adequately. My job, then, was to find someone who would enter into this adventure with me and accompany me in my scholarly journey without being in the remotest way acquainted with the topic. I found this someone in the person of Dr. Hans Urner (1901–86), Professor of Practical Theology at the University of Halle. This was not only a stroke of luck for me but also a human experience of the highest order which demanded my greatest respect.

I had the audacity, while I was just a beginning university student, to take part in a literary disputation with a professor of theology, and that person was Hans Urner. He published a magazine entitled *Zeichen der Zeit* (Signs of the Time), and in one issue a prominent figure in church music, Professor Oskar Söhngen, published an obituary tribute for the nihilist poet, Gottfried Benn, who died in 1956. In this essay he stated, in rather flowery words, that we could console ourselves "that when our bodies have disintegrated, the miracle of Easter will still take place." To counter this lie at the graveside—one of my main themes to this day—I felt compelled to write an article contradicting his words by using the scriptures. That was too much for Professor Urner. He placed his own reply next to mine in the above journal. He even dragged Dietrich Bonhoeffer's name into the discussion, albeit, very unfairly.

Sometime after this I met Professor Urner in my parents' home when I opened the door for him, having no idea it was he. I could not esteem him highly enough after this occasion, since, instead of walking by this impudent little upstart without even noticing him, he stretched out his hand to me as a generous gesture of reconciliation. This human magnanimity deeply impressed me and gave me the courage a few years later to ask him to be my doctoral supervisor.

The dissertation itself was given a "summa cum laude" and the exam over it earned a "magna cum laude." From 1963 I was allowed to include the title "Dr." before my name. In the meantime I had completed my vicarate (student pastorate)—in Leipzig rather than Halle because the Saxon church administration would not permit its ministerial candidates to serve a vicarate in a Lutheran Free Church. This was the opposite of my father's experience. He had been assigned as a vicar to a Free Church congregation so he could become acquainted with a different approach within the confessionalist framework.

By the time I came along, the Saxon church office had abandoned its generosity of granting a candidate the opportunity of expanding his horizons in such a way. Because I was not on Saxon soil but was living by the "waters of Babylon" in Halle, I had to serve as a vicar twice as long as other candidates to compensate for this deficiency. On the other hand, the church administration was generous in considering my age and number of children and waived its usual requirement for outsiders to take additional courses at its special Preachers' Seminary before they could be ordained.

NO JOKE—CHEMNITZ

My service as a pastor began at the Schlosskirche (Palace Church) in Chemnitz in 1964. This city was, and still is, the dumbest city in Germany. I decided from the very beginning, as soon as it was possible, but at the very least after five years, to leave this historical, spiritual, and cultural accumulation of nastiness and insignificance. But I have stuck it out here until this very day!

Children's worship service at the Schlosskirche

As noted earlier, Karl Marx had never been in this city and there was no connection with him whatsoever. Local communist officials had re-named the old Chemnitz as Karl-Marx-Stadt and expected it to become the model of a socialist large city. And then, of all places, a worship service developed here which became a model for the entire GDR. Christians traveled here from around the country to experience what we called the "Worship Service, Somewhat Different." Actually, there had been such a service here before I came, and I quickly became involved in it as I was a part of the city's clergy team and shared in the pastoral duties.

For that day and time, the really sensational elements of this alternative worship service were: a band accompanying the songs, prayer requests projected from slides during the time of intercessory prayers, a relaxed greeting at the beginning, and the absence of the traditional elements of a Lutheran service such as organ music and liturgical clothing. The services took place only once a month, and the Holy Cross Church on the Kassberg was always packed, also by members of the *Stasi*. Incidentally, their headquarters were only a few minutes away from the church. It was quite clear that this didn't fit into their agenda at all. According to Marxist doctrine, the phenomenon of Christian worship was supposed to die out, but here it proved to be very much alive and a magnet for thousands, first and foremost young people. This was bound to lead to difficulties. For me, they began with the death of Carla Totzauer.

Carla, about 14 years old and a member of the Schlosskirche, was killed in a shooting accident. She was taking part in an exercise staged by the *Gesellschaft für Sport und Technik* (Society for Sports and Technology or *GST*), with the scarcely disguised aim of training young people in conventional military tactics. A loaded weapon was lying unsupervised on a table which was unsupervised. A 14-year-old boy and friend of Carla picked up the gun and began playing around with it. Suddenly a shot rang out and she was fatally wounded. I had to officiate at her funeral service.

I was nearly out of my mind. I asked another pastor to pray for me as I entered the hall where her coffin was resting. The room was filled to overflowing with mourners, representatives from her school, public offices, the *GST* and *FDJ*, and who knows from wherever else. As I saw this mass of people—functionaries, schoolchildren, and banners—I was gripped with anxiety, but I had to say what I had intended to and had written down.

Right at the outset, I declared that even if all others remained silent, I, as a preacher of the truth, must speak the truth. First, I said that weapons do not belong in the hands of children. Next, I recited the Ten Commandments. After the Fifth Commandment (Thou shalt not kill) I stopped, and paused for a minute, or maybe it was only half a minute. I stared at the people in the audience and they at me. The silence at this point was the strongest sermon I ever preached on that particular commandment. And it was the longest minute of my life.

I then expounded on a passage of scripture and fixed my gaze on the face of one person. It was the girl's grandmother. She was completely distraught with pain, and with eyes wide open, she stared at me and hung on my every word. Afterwards she told me that she had thought all through the service, "Go for it, pastor! Tell them the truth! Tell them the truth!" That I did, and a few minutes later, before her open grave, I paid the price for so doing. When I had ended with the final prayer and the blessing, the principal of her school stepped to the graveside and assured the dead Carla that "she had died for peace, which had to be defended with weapons." [This was one of the most commonly used political slogans in the GDR.]

THE ATTEMPTS OF THE TEMPTERS

On the following Sunday, a "Worship Service, Somewhat Different," was scheduled. Presumably, the authorities thought we would make something big out of the incident at the service, but in fact we hadn't planned to do so. That would have been particularly provocative since Western journalists were in the city because of West German Chancellor Willy Brandt's summit conference in Erfurt with his GDR counterpart. Following mammoth governmental sessions, the worship service was forbidden. We refused to obey the order!

Superintendent Fehlberg and I were summoned to the city hall. In my 30 years as a pastor, I had never once been asked to come to a "conversation" at a government office. And this one, too, didn't actually take place. The superintendent went in alone while I had to remain seated in the outer office. Most of the time the conversation dealt solely with me, and the superintendent said over and over that all they needed to do was to call me in. I was simply sitting out there in front of the door as they discussed my case. When he came out after about an hour, he asked me, "What have you been doing?" "I was praying," I said. When we were back out on the street, he said, "They're going for the jugular."

The most obvious thing that occurred during this period of intense pressure was that more and more people came to the services. It became necessary to hold two services back to back in order to accommodate the crowds. All of this happened under the constant observation of the *Stasi* whose agents were present in each service. I learned from my *Stasi* file that in 1969 besides the full-time officers (regular *Stasi* personnel actually held military rank) the police assigned eight paid informants (*Inoffizielle Mitarbeiter* [unofficial collaborators], referred to in *Stasi* parlance as *IM*'s) to the first service, and seven to the second. Immediately following the event, Captain Decker and First Lieutenants Heimbold, Günther, and Weiss filed a report. In addition, the *Stasi* smuggled spies (*IM*'s) into our team. The most egregious of these was *Kantor* (Choir Director) Sauer (*IM* "*Klaus Müller*"), who not only led the choir but also was present at our team meetings. To show the kind of little "games" that the *Stasi* played, I will relate an action taken in 1970 that was referred to in the documents as "Detailed-Operational Action Plan 'chapel.'"

It was a common practice to use slides during the intercessory prayer times. The projector was placed in the center aisle of the church, and, as the *Stasi* reported, no one from the team kept an eye on it in the intermission between the two services. The slides lay on the table next to the projector. *IM "Klaus Müller"* had observed this in minute detail in his report. The *Stasi* plan went as follows: "With the objective of disturbing and hindering the *Gea* (*Gottesdienst etwas anders* [Worship Service, Somewhat Different]), it is proposed that, during the services to be held on 11/22/1970, a slide be exchanged for one that is already in the tray for the purpose of undermining the sermon that will be presented. The slide will be a pornographic scene." This slide should unleash a scandal "that would damage the reputations of the responsible functionaries and lay workers of the Lutheran Church in the Karl-Marx-Stadt area . . . as as well as severely harm the authority of Pastors Lehmann, Mendt, and Ackermann."

What I found particularly disgusting about the scheme was that it would bring our faithful brother, Volkmar Uhlmann, one of our most able co-workers, into the line of fire because he was the one who operated the projector. As was the case with so many of the "action plans" which I found in my *Stasi* documents, things turned out as the writer Bertolt Brecht so well described:

> "Yes, just make yourself a plan.
> Show how bright you are!
> And then, make another plan—
> Neither one will work."

Nothing worked, nothing happened. We held the worship service without even being aware of what disruptive maneuver God had prevented.

Even if we knew nothing about the "action plans" and the machinations of the *Stasi*, we were conscious that we were always under surveillance. Frequently, they let us know that by parking a car conspicuously right outside a place where we were holding a meeting. I noticed, too, such a car was parked in front of the church office at the Schlosskirche, and every time I drove away in my auto, it started up and followed me.

It was so clearly staged that I had to see it, and, indeed, I was supposed to. It was a means of intimidating us, which, at least at the beginning, never failed to do so. It completely unnerves a person when one is "accompanied," indeed, pursued, in this way. One time I feared that I would be arrested while en route somewhere, and I loaded my entire family into the car so as not to be driving around in town alone.

We tried to downplay this before the children, but they, of course, realized this wasn't a harmless paper chase. After all, being followed regularly by a car occupied by four men had to be threatening. We discussed the situation rather freely in the family, but we avoided telling the children everything we knew about the *Stasi*. The following incident will show how deeply the anxiety carried over to the children and how obvious the harassment was. We were downtown one afternoon and did not return home until twilight. Our eldest daughter, Constantia, was waiting for us in front of the manse and greeted us with the comment, "I thought maybe they had arrested you." It was the first thought that entered her mind when we were a little bit late. Any other child would have assumed that their parents had met friends, had a cup of coffee, or were tied up in a line in front of a store. Our daughter thought first of the *Stasi*. This fear that they instilled in the souls of our children was surely a criminal act.

WHEN ANGLO-SAXONS GO ANGLING IN SAXONY

For many years Americans regularly turned up in Saxony. They were Christians, pastors and their church members, who came to the GDR on vacation to meet Christians here. That there were people in far away America who were interested in us and sought us out in our prison was an overwhelming experience, a strong expression of brotherly love, a sign that we were not forgotten. The founder of this ministry of visitation was Pastor Walt James, a man whom I admired greatly. A genuine friendship developed between us. Until his death at over 90 years of age, we prayed for one another daily. To indicate my profound respect for him, I never addressed him in any other way than "father." Also, with some others who frequently came we had good relationships, in one case even a pastoral one. For some of these friends it was quite a surprise to meet a pastor in the socialistic city named after Karl Marx, one who had even written books about spirituals and blues, that is, American music. Some of them were the first African-Americans with whom I could speak about their own music.

Unforgettable was the way they showed their heart-felt feelings for us. The kisses, the embraces, as common as they are now but still unknown to us at the time, were customary gestures for them, especially when they were taking leave of one another. And I never in my wildest dreams thought I would be embraced by a foreign woman as we parted. Especially unbelievable was one of the African-American women, who, with a grandmotherly embrace, pulled me to her breast, while I stood there with my arms hanging limply at my sides and cast my gaze over her shoulders to my Elke, pleading for her pardon. Never had I, especially not in Elke's presence, allowed myself to be touched by a female.

This stubborn part of my nature and absolute correctness and distance in the presence of all women made all attempts by the *Stasi* to destroy our marriage fail. They even sent female *IM*'s for the sole purpose of tempting me. Strangely enough, I never actually realized that women with such intent were about their work. Not until the *Stasi* documents were available to us did I learn of their existence. That was good enough reason why I had observed the maintenance of distance between myself and any woman seeking counseling as an absolute law in my service as a pastor.

Another time, when an American group came our way, we wanted to show them the area around Karl-Marx-Stadt. An outing into the Erzgebirge hills was announced. As we gathered on the parking area of the Hotel Chemnitzer Hof, I noticed a car in which four smartly-dressed young men were seated and who were staring rather obviously into the air. When we started up, so did they. Because one of the Americans had forgotten his camera, we stopped and waited until he returned with it. The other car with the four men in it had stopped also. It was quite clear to me.

As we continued on, the conversation turned to the usual questions—how do Christians in the GDR live, is the church free, or do we feel oppressed and persecuted? I told the pastor who was interviewing me that he should look in the rear-view mirror or out the back window and tell me what he sees. "I see a car," he said. I told him that the car had been following us since our departure. Of course, that produced a rather dejected mood.

These men were in close proximity the entire day. They were at the restaurant where we had lunch reservations. The manager had set a small

American flag on the table before our arrival, a rather remarkable thing to do. Likewise, they were there as we peered into the glass display cases in an Erzgebirge museum. I really felt like James Bond when I succeeded in ditching them on our way home. I veered off on a small side street at a railroad crossing, and they could not catch up with us. When I later read their report, the four men had omitted this part of their spying activity, which for them was rather inglorious. They simply ended the report at an earlier point in the day.

Strangely enough, the visits from the Americans played no role in my *Stasi* files. On the other hand they focused on alienating people from the "*Gea*," as they called our distinctive service. The strategic objective of the *Stasi* was always to ratchet up the "differentiation process," that is, promoting differences among individuals in our churches, and, by this means, cause tensions and divisions among pastors and co-workers. They would play them off against each other and thereby decrease the effectiveness of the churches. How the *Stasi* must have rejoiced when this objective was reached without their involvement in the "Worship Service, Somewhat Different." I left the team because of sharp theological differences.

In the life that one leads
there is much that upsets God!
For man, as we're created,
has failings, Christians too.

We aren't better, but we're better off.
Jesus makes us free, and starts anew with us.
We aren't better, but we're better off.
Jesus makes us free, and starts anew with us.

To be sure, many folks imagine
that they are somehow better.
And think, since they're converted,
they can lord it over others.

Even the greatest hero of the faith
often falls into the pit.
And whoever thinks he's flawless
hasn't discovered himself yet.

Blues Music and Gospel Proclamation

Yes, we, too, fight among ourselves,
And some of us get weak.
Many things are merely pious "show."
Many things could be better.

Frequently an atheist is
much better than a Christian.
Yet a Christian's better off,
When he accepts forgiveness.

Even if the guilt is all too great,
Jesus makes us free of it.
We are free, even in the Judgment.
There's nothing better than this.

7

Only One Way

In the "Worship Service, Somewhat Different," a series on the Ten Commandments was scheduled. I was assigned to preach on the Sixth Commandment, "Thou shalt not commit adultery." I worked out the sermon and passed it around to the other team members for their discussion. The team unanimously rejected the sermon and expressed the opinion that I must not preach it. Superintendent Fehlberg gave the sermon to the other superintendents, an act which he was not authorized to do, and also made it available to the Saxon Regional Church Administration and Bishop Noth. All of them made a common front against me.

Since a convention of all the superintendents currently was in session and the representatives of the regional church were present, I was summoned to appear before the entire body. I felt like Luther before the Diet of Worms. I, one insignificant pastor, stood alone, facing the black phalanx of the church hierarchy, which also forbade me to preach the sermon in the "Worship Service, Somewhat Different." That evening I announced my resignation from the team and made it known that I would preach the sermon on one of the subsequent Sundays in the Schlosskirche, where I was the pastor.

My spiritual advisor, Superintendent Kruspe, told me that he would do everything in his power to prevent me from preaching the sermon. He was not pleased with the wording of the first sentence in the sermon, which he quoted to me almost verbatim. I replied that a good sign of the sermon's quality was that he still knew the first line by heart. I told him I had sat for years under his teaching and could not remember a single sentence from memory. I kept probing deeper, wanting to hear concrete arguments against it, but they were not forthcoming. He took shelter behind the bishop in a typical German servile manner and said, "If my bishop forbids this sermon, then it is incumbent upon me to do the same." Whereupon, I made reference to the fact that, as the ordained pastor charged with preaching, I had the right to do so at the Schlosskirche.

I then notified Bishop Noth that the time was past when an individual in the church could pronounce a ban in such an authoritarian way. As an adult and an ordained pastor I expected a firm, theologically-based reason for the action. So, the bishop ordered me to appear before him, but, once again, there were no theological arguments. Therefore, I stuck by my refusal to obey the ban. When nothing else was forthcoming, the bishop shouted, "Brother Lehmann, all of this is the result of your own vanity in wanting to preach this sermon."

THE SMELL OF RUMORS

Given my respect for Bishop Noth, I could not do anything right away after he made this charge. I had neither asked, nor in any way pushed, for the opportunity to preach this sermon. The team, of which both Superintendent Fehlberg and I were members, had assigned this to me. I did not understand what wanting to hear valid reasons for the ban on the sermon had to do with vanity. I did not grasp why the members of the team along with the bishop and the church hierarchy were all against this particular sermon. I had given it several other times—to parents of candidates for confirmation, church leaders, even a gynecologist—and none of them had raised any factual objections. I thought it especially significant that the medical doctor had no problems with it.

Well, you can imagine how the rumor mill in Karl-Marx-Stadt quickly cranked up: "Lehmann wants to preach about sex and the bishop has forbidden it. Who knows what kind of nasty stuff and liberal drivel he wants to talk about?" This happened at the time I was in the early stage of my work as a pastor and there was uncertainty as to where I stood. At this point, I really had a personal interest in preaching this sermon. That wasn't vanity, but rather my desire to expose such rumors to facts and the truth.

What was it all about then? The message of the sermon was, in its simplest form, no sex at age 16. "NO!" to premarital sex. I was ready to take a beating for my arch-conservative theology and ethics. But, I was not prepared to allow my reputation to be sullied by rumors without first having the opportunity to present my message. And, because I was convinced, out of a clear conscience, that I should never proclaim anything that was unbiblical, I did want to preach this sermon. How could this possibly be vanity?

The charge of vanity that the bishop made served as a lesson to me for life. To be sure, what happened was a miscarriage of justice, a misinterpretation of the whole matter. Later on, when giving a pastoral talk, I recalled this event and guarded against using my pastoral authority to cast my personal impressions and interpretations onto another person. As a pastor I have tried to say only that which I could back up with the scriptures and never to misuse my position as a preacher to make authoritative statements and judgments that really came from my purely personal opinion. Now I knew that a pastor, yes, even a bishop, can err.

On October 29, 1969, the "Worship Service, Somewhat Different" dealing with the Sixth Commandment, took place in the Kreuzkirche, and the building was packed. I was in the balcony and beside me was a high official whom the Regional Church Central Administrative Office (*LKA*) had sent to observe what was going on. What this man told me there about the effects upon young people of my statements on the topic of "Sexuality" was such outrageous nonsense that I am too embarrassed to relate it here.

Elke sat below with our three children in one of the front rows. One could cut the tension in the air with a knife as everyone awaited the announcement explaining why, not Pastor Lehmann, but rather another person would deliver the sermon. The explanation went as follows: Dr. Lehmann had declared his resignation from the team since it did not agree with the contents of his intended sermon. Once again, he did not provide a single objective argument or factual clarification which would have cleared me from all the rumors that gushed forth from the "rumor mill." The whole thing was presented in the hazy, imprecise manner of which many pastors are world masters, whereby they tell half-truths and hide from the whole truth. That I had left the team and that it was opposed to my sermon was quite well-known by now. Only—why? One learned nothing of the reason, in spite of tortuous statements.

This was simply too much for Elke. She jumped out of her seat protesting loudly—I understood only one word she said, "hypocrites"—and then marched up the center aisle towards the exit. Suddenly she stopped in her tracks. She had forgotten our children. She turned around, went back and grabbed them from their seats, and continued to shout "hypocrites," as she stormed out of the church.

The representative from the Saxon Church office stared down from the balcony dumbfounded. I made no comment. Then came the sermon, based on the same biblical text that I had chosen for my sermon. I couldn't believe my ears as the preacher recommended to the parents of 16-year-olds that they fix up a room in the attic to give them the opportunity to "get to know" their boy/girl friend in a more intimate fashion. He said this at the very time when the laws against sexual procurement were still in force in the GDR. Simply stated, apart from the biblical viewpoint on the matter, this was a bold invitation to break the law. I asked the church councilor whether he had heard that statement. Of course he had, but he remained silent.

In any event, following this sermon, I had a good idea why the team opposed my planned sermon. It was too traditional, too conservative. My rejection of sex at 16 and premarital sex disturbed them. That obviously was the critical point. Since a number of my colleagues exhibited liberal views in other matters and held positions that were quite at odds with my understanding of the Bible, it was no wonder they did not share my outmoded views about sex either. If I found it a shame that they lacked enough brotherliness and tolerance to allow me to preach my conservative viewpoint, at least now I knew what the crux of the whole matter was.

What moved the bishop and the Saxon church hierarchy to remain silent on the issue remains a mystery to me until this very day. I am firmly convinced that such people as Bishop Noth stood for the same position I did—no sex at age 16.

ONE MAN'S SADNESS IS THE *STASI*'S JOY

However, when people do not talk openly and honestly with one another, provide no objective arguments, and cannot discuss the matter theologically with the Bible in front of them on the table; everything remains in the realm of conjecture. This is why the bishop acted as he did regarding my message of "No Sex at Age 16."

I had posted my people at the exits of the Kreuzkirche, above all my friend, Peter Fritzsche, who had a booming voice. They screamed and shouted to the people coming out of the church, "Pastor Lehmann will preach the sermon that he wasn't allowed to preach here, in the Schlosskirche on November 9." I will never forget the stunned look on

Superintendent Fehlberg's face as he stood in front of Fritzsche, his hand propped behind his ear to hear the horrendous news.

The days leading up to November 9 were filled with the already mentioned conversations, endless debates, and the preparations for the worship service. In addition, I had only a few days to round up a band and get the equipment up and running.

While on the one hand the church leaders hindered me with everything they could throw at me, the *Stasi* aided me with every means at their disposal. Of course, the *Stasi's* intention was not to help me but bring me down. An agency memorandum recognized that "at the present time there are suitable opportunities to advance the process of differentiation among the groups [in the church] opposing one another. The attempt must be made to induce L. to take part in thoughtless actions, such as preaching the sermon in question on November 9 in the Schlosskirche. Then the *LKA* (!) would initiate a disciplinary action."

The measures to be employed were detailed in the document. *Stasi* personnel would monitor all of my sermons (even the regular Sunday ones). Seven informants were assigned to this task. *IM* "Peter" was to strengthen my resolve to hold the worship service on the ninth of November. He turned out to be Georg Brühl, an art and antique collector, who had placed an African sculpture at my place on loan, so that he would have an opportunity to visit me again. He has the brazenness, even today, of taking an active part in the cultural life of Chemnitz. He acts as a patron of the arts by making generous gifts from his collections. (I often wonder how he had obtained and hung on to them during the GDR period).

Additional measures to be taken were:

> Letters, already composed, were to be sent to a number of conservative pastors. They will demonstrate the methods and means Dr. Lehmann uses to discriminate against and malign other pastors and church musicians. In this way, this particular group of people will have something in their hands which they can put to good use against Lehmann. This is one more way to intensify the process of differentiation.... In the remaining time up until the ninth of November, two more letters are to be sent to Dr. Lehmann that will assure him that he enjoys the sympathy of the young people. This measure will serve our objective of encouraging Pastor Dr. Lehmann to preach the banned sermon on the ninth of November.

His doing so will result in a disciplinary procedure as well as further measures against him by the *LKA*.

These are unambiguous statements, with clear objectives and distinctly formulated motives. Unfortunately, I have not found any statements by my church superiors of similar clarity which could help me to know their real motives. Not to be overlooked is the fact that the archives of the Saxon church with regard to the *Stasi* are to this day still sealed and inaccessible for research purposes.

The worship service on November 9 took place without any disruptions. Presumably, it was a big disappointment for those who had expected a scandal or hoped to hear liberal views on sexuality.

A SHOCK AND NO CHOCOLATE

After word had gotten out that the church authorities had banned the sermon, people expected that I would rail against the usual position of the church in this matter. They hoped for a few stinging theses in the spirit of the sexual revolution of the 1960s ("Whoever sleeps twice with the same partner already belongs to the Establishment") and a license for sexual permissiveness. The fact that I supported the traditional standpoint of the church and preached a very conservative sermon was the real shock of the evening. Many could not understand that I did not subscribe to the modern sexual revolution but rather to the "outmoded" biblical teaching. At the same time, no one could see what there was in this rather conventional sermon that would cause the church authorities to ban it.

Years later I took the greatest pleasure in using this sermon once again. The editor of "*Sonntag*," the weekly news magazine of our church, asked me to write a series of articles for the youth page on the topic "Youth and Sexuality." I printed out this sermon, word for word. Perhaps it wasn't an especially noble stirring of my heart, but I must admit that it filled me with a great sense of satisfaction that the very same sermon that the church hierarchy had forbidden now appeared in the newspaper that the *LKA* itself published.

> Only one way, only one God!
> My friends, yes, so it is.
> Only one way, and he's called Jesus Christ,
> Who leads us to the Promised Land.

Only One Way

It's so easy to take the broad path,
No law binds you. Death wins in the end.

The Way, straight and narrow, leads through the dark valley.
But don't be afraid! It's the Way to the Light.

You'll not be alone as you walk on this path.
Many friends are here who'll be with you.

It isn't too late; turn 'round while there's time
But come along now. Take the first step.

8

With You Alone

THE FORM OF THE worship service as practiced in our church has always rubbed me the wrong way, and to this day I feel terribly out of place when participating in one. It simply isn't my world. I refuse to turn my back on the world in which I live by speaking a language that is so outdated. It is not my language at all where it concerns the most important things in life. My problem begins with the very first sentence in the liturgy. We recite, "*Our* help *stands (steht)* in the name of the Lord." Help! No one speaks this kind of German today. Nowadays people say, "*My* help *is (besteht)* . . ." But *stands (steht)*?

And so on and on it goes, from the hymns, readings, and prayers, right up to the Lord's Supper. Even the most reckless language innovators and those who pervert the biblical language to make it politically correct (for example, "and he gave it to his [male] friends [*Freunden*] and his [female] friends [*Freundinnen*] and said "Take and eat, this is my body"), stick with the "*e*" in the second person plural even though it is no longer used anywhere, and this with a stubbornness that will not cease. It is as if their salvation depended on saying, "*Nehmet, esset, und trinket*" (instead of "*Nehmt, esst, trinkt*") for the verbs take, eat, and drink.

Normal people cannot sing the hymns and liturgy because they are pitched too high. Many liturgical expressions are not understandable, or even erroneous, in modern German. I often wonder how ordinary people, who work all week and speak just like everyone else as they do their jobs, then in the Sunday worship service parrot words and phrases that, on any other occasion would at best be considered ludicrous. And since I have always been obsessed with the idea that a gulf should never exist between one's life and faith, I refuse to go along with this balancing act between present-day and archaic German. I cannot conceive why so many people faithfully and honestly sing the most impossible trash. As a result I have often just slammed my hymnbook shut. [This situation is analogous to the way many Christians in the English-speaking world utilize the language of the King James Bible as though it is some sort of heavenly speech.]

AWAY WITH THE POWDER BARRIER

A special problem for me is the robe. There were times in my life when I had the highest regard for the clerical gown—from whose fulsome sleeves one could sew the curtains for an entire regional church office building—such as when I was requested to officiate at funerals in non-church cemeteries. But I ask myself again and again why I, as a human being, must first put on a long black gown so that I can preach the Word of God. The trend for pastors nowadays is to adorn themselves in albs and stoles, which opens the way for expressing their individualism and vanity. In this situation I would prefer the Big Black Gown.

A Lutheran minister must struggle throughout his life with the Geneva collar that is integral to the clerical dress. It is difficult enough to put on correctly, but then one has to worry about its tendency to gradually slide down the gown during the sermon. Consisting of two separate white pieces of cloth that look like wide ribbons, it is highly-stylized to serve as a part of the liturgical garb although, in reality, it is nothing more than a "powder barrier," the symbolic remnant of a broad collar which was supposed to keep the powder falling from one's wig from landing on the black gown. The powdered wigs have long since disappeared, but the "powder barrier" remains and brings forth new blossoms again and again on the necks of women who are clothed with the pastoral office. I realize that the pastoral ministry of women is now widely accepted in Western churches, including many evangelical ones, but personally I still have doubts about its biblical validity.

Now, I have not only questioned many common practices but also given a lot of consideration to the kind of worship service in which I could feel comfortable. I have also thought about the non-Christians we are trying to win to Christ.

For many years, I have traveled around giving lectures about Negro spirituals. At Protestant academies, at conferences for pastors and church musicians and for bishops and candidates for confirmation, I have introduced the worship styles of African-American Christians and attempted to show that a worship service can be very different from ours.

Of course, we have to recognize that those in attendance at our services are becoming fewer, while in the black churches the number is increasing. I discussed, argued, proselytized, and waxed enthusiastic with the critical voices among the church musicians in articles (a typical title was "*Swing oder Zwang*" ("Swing or Compulsion") or "*Banjo contra Orgel*" ("Banjo versus Organ"). Most of the time I was greeted with rejection or mockery when I declared that it ought to be possible in the twentieth century to make music and to sing in the manner of the twentieth century.

Unfortunately, some even countered my assertions by wielding the cudgel of that distinctively Nazi expression, "foreign (*artfremd*) music." Even a writer in a 1969 issue of the church newspaper, *Der Sonntag*, swung it by declaring that Negro spirituals were "inappropriate (*artfremd*) for us Germans." The editor-in-chief rejected an offer from me to produce an article on the topic. His reason was that a discussion about Negro spirituals was "premature." That was five years after the publication of my dissertation. Perhaps the mildest comment that I came away with from our encounter was: "Herr Lehmann, we are eager to know what kind of a worship service you will actually conduct when you are a pastor."

Actually I was a pastor right then. But I did not belong to that group of people who, having just gotten out of the university, simply reject everything and think they know better. They want to make everything different, but in fact they don't. Rather, I kept my dreams to myself, kept my trap shut for years, and carried out my normal responsibilities in a most proper manner. I even asked our Choir Director Kircheis to practice the Lord's Supper liturgy with me. (This simply didn't work. When each of us realized it wouldn't, we mutually agreed to break off the attempt.) I didn't undertake any revolutionary changes in the regular worship service. I did try some new approaches in the aforementioned "Worship Service, Somewhat Different," but even this really wasn't what I had envisioned. And then, after seven years of pastoral duty, I knew something had to be done. My ideas were now fully mature. I recognized that all of this endless chatter had not produced anything and that the only one way to move forward was to put a real, concrete model into practice.

EVEN A NEW TUNE OFTEN MAKES MANY PEOPLE UNEASY

Superintendent Fehlberg, a member himself of the "Worship Service, Somewhat Different" team, admonished us pastors incessantly, year after year, that we shouldn't be content simply with providing the *Gea* as a service for the local congregations. He drilled it into our heads that we were obligated to hold a youth worship service at our respective churches. Except him, none of us, me included, were doing this. But then a situation arose that so challenged me that I realized the time had come to act.

It occurred at a meeting of the parish council in 1971. It was customary at one session to present the church statistics for the past year. The data revealed that there were fewer new members coming into the church through baptism than members who had died or formally left the church. The congregation of the Schlosskirche was shrinking. After hearing these devastating statistics, the stunned board members sat there with heads bowed and blankly stared into space. Silence. Then the chair asked if anyone had a suggestion how to engage this negative trend. I stood up and said that I had an idea. "I will start a youth worship service." (As the youngest of the three pastors at the time, I was responsible for youth ministry.) The sentence had hardly left my mouth when Choir Director Kircheis, with whom I had usually gotten along quite well, shot up out of his seat as if bitten by a tarantula and asked, "Do you intend that we will make music with guitars?" I answered "Yes."

But now the issue was no longer the shrinking congregation or the young people who belonged to this parish but never darkened the door of the church. No, the crux of the matter was the kind of music that would be used in the services and what would not be allowed. The description of the struggle that ensued and which kept me in a state of constant agitation for the next months would fill a small book. The church council itself was divided over the issue, but it charged me to work together with Choir Director Kircheis to develop a common liturgy and musical form.

Nothing came of this since I refused to compromise. The regular worship service with its liturgy, organ, and hymnbook had failed. That was obvious and was the starting point for everything else. Of the thousands on the church roll only a small percentage actually took part in the worship service and other church activities The largest part of the confirmed and baptized young people never attended any services, to say nothing of the thousands of non-Christians who lived in our parish. In this situation I wanted to make a special offer to the young people here. I intended to replace the very things that had scared them off—the formalized liturgy and hymns accompanied by the organ. These had not proved to be a help but rather a hindrance.

I could not really come to terms with our choir director, who was the music minister of the church. In those areas where I needed his assistance the most, he could not do anything to help me. I was able to put a band together from scratch comprised of novices and musical upstarts. But Kircheis was neither ready to help or capable of doing so. He couldn't even tune a guitar. This was the case because the customary one-sided education program for ministers of music provided him with absolutely no understanding of the contemporary popular music scene familiar to the young people in his own congregation. He could only cater to the higher tastes of those who loved Bach. As a result, we had to do without the services of the church's trained and salaried music expert and manage on our own with our lay orchestra.

Youth worship service at the Schlosskirche in the 1970s

Since I was not prepared to mix the old and the new, the problem became increasingly acute. Even the Saxon Church Office looked into the situation. I had to appear before the higher authorities, but that didn't help matters any. I insisted on using guitars. As a result, people accused us of "unbrotherly" conduct since the *Kantor* was not included in the plans. "We" consisted of the co-workers from the *Junge Gemeinde* with its leader, the congregational staff assistant, Brigitte Vogel. The charge of "unbrotherly" conduct, made by the church council, was a heavy burden upon our shoulders. We reflected at length on the matter, discussed it, and prayed that a blessing might accompany our intentions. After thorough consideration, we decided simply to accept this charge rather than do nothing for the youth. It was clear to us: The command to evangelize was more important than matters of church tradition and questions of musical taste. Young people must come to know Jesus. Through *him* they will be saved, rather than by a hymnbook.

Of course, I wasn't so naive as to assume that I would get a medal if I, as the sole person on the pastoral team and the local church council, undertook measures to confront the statistical trend of shrinking membership. This much I knew from my experience in the church: anything new will at first be rejected. But I had not counted on such a determined campaign against me, beginning with the very first worship service and then intensified by the actions of the *Stasi*. I had hoped for support, or at least to be left alone to experiment in this way, and that they would give me a break and not harass me. What I was unprepared for was the massive resistance by our own church people.

LET'S GO WITH RUMPELSTOLZ AND CO.

While I was involved in a war of nerves with people from the parish on up to the central church office, I had to solve a lot of practical questions such as who would play the guitar and which songs would we sing? For years I had sought a person who played the guitar, who could sing with all kinds of people, and with whom I would have a close spiritual relationship. God has always sent me the right people at the right time.

The story began with Reiner Schöne. I met this giant of a man, six and a half feet tall, at one of the jazz festivals in Buna, when I announced that his band from Weimar was to perform next. I was immediately enthusiastic about him since he played the banjo. A friendship developed between us that lasted over decades, walls, and borders. My blues idol at that time was Snooks Eaglin, and because of his blues-sounding voice, I nicknamed Reiner "Snooks." And so it remains today even in our correspondence. He was the one who sang my first song. I had written a text to the jazz piece known to every child, "When the Saints Go Marchin' in." This song, "There is a Word in This World," contains, in a nutshell, my entire theology. Snooks sang it in a "Worship Service, Somewhat Different." Incidentally, at my request he sang it immediately followed by the powerful medieval hymn, "*Mitten wir im Leben sind von dem Tod umfangen*" (In the Midst of Life We're Surrounded by Death) from the hymnbook.

Unfortunately in 1971 he couldn't help me. By then he had been living in the West for some time and had made a fantastic start in his career by playing the main role of "Hair." Later on, he also performed the lead role (Christ) in "Jesus Christ Superstar." We had discussed the latter opportunity a great deal, and it was my arguments in favor of so doing that was the impetus for him to accept the part. Still later, Schöne gave me a melody to which I wrote the text "*Doch wir stehen wieder auf*" (Yet we are standing up again). This became the Saxon hymn during the time of the *Wende* (turning point), the popular name for the East German revolution of 1989. The song was sung by thousands, who, at the moment the first notes sounded, automatically rose to their feet to sing it.

Youth worship service at the Schlosskirche in 1972

Since Snooks was no longer available when I began the youth worship service, I looked for a musician who fulfilled my wishes. I found him in Detlef Bretschneider. He attracted my attention when I gave a lecture on Negro spirituals at an instruction session for confirmation candidates. While most of the youths were bored and clearly indicated their lack of interest, I noticed this lad paid attention, hung on my every word, and, most importantly, absorbed what I had to say like a sponge. After his confirmation, he played guitar in the youth group of a nearby church.

When I asked him if he would join me in the youth worship service, he immediately accepted. With him as my number two person, we made our start. He continued singing with us until the day he was drafted into the army. To enhance our effort, he assembled a group that was called the "*Schlossband*" (Castle Band) that consisted of a banjo, a washboard, and later, a bass. The washboard was, of course, the optical and musical show-stopper. The reason for this was quite simple; we had no money for a drum. Moreover, such an instrument is normally too loud to be played in a church. Over time I have learned that when it isn't played by a trained percussionist but by an inexperienced layperson in a large church structure, the sound of the constant beating becomes rather mushy. But, for the purpose of a decent foundational beat, I found grandma's washboard from the attic was just the right thing: cheap, original, and easy to transport. In other words, we had formed a skiffle group, that is, a primitive jazz group that played on simple and unconventional instruments.

Interestingly, a washboard was generally used in the early skiffle bands in America. According to the name plate on its back, the instrument used in our band was made by the firm Rumpelstolz & Co. Moreover, the German word *rumpeln* (rumble) was applied to the style of Dixieland music that jazz artists often played.

Accompaniment of congregational singing was the only task for the band and it existed just for this worship service. It was not intended for concert performances although I found it a real pleasure to listen to this jazz-type music. Over the decades various musicians were a part of this group. Wolfgang Tost, the successor to Detlef, spent 33 years with the band. Try to imagine for three decades giving up one's personal and family life every second Sunday of the month for a rehearsal in the morning and the services in the afternoon and evening, and all of that without receiving even a single cent for one's labors. I doubt that such a thing as this exists nowadays among young people, where the desire for the limelight is just as great as the craving for money. It also was clear that the youth service could only have lasted as long as it did because it was put together by people whose hearts were totally in it. Without this handful of engaged individuals who made this event their own, it would never have functioned at all.

My last youth worship service in the Luther Church

The fact that this youth worship service took place 240 times (I was present at 200 of them), is probably unique in the history of youth ministry. At the beginning I thought that we would be able maintain these services for one or two years and then it would have run its course. Young people always want something new. One has to get fresh inspiration after a few years. But yet it kept on going, year after year, always in the identical format as in the beginning.

AGAIN AND AGAIN NEW SONGS

I soon wearied of the songs that we had sung in the "Worship Service, Somewhat Different" with such great enthusiasm ("Thanks for This Good Morning," "A Ship That Calls Itself Church"), and I began looking around for something new and different. I knew from my work with spirituals that church music existed whose melodies were well-known throughout the world, easy to sing, and quite inspiring. Since I was no musician myself and didn't know anyone who could compose such pieces, I took the melodies of spirituals, blues, and Beatles songs, and wrote new texts for them based on the theme of the original songs. They were not translations; "There Is a Word" exemplified what I had already done. Among my new songs were *"Freunde, kommt, singt Hallelujah"* sung to the chorus of the Battle Hymn of the Republic, "Glory, Glory, Hallelujah"; "Down by the Riverside" became *"Ich will froh sein und leben"*; and "Lord, Lord, Lord, You've Been So Good to Me" became *"Gott, Gott, Gott, du bist so gut zu mir."* I changed Bob Dylan's world-wide hit, "The Answer, My Friend," to *"Die Antwort, mein Freund, gibt Jesus nur allein."*

To develop song texts required hours, sometimes days. Some I kept reworking for as long as ten years until I felt they were ready for publication. For the first youth worship service I had to compose a whole series of songs within a relatively short period of time. *"Die Antwort, mein Freund"* I wrote in a few minutes. I was so inspired that the text itself simply flowed out onto the paper. This occurred in spite of what surely was an impossible situation—I had opened the window to air out the place, a draft blew through the room, the curtains fluttered, and the typewriter was covered with papers. Everything seemed in disarray as if haste was the watchword, and then, suddenly, the lines came together.

Over the years a vast number of songs were written expressly for this service, were sung here publicly for the first time, or became known because of it. During the GDR period it was virtually impossible to get new songs published. Only by singing them did people become familiar with them. Many of them made their way over the border into the West. The youth worship service was the most important incubator for new songs.

What enabled this were the musicians I invited, one per worship service. Each performer had 20 to 25 minutes to present his message. With one exception, and that turned out to be a disaster, I never let vocalists perform whom I did not know beforehand. Of course, I also had to hear them sing. Not every musician, not even every Christian musician, fit into our worship service. I never asked in advance about the precise details of what they intended to sing. They had absolute freedom here. This, of course, assumed a certain level of confidence and that we were on the same spiritual wavelength.

Youth worship service at the Schlosskirche in Karl-Marx-Stadt, 1972

It wasn't simply a matter of singing songs. Rather, I needed songs that strengthened faith and that were attuned to my evangelistic sermons. The musicians came from the various regional and free churches in the GDR. Many of them were appearing on a larger stage than they had ever been on before and for the first time gained recognition, at least in Saxony. For the Christian music scene in the GDR, the worship service was an important crystallization point. Significant fruits of these services after the *Wende* included the Lichtenstein Music Festival that started in Saxony and the annual "*Gottwillalle-Tour*" (God Wants Everyone Tour), in which leading musicians engaged in evangelistic efforts all over Germany.

Jörg Swoboda had gotten his start as a singer/composer a few years before joining the team. He was the first songwriter to do so and remained faithful to the end. He began his career as the pastor at a Baptist congregation in the town of Lichtenstein, located about 15 miles from Karl-Marx-Stadt. A mutual friend, Andreas Wachter, had told him about me and arranged for him to contact me. One day the door bell rang. When I answered it before me stood a strapping young man with a guitar case who introduced himself as Jörg Swoboda. It was love at first sight. I had long dreamed of finding a musical partner who was good-looking, could sing well, could play the guitar, related well to people, and most importantly had the right theology. It was a wish fantasy that I could scarcely hope to see realized. And yet the fulfillment was right here on my door step.

Into the living room we went, and he unpacked his guitar and sang several songs. This was it! He was the one for whom I had been looking. After he had departed, Elke (unlike Sarah [Gen 18:10] who eavesdropped from behind the door) was in the room listening to Jörg's singing and said, "We'll take him." That was the beginning of a lifelong collaboration and friendship. As a duo we held evangelistic meetings from Karl-Marx-Stadt to Canada, struggled together on a variety of occasions, and even lollygagged as tourists in New Orleans. But most significantly, we composed a great deal of music together such as the *Christival* Song of 1988, "That Your Word Might Take Root in My Heart." (I will say more later on about this large evangelical youth congress that takes place in Germany every few years and draws thousands of people.)

Jörg later wrote the following about me: "True to the Bible and powerful with words like Spurgeon, faithful like Jonathan, untamed like John the Baptist, like a loving mother to those who are beaten down, as vicious as a watchdog when it came to theological hot-shots with over-inflated ideas of their own importance, precise like a senior nurse, absolutely without respect for those godless types who deified themselves, [and] as humorous, even satirical, as a cabaret performer."

The musicians gave each worship service its own unique tone, whereas everything else in the service took place in the same form and sequence: an introductory song played by the band and sung by the congregation, my greeting, a song by the band, introduction of the guest musician, 20 minutes for his performance, another song by the band, the sermon, a prayer ending with the Lord's Prayer, a clos-

Three musicians (l. to r.): Lutz Scheufler, Jörg Swoboda, Wolfgang Tost

ing song by the band, and finally, a benediction. That was all! It was a completely straightforward, unsensational affair.

With You Alone

Because of the many pillars in the splendid Gothic Schlosskirche where these services were inaugurated, most of the attendees, whose numbers reached into the thousands, were unable to see much or even anything at all. This precluded the use of visual elements in the service; we were totally dependent on what could be heard. There were no visual presentations, pantomimes, or other such things that enrich many a service today. This concentration upon the spoken word, forced upon us by outward circumstances, was actually our strength.

Another factor, the very presence of such large numbers, proved to be especially important in strengthening one's faith. Anyone who wanted a seat had to come at least an hour early. That was the first thousand. The remainder, also approximately a thousand, had to stand. The center aisle from the door to the altar steps was jammed. I had to struggle to find a path from the sacristy to the pulpit, and I looked like a stork as I tiptoed through the mass of young people squatting in my path. Moreover, the sacristy, where we met to prepare for the service in prayer and partaking of the Lord's Supper, was crammed with up to 60 people. Charismatics would have had no chance here. There simply was no space for any to lift up their hands. As it was, it was difficult to partake of the communion bread and cup and to pass the elements on to the next person.

Youth worship service in the Petrikirche, Karl-Marx-Stadt, 1980

NO CHATTERING, NO IF'S, AND'S, OR BUT'S

Now, try to imagine what it meant for those young people who met with a small group of others once a week on youth night, and who were always being told that the church was dying out, and that Christianity was at the tail end of society. Then, they came into this huge stone church which was bubbling and throbbing with the sounds of thousands of young people. This experience—"Hey, we really aren't alone here"—was the first thing that strengthened an attendee's faith, even before I had opened my mouth. Then a yet greater boost in spiritual awareness came as the band cut loose and the mass of young people responded in song like a thousand-voice choir. All in all, each service was a unique experience, something that was true not only for the participants but also for me.

I prepared for each service with a maximum of effort. I read my sermon beforehand to a small group, and we then discussed it. That was of great help to me, and I got a lot of useful feedback and stimulation. My reactions were varied. Often when they said, "You can't possibly say it that way in this sermon," I accepted that criticism and changed what I was going to say. Other times I just responded: "You can say what you want, but I am going to do it Sunday just this way and no other, regardless of what happens." Once I read the statement by a noted preacher: "A preacher must be ready to go to the scaffold for his sermon." That was my view as well. There were truths that I had to say clearly and directly, and I had to reckon with the possibility of arrest. I never understood how it was possible for colleagues to carry out their duty as preachers without taking the consequences into account.

The preacher

As a preacher of the truth who lived in a system of lies, proclaiming the truth openly was bound to lead to conflicts and consequences. From the outset of my ministry I had decided that the main emphasis of my pastoral work would rest upon the sermon. That meant that I would not be able to make as many house visits. As a pastor, one cannot do everything. Each person must figure out where his or her special talents lie and emphasize them. With me it was the sermon. Since I spent many days in intensive preparation for each sermon, I often questioned myself about whether this huge amount of time was justified. I was helped very much by the Saxon church's youth administrator, Werner Morgenstern, who said to me one time: "You reach more young people with one sermon than I do in half a year." And so during my preparation time I continued to sharpen my ideas, smoothed out the language, and struggled for clarity.

The operative principle for me was: Nothing must take place in the service that is unintelligible to a non-Christian, or assumes any kind of prior knowledge. This principle held true not only for the sermon, but for everything—beginning with the first words of the greeting, to which I likewise gave great effort and often spent hours in preparation. The same held for the offertory. I devoted a great deal of time to explaining what kind of an outreach action the collection would finance, and this required research on my part to insure my facts were correct. Then all this had to be presented with humor and jokes to produce a successful result.

The collections themselves were a phenomenon. The largest single offering brought in 10,000 East German marks. The grand total came to over a half a million marks. The ones throwing money into the baskets were young people, truly sacrificial givers. The sermons were always evangelistic. The object was to interpret a Bible text carefully so as to make the message one that awakens and strengthens faith. One need not artificially pep up the words of the Bible with all kinds of gimmicks. The more carefully the Scripture passage is explained, the more effective it becomes, and its absolute relevance will leave the listener breathless.

I learned from a music teacher, Gottfried Schmiedel, that an hour in which a person doesn't laugh at least once, is, from a pedagogical standpoint, a total waste. That was true also for the youth worship service. There was always some sort of humor in the greeting, and certainly in the sermon. It almost always began with a joke and often was spiced with political humor.

Everything, even the song selections, lay in my hands so that every evening was virtually identical in structure. There were to be no surprises. The youth service became a kind of trade mark for me and came to be called the "Theo-Worship Service." The totality of my pastoral service was focused on this time period—always the second Sunday of the month. Invariably I spent the evening before in my study. Even the day itself was determined by the evening service. I sat around in my room in my apartment, went to hear the band practice in another room, and ate spaghetti with them at noon. Those were the only contacts I allowed myself until I appeared in the church in the evening.

I was always the one who preached—except when I was hospitalized because of my heart operation. The person who filled in for me then was the youth administrator, Rainer Dick. All other times, I was there. Frequently people asked how it was that in nearly 30 years I almost never was absent from these services. My response was simply: on the second Sunday of the month, the youth worship service took place. *Period*! It didn't matter whether I had a cough or a cold. Moreover, the maxim I learned from my father held true: "Pulpit wood has healing qualities." Not being there just wasn't an option.

At the beginning, the service started at 6:00 P.M. Later on, in fact, for most of its duration, duplicate services at 5:00 and 6:00 P.M. took place. Because of construction work, we had to move out of the Schlosskirche into the Petrikirche, located on the Theaterplatz directly in the center of town, and then once again, for the same reason, we relocated into the Lutherkirche. Wherever we were, people could be sure that the service was exactly the same as at the beginning. I assume that this regular and simple format was one of the main reasons for the length of time that it existed. Nothing "wears out" faster than constant changing of a group's meeting format. It tends to drive people away. For the sake of orientation, people need a certain degree of familiarity. That something exciting, surprising, and sparkling took place was not because something new and different was always occurring. Rather, the attraction and curiosity were based on the content of the service

In front of the Petrikirche
before the youth worship service

The young people gradually became accustomed to the style of the band, the music, and the preacher. Even the washboard lost its drawing power as the controversial meeting came to be accepted as a regular part of normal church life. What was always new were the contributions of the musicians, who often risked their necks with their off-the-cuff comments and song lyrics. And then, of course, there was the sermon.

THE *WENDE* AS A BEGINNING BUT NOT A CONCLUSION

The youth worship service survived the *Wende*, the "Revolution of the Candles" in 1989. In fact, it did much better than all the other church (and many secular) enterprises known to me. There were voices filled with malice or worry that questioned whether the whole thing would continue after the *Wende*. What lay behind these expressions of concern was the idea that the masses had come merely because I had laced my sermons with political barbs and remarked about current political events. The assumption was that following the demise of the political foe, this attractiveness of the youth worship service would vanish. But, the essential factor was not that once in a while I made a few choice comments, but rather that I preached the message of God's judgment and grace and called upon the hearers to be converted.

Another view following the *Wende* was that we could throw away the old manuscripts, sermons, etc. Everything now had to be done differently. However, I threw nothing out and did not do anything differently. To the contrary, I feel quite gratified that I did not find it necessary to change my message after the *Wende*. Apart from a few dated references, I could preach the same sermons today that I did in the communist period. I not only made use of jokes but also explained the Bible. The message of the Savior of sinners who rescues lost human beings is absolutely independent of political jokes and changes. Because my sermons were strictly biblical, in the GDR they were de facto political statements.

The changed political situation did not render the sermons invalid since they were explanations of the eternally valid divine truths in God's commandments and offer of salvation. Moreover, I am convinced that the outer form cannot at all be separated from the contents. Therefore, one cannot factor out the individual motives as to why this worship service attracted so many people. It was the event as a totality, and the contents are just as important as the packaging.

In the first years of the youth worship services I tried an experiment. I preached the same sermon in the evening youth service as I had in the regular morning congregational worship service. The only difference was that in the morning, I used the formal second person pronoun, *Sie*, when

I addressed the churchgoers, and in the evening, the informal, *du*. Also, in the morning, a time when the young people were still sleeping, I was wrapped in my black garb, surrounded by the sounds of an organ, and bound by the language of the liturgy. All of that, including the hymnbook, fell by the wayside in the evening. I proved for about a decade that I could reach an audience ten to twenty times as large with the identical sermon by changing the format and time. From a business standpoint, you could say I was able to deliver the product "directly to each person" and reach 20 times as many of them simply by changing the packaging. I am just as gratified about of this result as I am sad that so few churches were willing to emulate this worship service.

The first youth worship service in September of 1971 was accompanied by a considerable amount of tension. Would the band succeed in getting the young people to sing? The band had never done this and the songs themselves were new. And, would anyone come? The *Junge Gemeinde,* the youth congregation, carried out an action deserving of high praise. They went through the church roll and looked for the names,

Youth worship service at the Petrikirche in the 80s

by date of birth, and addresses, of those who had been baptized and confirmed, but who were not active in the life of the church. They then wrote hundreds of letters, all by hand, inviting the recipients to the new service. There were times when the meeting room of the *Junge Gemeinde* looked like a post office at Christmas. How would the young people from the Schlosskirche congregation react? This worship service had been designed for the youth of that church. But where the 500–600 young people came from who were at the first youth worship service still remains a mystery to me. From the very first, this was not an internal affair of this one congregation but rather one of national significance.

With You Alone

The singing of songs that few had ever sung before went well from the beginning. And the spark leaped over to the next service. Ambe, who was playing the washboard, jumped up and down like the fairy tale character Rumpelstiltskin. Gunter plucked away on the banjo like an old jazz pro. Detlef with his guitar led the singing as though he, a cook by trade, had never done anything else in his life. I was absolutely amazed at these guys who were playing together for the very first time. And not only that. These were all new songs that they were singing before hundreds of young people.

This interested me, since on that same day during the morning worship service I had watched as our very enthusiastic music director was unable to get the Schlosskirche attendees, all of whom were well-acquainted with singing, to learn a simple canon (round). What the band did had little in common with musical quality. By today's standards the sound system was little more than "junk." But, the passionate engagement that these guys demonstrated was outstanding. The quality of the music, of course, gradually improved, as well as the technical quality of the equipment. Still, when I listen to the old tapes, I always have the impression (perhaps it is just nostalgia, I don't know) that this enthusiasm was never again quite the same.

Lutherkirche: the 150th youth worship service

At the Monday morning staff discussion of the Sunday's events after this first youth service, not a single word was said about the youth service. It was eerie—the church had been filled with young people and everything had gone peacefully—but everyone acted as though nothing special had happened. Only at the end of the conversation did the senior pastor ask me for the collection taken up at the service. I refused his request since according to the church rules collection funds designated for specific purposes may not be commingled with other monies. *The cold cash!* That was the only thing that my church wanted from this service.

But the discussion became more intense in another area. The same superintendent, who had insisted that we offer a youth-oriented worship service in the churches of our district, pounced on me and called the service in the Schlosskirche my "solo project." He wrote me a letter, somehow rather appropriately for him, on the day before Christmas which said, "What you are now experiencing is, in truth, nothing other than the consequence of what you yourself have done." He was referring, of course, to my "solo project." He then informed me "that a sensible pastoral activity, one that would be blessed, could only occur when it proceeds from community effort, from the group." By this he meant the church hierarchy, the pastoral staff, the Team.

He undoubtedly did not understand when I explained to him that I prepared the services together with a small group of young people (he referred to them as "minors," therefore unqualified) who were in our home almost day and night. I was not aware of any pastoral colleagues who had given up family and private life to such a degree to work together with a group. Moreover, I never knew a pastor who, as I would do for several decades, presented his sermon ahead of time to a group of church members and discussed it with them.

The team from "Worship Service, Somewhat Different," also had their "two cents" to add. They invited me to a discussion where they accused me of offering competition against the main group. To defuse this nonsense, I preached again several times in that service, but I had to stop when the theological trenches between us became too deep. The *Stasi* had taken note of this with great satisfaction, since this rift greatly aided them in their "differentiation process." The *Stasi*, however, didn't just see us as a pastoral team torn by divisions. They took an active part in the process and turned up the heat by sending anonymous letters that defamed my character.

> I'll go through life with you only.
> Only with you can I exist.
> Jesus, I trust you.
> You are here, stay by me, lead me on.
>
> Only with you through all my sorrow.
> Only with you to eternity.
> Jesus, I trust you.
> You are here, stay by me, protect me.

With You Alone

Only with you can I endure.
Only with you can I come home
Jesus, I trust you.
You are here, stay by me, bless me.

9

That's When Freedom Will Really Be Ours

I HATE SPIDERS. AND, of all things, that's what the *Stasi* labeled my file: "Operational Procedure-Preliminary Stage, 'Spider' (*Spinne*)." And so this term is inscribed on my *Stasi* documents. I really would like to know how they hit upon this idea. Maybe it was because they had discovered "a web of numerous contacts to whom L. has access in many areas of the arts and cultural life, young people, education, etc." What one in the West might call the "executive summary" for my file opens with a graphic representation of the network of people with whom I was associated. The list ranges from "*dekatenten Jugendlichen*" (decadent youth—the *Stasi* had a spelling problem; their reports almost always used the spelling *dekatent* instead of the correct *dekadent*), to pen pals, people from the jazz scene, such as those from the Jena jazz band and the jazz club New Orleans, USA, and singers from Fred Frohberg to Pete Seeger.

The first detailed operational plan "because of suspicion of verbal anti-government propaganda as outlined in Paragraph 106 in the Civil Code of the GDR" has the following "points of emphasis":

1. The acquisition of evidence as well as possible clues showing verbal anti-government propaganda, along with infractions of other criminal laws.

2. The introduction and achievement of effective measures that lead to compromising the character of Dr. L. as a citizen of the GDR, and as a recognized representative of reactionary church circles in Karl-Marx-Stadt.

3. The introduction and achievement of a number of carefully-conceived operative combinations which will compel L. to surrender his position as a pastor in the Lutheran Church in Karl-Marx-Stadt or to completely give up his service as a pastor.

That's When Freedom Will Really Be Ours

THE MONKEY WANTS TO GET ON MY BACK

As I pored through the thousands of pages of my *Stasi* documents I discovered remarkably few false entries or errors (wrong names or dates), and even fewer fabrications and ridiculous lies. Still, there were exceptions. For example, I found a note regarding a conversation from *IMV* "*Klaus Müller*," actually our Choir Director (*Kantor*) Eckard Sauer. [An *IMV* (*Inoffizieller Mitarbeiter Vorlauf*) was an individual who cooperated with the *Stasi* but was not yet formally recognized as such. He was sort of an "agent-in training" and eventually would become a paid informant, an *IM* ("unofficial collaborator").] "Lehmann had said that his vacation this year did not go very well. In the vacation facility run by the *FDGB* [*Freier Deutscher Gewerkschaftsbund*, the GDR's state-controlled labor union] the crooks took advantage of him. In addition, he said that he had to buy winter fuel this year himself. In previous years [he] had surreptitiously taken the fuel from the church." As a professional church musician Sauer knew quite well that I, as a pastor, was not a member of the *FDGB* and would never have been allowed to book space in any *FDGB* vacation facility.

To compromise my character, the *Stasi* conjured up some silly, mischievous things in addition to the really profound, devilish, malicious acts. Let's start with the relatively harmless things. For example, one operation was described like this:

"Using a children's play printing set, [we will] create the following lines:
1. 'Come to Pastor Lehmann's tonight, for we will have group sex'
2. 'Sex at 16 is very nice. You can see it at Pastor Lehmann's.'"

The police then stuffed the mail boxes of homes in our immediate neighborhood with these rhyming couplets [in German] and several others hand-printed on plain school paper.

"What we intend to accomplish is to make L. the laughingstock of the Christian community. As a result of the combination of these actions, [we expect] the following to occur: The school located in the area of the church and the Central/North Adult Education Department of the city will lodge a formal complaint with the church, alleging that since the contents of these documents do not coincide with the moral standards of our socialist state, the culprits must come from the *Junge Gemeinde* of this church."

If these couplets seem inane, the *Stasi* anonymously circulated other bits of verse—one was based on a poem in the style of the nineteenth-century Romantic poet Eduard Mörike, obviously composed by someone who had literary training—about Elke and me. It hit so far below the belt that I can't quote it here.

The left-wing satirist Kurt Tucholsky had wrestled with similar kinds of character defamation during the Weimar years and worked out some formulas to determine who had composed such bitter verses against him. He concluded that someone had to consciously sit down and write these things. But who was it? Naturally, I had the same question about these filthy poems. Who goes to the trouble to do such a thing? Who has such a sick mind? Who in his thinking is so *kaputt*, amoral, and possessed of the lowest possible vulgarity? Yes, it was certainly the *Stasi*, but what specific individual put these vulgarities on paper?

He was, as I learned from my own as well as other *Stasi* documents, IMV "Kaufmann," the code name for Pastor Carl Schmid, one of the five Karl-Marx-Stadt pastors who had been assigned as *IM*'s to spy on me. Comments in my *Stasi* record indicated that Schmid had received numerous awards from the GDR—the "National Medal of Honor in Bronze," another medal honoring 30 years of faithful service in the *Nationale Volksarmee* (the East German army), and medals commemorating the 30th anniversary of the founding of the GDR, and 30 years of the *MfS* (Ministry for State Security, i.e., the *Stasi*). He received a monetary award of 5,000 marks during the celebration in 1980 honoring the 31st anniversary of the GDR and a bonus of 1,000 marks for 25 years of service as an *IM* as well as an additional 350 marks tacked on to his monthly pension. (As a pastor one earned a maximum of 650 marks.) These entries alone show that this man could not have had anything resembling a conscience. He was the one who sat in his pastoral study and thought out these horrific verses. Presumably, he even smirked as he wrote this filth down.

Together with Pastor Schmid there were three additional pastors who were responsible for keeping track of me in Karl-Marx-Stadt:

IM "*Matthes*," really Pastor Löbel,

IME [*IM in besonderen Einsatz*, an informant who was given special assignments] "*Schiller*," really Pastor Müller

IMB [*IM zur Bearbeitung*, an informant who worked directly to penetrate alleged oppositional circles] "*Friedhelm*," really Pastor Leonhard.

From my colleagues at the church was the aforementioned *IM "Klaus Müller"* (Choir Director Eckhard Sauer).

But above all was one of the most disgraceful creatures I have ever known, *IMV "Steinert,"* actually Armin Schwarze, who served as Church Music Director in Aue, a town about 20 miles away. This *Stasi* lackey was assigned "to spread the rumor that L. is cooperating with the *MfS*" and to communicate his amazement that, in spite of my "negative comments" I had never been called to account by the state authorities—thus meaning that I must have a "patron" inside the state apparatus.

This supposition that I was working as an "informer" for the *Stasi* was also spread by other *IM*'s, and an action plan was developed which specified the following: "An anonymous letter will be sent to Supt. Fehlberg arousing the suspicion that 'Spider' is collaborating with the state authorities. The basis for this would be that 'Spider' had [illegally] sent out 700 invitations [to an event] and was not punished. The author of the letter would suggest that there must be a Christian who still works for the government and knows something about 'Spider.'"

BROTHERLY LOVE AND SIDESWIPES

Anonymous writings were an especially important and effective measure utilized by the *Stasi*. So, the *Ökumenischer Arbeitskreis* (Ecumenical Team) sent a letter addressed to all pastors, the Saxon Church office, the Confessing Church [a group that countered anticommunist tendencies in the church], the Home Mission office, and the Task Force on the Church and Religious Confession. The "Ecumenical Team" actually was a fabrication of the *Stasi*, as the document frankly admitted: "Most of the pastors and lay people accept the fact of the existence of the organization which, really, we created." The author of the various phony letters was *IM "Kaufmann,"* namely, Pastor Carl Schmid.

The *Stasi* observed closely the reactions of the pastors to whom the various anonymous letters were sent raising suspicions about my marital fidelity, trafficking in hashish, sex- and drug parties, collaboration with the *Stasi*, etc. The report went on to say: "Within the framework of so-called 'ecclesiastical brotherly love,' pastors stand behind 'Spider' in pastoral discussions regarding church policy and other matters (in order to preserve the appearance of brotherliness). In individual conversations between pastors and other individuals one can be glad that we have defamed 'Spider' in this way. This also lends credence to the charges against him." I find it personally gratifying that the pastors, outwardly at least, backed me. Less gratifying is what many of my colleagues said against me amongst themselves which, of course, I cannot verify.

So I read in the *Stasi* intelligence report:

> Fehlberg states that the charges against "Spider" could be true [and] that he himself believes them to be true. "Spider" could very well be involved in sex orgies and drug smuggling.... In this connection, he directed youth pastor Hermsdorf to look after "Spider" and to keep a close eye on him.
>
> Pastor Böhme in Hainichen [northeast of Chemnitz] declared that the allegations against "Spider" probably do correspond to the truth. He had joined "Spider" on a vacation trip on the Baltic and determined that his family life was a shambles.
>
> Pastor Pirl, Karl-Marx-Stadt, is glad to see the charges against Le. and likewise he believes, based on personal conversations, that the strong possibility exists "Spider" has taken part in such activities. ... Pirl said that "Spider" has only himself to blame. Whoever engages in such activity shouldn't be surprised [at the outcome].
>
> Pastor Ackermann . . . doesn't like "Spider's" worship services and is working with the *ESG* [*Evangelische Studentengemeinde*, Protestant Student Congregation] to counter them. Pastor Kluge at the Karl-Marx-Stadt Schlosskirche is the only one who, on the basis of "brotherliness," tries to justify "Spider's" actions.
>
> Pastor Fraustadt, Karl-Marx-Stadt, stated he is of the opinion that the charges leveled against Lehmann are true.... He believes that "Spider" is training the young people to be obedient subjects dependent on him and are, therefore, not true Christians. As a result, he totally rejects "Spider's" methods.

Besides Pastor Kluge, only Pastor Epperlein stood up for me. The others were silent or reacted as described above. The *Stasi* had achieved its goal of my defamation and isolation. Superintendent Fehlberg well summarized the situation within the pastoral staffs in Karl-Marx-Stadt: "So much mistrust has been sown that currently no pastor trusts any other one." In fact, Pastor Kluge suggested that to be consistent we should cease addressing each other as "Brother."

That's When Freedom Will Really Be Ours

BEAUTIFUL COUNTERFEITS IN *STASI* GARB

The destruction of confidence and the fact that, in the end, almost no one trusted anyone else was a catastrophe. Naturally, this was a clear victory for the *Stasi*. And yet, I would have to say that this mistrust was, in fact, justified, and far too many of our colleagues were not careful about whom they should trust. We must remember that there were four pastors in our midst who, at the behest of the *Stasi*, had themselves brought this entire loss of trust into our workplace. Regarding Löbel and Schmid, word had already seeped through that they were working for the other side, but we did not yet have hard evidence for this. About the others, including many of our own church colleagues, we didn't have a clue. In any case, I learned from the *Stasi* period that one cannot rely on anyone because every individual is capable of almost any conceivable act.

Of course, one can't live with such a weight of mistrust on one's shoulders. Therefore I risked trust time and time again and, in so doing, I found people who did not disappoint this confidence. Without such people in my life I would not have been able to hold up during this time. But I also experienced a situation where the person in whom I had placed the most trust and could under no circumstances imagine him committing a betrayal, that very one turned out to be a betrayer. My understanding of human nature, of which I thought I had a good portion as a pastor, totally failed me here. My disillusionment about human nature, in spite of the scriptural warning "the inclination of the human heart is evil from youth" (Gen 8:21), was as great as my shock over the satanic power of the *Stasi*, who was able to distort the thinking and actions of such people.

As stated in my file, the anonymous letters of the *Stasi* were written "with the objective of harming 'Spider' in every aspect of his person." It goes without saying that all of this had its effect on me. The *Stasi* evaluated my situation in this way: "His fears are leading him to believe that both the state and the church are gathering material to annihilate him. By means of these operational measures 'Spider's' nerves were so strongly attacked that in further actions to be undertaken special emphasis will be placed on this fact.... 'Spider' must be forced to liquidate his service as a pastor in Karl-Marx-Stadt, or even in the church at large."

The *Stasi* plan to achieve this goal included several objectives. I was to:

- become entangled in a sexual crime,
- be put under suspicion of larceny,
- be made an accessory to criminal acts that had been committed with my knowledge.

Furthermore:
- In my neighborhood acts of vandalism would take place,
- Elke was to be tempted into engaging in extra-marital relations, and I, likewise, was to be seduced by a female *IM*,
- I was to receive telephone calls threatening me with bodily harm and the destruction of my health.

Stasi Colonel Gehlert suggested that I should be conscripted into a reserve training unit, or as he specifically put it, "that Dr. L., at an appropriate time, will be assigned to the *NVA* (GDR army) post at Marienberg in the Karl-Marx-Stadt District [20 miles south of the city] so that additional measures can be carried out that will bring about his assimilation into a solid military collective of dependable and convinced members of the *SED* Party and the Free German Youth. Through his assignment to the *NVA* unit in Marienberg, the conditions are in place for an active operational handling of Dr. L.'s case."

Finally, the *Stasi* determined that: "The next invitation that Dr. L. receives to go to the *Kapitalistisches Ausland* [capitalist world abroad, the GDR bureaucratic term for non-communist territories], or to West Germany, will be approved. However, travel permission will be denied to any others invited to the same event. The reason to be given is that only trusted citizens and those well-disposed toward the state may receive permission to travel abroad. This operational measure will inevitably compromise L.'s character and motives and effectively serve to confirm the rumor that L. is, in fact, a *Stasi* collaborator.

The plan specified another action:

"On December 5, 1971, the electricity will be shut off in the area of the Schlosskirche from 18:20 until 19:30. This period coincides with the time that music will be playing and the young people present will become quite restless as a result of the power outage."

The higher-ups in the *Stasi* rejected this scheme as well as one proposed by someone in the Central Committee of the *SED* in Berlin. This one called for "systematically delegating hundreds of [uniformed] *FDJ* members to attend the service in the Schlosskirche. The presence of so many people will lead to disturbances and thereby give the state authorities a reason to forbid the service."

The plan virtually took on the character of a detective novel:

> *IMV "Klaus Müller"* will plant a wallet in L.'s apartment at a time when many young people are expected to be present. This wallet will contain a goodly number of secretly marked West German DM bills. Should a purchase be made in an *Intershop* [a special store in the GDR which only accepted Western money] with this currency, the buyer will be immediately taken into custody and turned over to Department K.[the criminal police]. It is immaterial whether the L. family or a young person from his group makes the purchase. Through follow-up measures of Dept. K, L. or the other person from L.'s circle can be charged with violation of the foreign exchange laws, and judicial proceedings then instituted for the punishment of L. or his friend. Following this, the possibility will be considered of preparing a thorough report on the attitude of the pastor and sending it to the Regional Church Central Administration or to Superintendent Fehlberg.

It went on to propose that during one of the youth worship services, an *IM* "will pour out in the church a quantity of butyric acid provided to him. [The noxious-smelling chemical] will cause a considerable disruption of the service. Dependable *IM*'s will paste bills advertising church events on cars parked on the Theaterplatz [the square adjacent to the Petrikirche] with the objective of encouraging citizens to file formal complaints about property damage. Selected *IM*'s of Section Ref. XX/2 [as mentioned earlier, the *Stasi* department responsible for oversight of the church] shall be used to discredit L.'s church service through obscene behavior and tossing trash on the church grounds and adjoining properties. This will evoke negative reactions by sincere Christians and pastors as well as the appropriate parish council."

Later, the *Stasi* wanted to try, "if the occasion presented itself, to charge [him] with customs violations or implement punitive measures as a result of other offenses committed against existing laws."

Finally, "according to the instruction received from the Comrade Minister [of State Security]," I am to be summoned to a discussion in the Karl-Marx-Stadt District Police Office that will accomplish the following: "It will be communicated to Pastor Lehmann that he must reckon with the fact that the state apparatus intends to initiate an investigation to determine whether he is strictly adhering to the ordinance concerning public meetings. Should Pastor Lehmann, in spite of this situation, again become involved in state matters or in his worship services go above and beyond purely religious topics, then a criminal proceeding will be brought against Pastor Lehmann."

A mini-detective story of a special kind was a clever speed trap designed just for me. The *Stasi* knew that I intended to drive to an evangelistic campaign in Hohenstein-Ernstthal, about ten miles away, and some agents put on traffic cops' uniforms and positioned themselves along the route. They planned to stop my car, an East German built Wartburg sedan, charge me with speeding, and confiscate my auto papers. However, I wasn't in my Wartburg, whose license plate number they had and for which they were watching, but in the passenger seat of the Wartburg of the singer for the meetings, Gottfried Schreiter. He had a Dresden district tag on his car and the *Stasi* did not notice us as we drove by. So none of these plans functioned. I felt as though I were Daniel in the lions' den. God had again and again delivered me from the jaws of the *Stasi* and kept me safe.

Fortunately for me, I knew absolutely nothing about these plans. I only found out about them later as I saw them detailed in the pages of my *Stasi* files. It then came to me that I was like the horseman in the 19th century ballad by Gustav Schwab who rode across the frozen surface of Lake Constance. Only when he had arrived at the shore safely did he realize what danger he had been in—the ice was only an inch thick.

JUST ONE REFRAIN—LET US BE FREE

The *Stasi* carefully noted every one of my political jokes and every social allusion and understood them very well. Their great concern was, as one document noted, "that Pastor Lehmann remains below the criminal radar, albeit coming very close to crossing the line. He uses his sermons in a skillful way to attack the societal relationships in the GDR without overtly doing so in an inflammatory manner. He addresses individual issues and leaves it to the listeners to draw their own conclusions about them."

For example, a sentence was quoted from a sermon on the Good Shepherd (in which I used the *Stasi* to represent the missing sheep dogs in Jesus' parable): "Jesus isn't a party boss who is so anxious about his power that he lines every critic up against the wall." The document goes on: "A direct slander of societal relationships in the GDR was committed by Lehmann on May 9, 1982, when he stated: 'Talk with those who lie at your door, who were shot down, or who were placed on a cross, not to mention those whom one can no longer question at all because they are in prison or are sitting in an [insane] asylum because of their political or religious persuasion.'"

Absolutely correct and on the mark, however, is this evaluation by the *Stasi*. "The political views of Lehmann can be summarized as a consistent rejection of the socialist state, the basic belief that freedom in the GDR is limited, and everything must be done to utilize the existing possibilities in the GDR to struggle for freedom. His veiled attacks are directed towards the socialist policy of military training for our youth and our educational policies." Marvelous! Struggle against the lack of freedom as the foundation of my work and life—I couldn't have said it any better!

The *Stasi* recognized that the theme of freedom not only was the foundation of my preaching but also of my book and songwriting activity. "In this connection, we must look at his written works. They deal with the history of the Negro spirituals and how they are derived from the Negroes' history of oppression in America and this leads the reader to assume that L. is drawing comparisons with the socialistic GDR." They got it right again! That is precisely why I got into this kind of music and have propagated it. How did the African-American Christians through their music react to the oppression that they were experiencing? What did this longing for freedom, expressed in their songs, practically achieve? All of this is what I researched in the history of these Christians and wrote about up to the civil rights movement under the leadership of Dr. Martin Luther King, Jr. His book *Stride Toward Freedom* fascinated me, and I have quoted from it often. However, while I hid, so to speak, behind the words of others and talked in a roundabout way, Elke minced no words on this topic.

It was once again an election Sunday, and once again the Lehmann family did not show up at the polls. So, the customary agitators rang our doorbell and demanded that we go and vote. A heated discussion ensued. One of them said, "You are doing very well here in the GDR. I see you have a large apartment, and you also have a car—What do you really want?" Whereupon Elke screamed so loud that her voice resounded through the stairwell, "We want freedom, freedom!"

True freedom is only possible when one is in union with Jesus. That was the real theme and goal of my sermons. And I feel extremely gratified that the *Stasi* recognized precisely that point. They judged that the purpose of my sermons was always to convince the young people "to turn themselves over, unconditionally, to Jesus." What a beautiful testimonial: "Lehmann called upon the youth—with great urgency—under all circumstances, regardless of one's position, to turn their lives over to God."

Sadly, many of my church colleagues did not see matters in the same way. Of course, I never expected that everyone would agree with my way of doing things and every one of my basic theological beliefs. There were enough heated discussions and theological in-fighting as it was. What I could not fathom was why those colleagues who held theologically different positions than I did refused to stand with me when it came to our relationship with the state. Instead, they ran unscrupulously and zealously to the representatives of the state with their negative opinions about me.

Of all of these people Pastor Eggert took things to their greatest extreme. (Incidentally, after the *Wende*, he did a stint as the Interior Minister of Saxony). Although not an *IM* himself, he talked freely with his *Stasi* contact who sought his opinion about a particular youth evangelization effort I was planning to hold, as he believed "that this occasion would not be in the best interest of the church." He told the agent that he had posted no advertisements for it, he was "against this type of presentation," and he had attended one of the meetings but left it early in protest.

The contact summarized Eggert's assessment of the youth campaign as follows: "He regarded Lehmann as a blasphemer; his knowledge is primitive and has nothing to do with theology; his supposedly scholarly explanations are comparable to those made by the emcee at a bad variety show; [and] one can't bring people to God while threatening them with the end of the world."

BEST OF ALL, GET RID OF HIM IN THE WEST

In the fall of 1972, I was summoned by a high level official of the Regional Church Central Administrative Office, von Brück, to Dresden. When I returned home, I told Elke about the conversation. I related that von Brück had talked with me for an hour, but I really didn't know what he was after, what he wanted to get from me, or why he had called me in. Most of the conversation dealt with the relationship I had with my brother Johannes, who had been living in West Germany for a long time and with whom

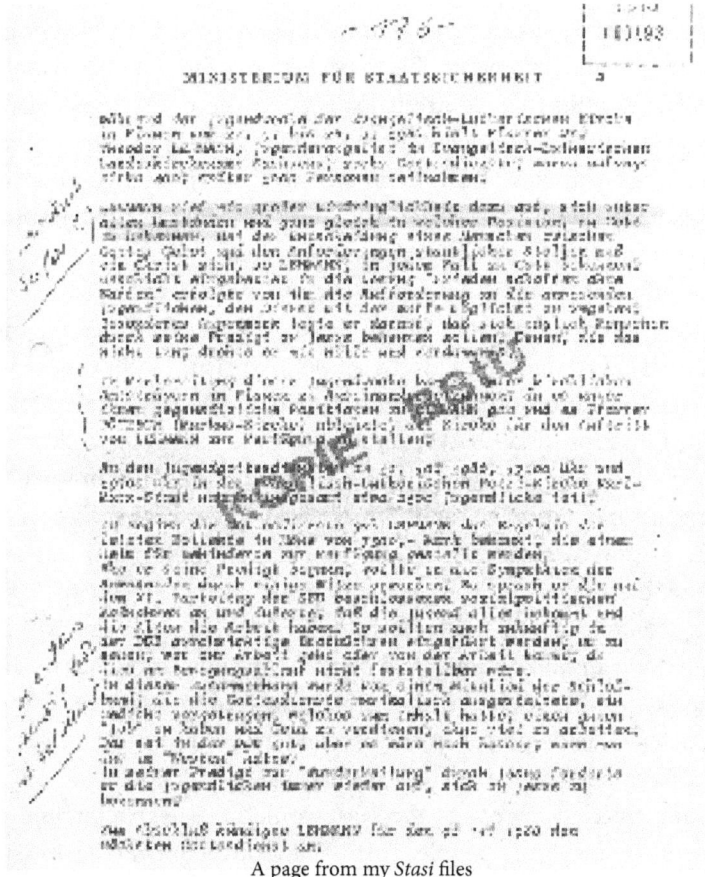

A page from my *Stasi* files

I had very weak contacts. Why was he interested in this? It was all so mysterious. Since I learned after the *Wende* that von Brück had been on the Stasi payroll as *IMB "Zwinger,"* I assume that he had been assigned to find out about my relationships with friends and family in the West. Presumably, the *Stasi* was looking for people whom they could use to facilitate my emigration to the West.

Then, on November 9, 1972, soon after that strange conversation, City Councilman Hahn came by my place, laid some papers in front of me, and said that my application to resettle in the Federal Republic had been approved. I told him I had never applied to emigrate and left the papers lying on the desk, untouched. Hahn was dumbfounded that I didn't jump at the chance to leave and didn't even want to know anything why I was not interested in leaving. It could be that his astonishment was in earnest and that he was simply an unwitting but obedient messenger. In any event, I found in one of the papers in my file dated November 9, 1972, the comments that Comrade [*SED* party member] Trinks had telephoned and said that "a document from [East] Berlin had arrived granting permission for Pastor Dr. Lehmann with his family to emigrate to West Germany." Nothing else was disclosed, "in order not to compromise certain matters regarding conspiratorial actions."

As soon as Hahn put the papers back in his pocket briefcase and left my home, I jumped into my car and drove to Dresden to see the bishop. He said that this could be the last step before prison. Either there would be an arrest or there would be calm. The Saxon Church Office sent a letter to the Office of the *Bund* (Federation) of the Evangelical Churches in the GDR "requesting that Manfred Stolpe, senior councilor of the Church *Bund* consistory, do everything in his power to get to the bottom of the puzzling events of November 9, 1972." This man, however, was far too busy with his own numerous conspiratorial contacts with the *Stasi* to take time to look into my case. Herr von Brück told me later that "church circles in the Federal Republic" had desired my emigration, but he did not say a word about my older brother who now lived in the West.

I never considered for even a second re-opening the matter. First, I would have been agreeing to a lie because I had not made any such application. Second, a move to the West would have been a terrible disappointment to our young people. Third, without the formal permission of my church this wouldn't have been possible anyway. But, really, the most difficult point was the second one. I had been ordained and appointed as a pastor in Karl-Marx-Stadt and I could not and would not abandon either the Schlosskirche congregation or the youth who depended on me. There was no further discussion of the offer to emigrate. But that evening we had a very disturbing experience.

I stood with Elke at the window and watched as a large moving van parked directly beneath our window at the front of the manse. The tractor drove off while the trailer section was left behind. We knew that no one was planning to move either into or out of the manse. We therefore assumed that they intended simply to haul us and our stuff away in the night. Anxiety and helplessness overcame us. Maybe we would be sitting in Düsseldorf (West Germany) in the morning, and this whole miserable situation would be behind us.

What we didn't know was that a sizeable painting from the Schlosskirche was being taken to Dresden for restoration. Because the driver could not maneuver the trailer section of the vehicle into a position in front of the church, he decided to leave the van behind and haul the painting in the cab. Since I had been in Dresden that day and stopped off in Halle at my father's place on the way back, I had not been at the manse and was not informed about the action. The hours of waiting in the night were a test of our nerves. At some point we finally fell asleep. Next morning everything became clear. There was no arrest. The struggle continued.

OUT TO PASTURE! NO WAY!

In official conversations between the church and the state my "catalog of sins" was always presented to my church superiors. Since the *Stasi* could not admit that its agents had tape-recorded all of my sermons and were therefore well-informed about them, I discovered later in my documents that it was "arranged that a 'tape recorder would be found with recorded cassettes' and the items would be handed over to the district council by someone in the state police (*Deutsche Volkspolizei*)." Thus, the *Stasi* had a conversation with Church President Domsch and Senior Councilor von Brück from the *LKA* and told them the police had found a shopping bag at the Karl-Marx-Stadt main train station that contained cassettes of my sermons. Domsch and von Brück were oblivious to the lie, so that the *Stasi* was able to note: "They had no questions about this matter." When the *Stasi* played the critical portions of my sermon tapes, however, a difference of opinion about me arose between Domsch and von Brück. While Domsch tried to defend me, von Brück stabbed me in the back. "Von Brück accepted our concerns and said that Lehmann's statements had gone to the very edge, perhaps even somewhat beyond it."

Apart from this derailment, I would have to say that my church did stand behind me in our confrontations with the state. For example, the *Stasi* officials referred to the case of Pastor Michael Wagner who had gained the displeasure of the authorities for his youth work, and they expressed the wish that the *LKA* should see that such situations did not occur again. They ended the conversation by thanking the *LKA* for its "proper handling" of the Wagner case and advised it to discipline him. *IM "Zwinger"* (von Brück) soon reported to *Stasi* Major Rossberg "that the church leadership has Wagner in check and will help to limit his negative activities." Moreover, should it detect further negative activities it will inform the State Security authorities. The *LKA* finally yielded to the *Stasi* pressure and removed Wagner from his parish in Meerane, a town 20 miles west of where I lived. That was the *Stasi* objective in my case as well—moving me out of Karl-Marx-Stadt—but this time they weren't successful.

This conversation had an interesting sequel. In a memorandum dated March 10, 1978, included in this particular file, is the following:

> It was apparent that during the conversation Comrade HOYER [a subaltern in the district council's office of church affairs who talked directly with the Saxon church] and the official responsible for church affairs, Comrade MÜLLER [the chief], did not follow the instructions that the First Secretary of the SED District Administration, Comrade LORENZ, had given them. In regard to this matter, the district leader emphasized that in the future [*Stasi*] Department XX will have to step in to make certain that the prescribed line is followed. If a course of action has been decided, then it is to be carried out. In the future, they will do what the district chief has authorized.
>
> In the future, to obtain a more accurate understanding of the content of conversations between Comrade HOYER and representatives of the *LKA* Saxony, the head of Department XX shall make sure that the operational technology of Department 26 is utilized.

This meant that future conversations would be overheard with "bugs" and microphones so that the bosses could see whether their demands were followed, or, on the contrary, things were not in accord with the party line. Total surveillance!

In addition, a memo of March 3, 1978 contains an extremely interesting item. At the time the above-mentioned conversation had taken place, I was hospitalized because of my heart attack. Domsch and von Brück informed their conversation partners about this, and they hypocritically expressed their deep concern, although they were quite aware of my situation. In the memo was the following very revealing statement: "In regard to the illness (heart attack) of Pastor Theo LEHMANN, the leader of the district administration stipulated that the head of Department XX must make sure that LEHMANN receives the customary treatment for his particular condition. That means that the doctors dealing with his case must do whatever they professionally would normally do, i.e., for whatever they as doctors could be held responsible. In no way should it become apparent that we are behind any medical treatment administered to LEHMANN now or later that will lead to his becoming an invalid."

So, they would be happy if I became an invalid! Apparently there were compliant doctors who worked closely with the *Stasi*. In any event, the hospital's senior staff physician handling my case, Dr. G. Voigt, was not one of these creatures. There was never any talk of my being left an invalid. What neither the *Stasi* major nor the leader of the district administration knew was that Someone Else stood behind me. He was not only my doctor but also my Savior, and who would keep me from becoming an invalid. He was the One Who commissioned me and used me as His preacher. The *Stasi* plan to shut down my professional life was destined to fail.

GOOD WEATHER FOR A BOMBING

The disruptive actions by the *Stasi* continued. Prior to the Christmas youth service of 1979, I received a telephoned bomb threat. Then on the fifth of December came an anonymous letter that stated: "An inner voice compels me to write to you. In a dream a few days ago I saw you lying in a pool of blood in front of the altar. A servant of Satan had stabbed you in the back and killed you.... The dream was an omen to me that someone would do a terrible thing to you on one of the next days.... Pay close attention to the balconies. It would be best if they were closed during the service. Do not turn your back to the congregation."

Of course, I discussed the matter with the Regional Church Administrative Office in an emergency session. It went like this: If we report the matter to the police, we give them an excuse to forbid the service—to guarantee the safety of the worshipers. On the other hand, are we required to report the threat? And, what if something really does occur? It was a difficult decision. The *LKA* decided not to report it and let the service take place. A senior councilor from the *LKA* came with a bullhorn. I asked a colleague and a physician to stand immediately beside me. Although I experienced incredible fear, I went ahead and preached the sermon. No one suspected anything. Nothing happened; everything went fine.

Now the *Stasi* had a problem. They had made up this bomb threat. (File document: "As a preparatory action, an anonymous telephone call will be made about the service on December 9, 1979. The caller will only say, 'On Sunday, a bomb will explode in the Petrikirche.'") They had intended to charge the church with failing to report the call to the authorities, but they obviously could not admit being the source of the call. Thus, they had to conjure up an explanation as to how they had become aware of the threat. They decided, therefore, to send their *IMV "Karl Heinz"* (Andreas Czech) to the criminal police department. He admitted there, voluntarily and quite casually, that he had called me with the bomb threat. Now the state partners in the church-state conversations could refer to the report of the criminal police.

One consequence of the bomb threat was our decision to hold the youth service twice, at 5:00 and 7:00 P.M., to accommodate all those who wished to attend. This eliminated the seating problem, especially the central aisle crowded with standing youths.

I especially remember one service in the Petrikirche, where the center aisle was packed and the main doors were opened wide so that those standing in the rear entryway and outside could hear something of the goings on. What the people inside did not realize was that during my sermon several police vans drove up on the Theaterplatz in front of the church and uniformed personnel jumped out of the vehicles and posted themselves around the entrance to the church. This took place behind the backs of the listening youths, but I could see what was happening. I continued to preach, but at the same time my knees were knocking like a world champion. At the back of my mind was the thought that the church may be stormed and that the young people as well as I will be arrested. I am amazed to this day that God gave me the strength and calmness to continue preaching even more resolutely at the very time when things outside seemed to be coming to a head. Once again, nothing actually happened.

Following another worship service, I discovered a large silver Star of David along with the word "Judas" painted on the hood of my bright-red Wartburg car that was parked next to the church. The remainder of the silver paint was poured into the tank of the motorcycle of one of our coworkers at the church. Beginning with the next youth Sunday, my friend,

Reinhard Grütz, stood guard over my car. He ostentatiously positioned himself behind the windshield with a camera in hand ready to shoot.

HERE THERE'S NO BEER, MAN

Although the Saxon Regional Church generally protected me, unfortunately there was an exception. In the GDR there existed no possibility to publish evangelistic sermons for young people. But there was a publisher in the West who was willing to do so. In such a case the manuscript had to be presented first to an appropriate GDR publisher. If this publisher declined to publish it, then an application could be made to the "Copyright Office" to permit publication abroad. That is an Orwellian term for an institution whose job was to keep me as an author from exercising my right to publish a book. Officially, at least, there was no censor in the GDR.

The publishing house that specialized in Protestant church literature, Evangelische Verlagsanstalt, eager to show deferential obedience to the authorities, rejected my submission with the explanation that my "speeches" were just that, "speeches," something meant to be heard, not read. Now, really! So I decided to apply to the Copyright Office, but from it one seldom received written reasons for rejection. I did hear from someone I knew at *EVA* that I was accused of offending the sensibilities of believers.

However, I was able to get an appointment with the director of the Copyright Office, a very pleasant communist who had been in a Nazi concentration camp. He received me at the Leipzig Book Fair with the words, "You are the second Biermann case." [Wolf Biermann (b. 1936) was a well-known writer and ballad singer in the GDR who, although a communist, had many run-ins with state officials. When he made a trip to West Germany in 1976, the GDR officials at the border crossing would not allow him to enter his own country. He, in effect, lost his citizenship and had to remain in the West.] He had published a book in the West without receiving permission from the GDR authorities, but he was, as the director pointed out to me, a member of the PEN Club, the prestigious international organization of literary personalities. He had a name, whereas I was a nobody without any popular support. When I asked him what would happen if I were to publish a book in the West like Biermann had, he directed my attention to the law that stated in such a case, the penalty was prison for up to one year. I let that plan drop.

A year later I resumed work on the project and wrote another volume of sermons. Once again, all of my effort was in vain. The authorities rejected it because "the production of these texts would harm the prestige of the *Bund* of the Evangelical Churches in the GDR (*BEK*) and would not be in accord with the church policy of the GDR." That was too much for me! Since such an august authority as the *BEK* was involved, I decided not to follow my usual practice of protesting immediately and instead turned to my Regional Church with the request that they clarify this matter with the *Bund* in Berlin. It was simply too hot a topic for a petty cleric like me to handle. I was, after all, a pastor in this church that belonged to the *Bund*. I had preached the sermons openly and they were heard by thousands who were members of this very church. I made the point that the church ought to stand behind me as one of its pastors. Finally, the charge that I would harm the image of the *BEK* was no small matter.

That was the first and only time in my life that I specifically requested my church to defend me. It was an error and a bitter disappointment. Herr Stolpe was indeed asked to resolve the matter, but he had no inclination to get involved in it. When after a year nothing had happened, I inquired at the office of the Regional Church about the disposition of my request. I got a letter informing me that nothing could be done and that my manuscript had been turned down, because—I couldn't believe my eyes—"the texts would harm the prestige of the *Bund* of the Evangelical Churches in the GDR." I was supposed to turn to the *BEK* for help? That was the reason I made my request to the *Landeskirche* in the first place. The starting point thus became the final stroke. I had gone nowhere at all.

My reply to the *LKA* began with the words, "Never in my life have I felt so ridiculous as your letter has made me feel." They had left me standing out in the cold. I learned through this and other experiences not to rely on men. It became clear to me that one who is a pastor often has to stand completely alone, dependent on God and protected solely by Him. When one grasps this for the first time and thinks it through, it is staggering. However, I gained strength from the whole process. Because of my absolute dependence upon God, I became more independent and courageous in my dealings with men.

At this point I would like to tell of two actions taken by the *Stasi* which affected me greatly, but Elke even more so.

That's When Freedom Will Really Be Ours

A WAGNER *FESTSPIEL*

At the beginning of the 1960s when I still lived in Halle, Dieter Wagner from Karl-Marx- Stadt paid me a visit. He had heard that I was writing a book on Negro spirituals (the grapevine in the GDR among jazz enthusiasts functioned particularly well). I got to know him as a very passionate jazz fan and equally passionate opponent of the GDR regime. He became, during the course of time, one of my very best friends. He was the first with whom I would share a new political joke, a new book from the West, or a western magazine. His heterodox political views gained him four years in a *Stasi* prison. On the day of his release—his wife in the meantime had divorced him—we ate breakfast together in his apartment. While his mother was standing next to us

My wife and I with our informant "friends," 1974

at the table, he said to me, "In order to get out of that place, you have to sell your own mother." I didn't know how serious he was when he told me this. He had sold his soul and become a *Stasi* collaborator, with the code name of *IM* "*Albert.*"

I was never in a prison, much less one run by the *Stasi*, and I never suffered four years of incarceration. For this reason I am not pronouncing any judgment upon Dieter's fall. I was unaware of it and did not notice anything particularly unusual about his behavior. As far as I was concerned, he had been, and remained, my friend. He was the same passionate jazz fan and opponent of the government that he had been since I first had gotten to know him. Elke and I also developed a friendly and heartfelt relationship with his second wife. Unfortunately, his wife Steffi was *IM* "*Irmgard*" and her target was Elke. Like Dieter she was an atheist, but one day she was confirmed as an adult and worked as a congregational deaconess of the Methodist Church in the city. (Incidentally, the church building was adjacent to the main *Stasi* office and the pastor had a cozy relationship with the *Stasi* chief there.) At the time I rejoiced about the decision she had made. That her conversion was not genuine was demonstrated by the fact that she never confessed her spying activity to us. Incredibly, she not only continued it but even extended it to our daughters.

There was an openness and genuine friendship between us. We spent our holidays and birthdays together. For decades we had the custom of eating goose giblets at midday on Christmas Eve at our place—in a pastor's house, on this day when so much else is going on. Once, when Dieter too sick to come to our place on December 24, we drove over to his home with a large pot of the giblet noodle soup. Since we trusted them implicitly, we gave them our house key whenever we went on vacation. Yet he sat at the very same table where I am sitting right now writing these lines and drew a map of my study for the *Stasi*—where the bookcases were, where I kept the cassettes from the youth worship services, etc. The *Stasi* even had the keys to our home, presumably with Dieter's aid. For decades he gave them detailed reports about each of our meetings and included facts, statements I had made, and his evaluations about me.

Whenever I visited him after the *Wende,* he always asked me if I had applied to look at my *Stasi* files. My answer satisfied him every time: "No, I don't want to see them. Above all, I don't know how I should deal with the informers—should I smash their faces in, or what?" I can honestly say that I am glad that Dieter died before everything came out. I really don't know how I would have dealt with him after 30 years of friendship and informing on us. I would not have known what to do—I would have been totally at a loss. Another case, which went even further back, concerned a friend to whom I had become especially close, whom I loved like my own son. It took years before a genuine reconciliation and forgiveness took place.

I am glad that I did not have to settle matters with Dieter. He must answer to God, and I am no longer in the picture. I sat at Dieter's deathbed and I prayed very loudly the Lord's Prayer. He was silent and said nothing: no confession, no apology.

After his death an article appeared in the paper paying tribute to him and his achievements. Yes, he had an important role in the jazz scene and had played in the city's jazz club. The author of this obituary was his long time friend, Peter Moosdorf. When Peter read his own *Stasi* files a few weeks later, he was knocked for a loop when he saw the informant's report in the handwriting of his friend Dieter. Moosdorf, too, had not suspected anything.

Purely out of uncertainty and indecision about how I should proceed, I had decided at first to do nothing. For several years I didn't have the courage to apply to view my *Stasi* files. I feared that I did not have enough time and strength to work through all of them. The most difficult question for me was what I should do if I discovered acquaintances among the informers. Should I slap them on the ears, forgive them, write some nasty letters, give them a tongue lashing, or simply ignore everything? How does one deal with a situation like this? In the hardest cases, the necessity of speaking with the informants was no longer an option (also a cause for thankfulness) because most of them had already died and now only had to answer to God. But, when I heard from Peter Moosdorf of Dieter's betrayal, I said to myself, "It can't get any worse than this." And so I applied to see my file.

Because of the backlog of requests, I had a year to prepare myself for receiving the materials to read. But when I opened the document file and saw the reports, page after page in the handwriting of my friend Dieter that I knew so well, it was as if someone had slugged me with his fist right in the middle of my face.

On the morning of the day that I went to view my papers at the Gauck Commission office, the agency charged with handling the *Stasi* documents, I read in the *Moravian Book of Daily Texts* the Scripture verse for the day: "You have heard that it was said, 'You shall love your neighbor and hate your enemy.' But I say to you, Love your enemies and pray for those who persecute you, so that you may be children of your Father in heaven (Matt 5:43–45)." I knew the path I had to take. And it was the first reason I had to be thankful. I didn't need to choke on rage because of my wounds or let myself be consumed by hatred.

I don't know how I would have survived the following days if I hadn't had Jesus to talk to. For what lay before me was not only a mountain of documents, but also an absolute hammer, whose force I could not possibly have imagined. I had never thought I would need so much time and energy to somehow cope with this journey into the past. For weeks I was grumpy and insufferable, and for those around me, especially Elke, I was a real burden.

Afterwards, I asked myself, among other things, how it was that I hadn't noticed anything about Dieter. We always suspected some people of being informers, and it was a very positive moment when we found out from reading the documents that a few persons whom we had suspected were, in fact, not informers. On the other hand, I had already clearly recognized some people as informers. Often individuals came to me as adults and sought to be confirmed, and then they participated in the confirmation class for adults. I correctly surmised that some came at the behest of the *Stasi* to hear what I would say, since they could ask questions and everything took place in a relaxed, conversational manner. But with Dieter I noticed nothing.

There were a couple times when my suspicions were slightly aroused. It struck us as unusual that Dieter frequently came over to our place precisely on the Sundays that we were holding the youth service even though he well knew that I had not a minute of time for private matters on these days. The room was full of young people (that, of course, was what he was instructed to find out about). And then I got suspicious when he bought himself a car. I knew how much he earned as a bricklayer foreman. But he explained it to my satisfaction by saying he had inherited the money.

We, Elke and I, could not bring ourselves to utter the word "betrayal," and I couldn't even get myself to think it. The very idea that our friend of so many years could work for the *Stasi* was simply grotesque, impossible. That just could not be! I was ashamed of the thought and repressed it as best I could. It was so out of the question that, in the end, I thought I was seeing ghosts and losing my mind. Dieter working for the *Stasi*—that just could not be! I could not believe it, or even imagine it. I drove it out of my mind and everything remained between us as it always had been.

Today I wonder why I wasn't more suspicious. When he visited us, he always went to the toilet before he left for home, and he always spent at least ten minutes. Since we always kept interesting reading matter there, I thought—or should I say if I ever really thought about it—that, as an avid reader, he was simply reading something that caught his attention. Today, however, I believe he was jotting down important points (facts, quotes) he had observed. The usual parting ceremony was that I walked with him to his car. We embraced, waved goodbye, and expressed thanks for the nice time we had had. Really! And at the same time he was writing things about me which could have landed me in prison, the very place where he himself had suffered. I cannot make any sense out of this. It is incomprehensible, inexplicable, monstrous—even schizophrenic. That is for me the most frightening thing about the whole matter. I can't call it anything else but diabolical.

A HARSH PUNISHMENT

The *Stasi* was interested in every detail of the life and habits of their victims. Thus, Dieter was a welcome source of information with his intimate knowledge of our private and family life. Concerning the use of alcohol in our lives he kept a very precise record, but he also wrote quite truthfully about me: "When he drives, he never drinks a single drop." Unfortunately, that was not the case with Elke.

She never denied having drunk alcohol on the day in question. I had gone to a youth evangelistic campaign in Zittau, at least three hours away on the Polish border. Elke had remained home, and according to her own statement she had drunk some red wine and whiskey during the afternoon and then later drove to see some friends of ours, the Heinkes. She stayed at their place for two hours, without having anything to drink. Both Heinkes testified that they did not observe that she seemed to be affected by the alcohol she had consumed earlier in the day. On the way home she stopped at a gas station and filled up. The attendant stated that she had not noticed any signs that Elke was under the influence of alcohol. She then continued on, but failed to stop at a stop sign because at this time (10:30 P.M.) hardly any cars were on the streets of Karl-Marx-Stadt.

According to her, she was driving around 70 km/h (44 mph) on this completely empty street, where 60 km/h (37 mph) was the speed limit. She had been seen by two officers in a police car who stopped her and made her take a breathalyzer test. The police report claimed that the test result was a blood alcohol figure of 1.8%, and they concluded that, "at the time of the offense, she most likely had a blood alcohol concentration between 2.2–2.4 mg/G." Even the criminal police interrogator questioned this figure because a person with such a slight build as Elke would not be able to handle that much alcohol or even be able to drive the car. Still, because the GDR had such stringent laws on driving under the influence of alcohol, Elke's driver's license was immediately confiscated, and we awaited the further legal procedures customary in all such cases. But things turned out quite differently than we had expected.

After I had gone to a convalescent facility at Bad Elster, a spa south of Plauen near the Czech border, for additional treatment because of my heart attack, a police vehicle unexpectedly showed up at the front door. They picked up Elke and took her in for questioning. She had no chance to tell the neighbors or was even allowed time to lock up our apartment since some workmen were in the building making repairs. She was interrogated the entire day. She asked the police to let her call our neighbors so they could close up the house, but permission was denied. She was treated like a common criminal. She had already arranged to fly to a health spa in Hungary within the next few days, since the GDR state health plan did not cover such treatments for a pastor's wife. Because of this situation some friends in the West had helped her to be able to enjoy a little time away. However, the trip fell through because the police confiscated both her personal identification papers and the airline ticket.

And then, a few days later, an auto full of policemen pulled up in front of our house and—without a search warrant—they crawled around under Elke's car in the garage and checked it for road-worthiness. Communications between us at that time were extremely difficult. There was one public telephone in Bad Elster, and it always had a queue of patients in front of it. The same was true with the telephone inside the main building of the spa where my room was. It likewise was always blocked by a line of people waiting to call.

As we later learned from Elke's *Stasi* documents, this is the how the game was played. Department XX of the *Stasi* received the following message:

> Comrade Major General:
>
> Attached is information about the wife of Pastor Lehmann (charged with driving while intoxicated). Contact the local judicial authorities and demand indignantly that the maximum punishment be administered.

The problem here was that the imposition of the maximum punishment for driving under the influence of alcohol required proving that the action of the offender endangered the lives of other people. However, the police report on the incident stated:

> Based on a review of the situation carried out by the leader of Section K3 at the VPKA (State Police Headquarters) in Karl-Marx-Stadt, [Police] Captain General Lapka determined that a preliminary investigation in accordance with Paragraph 200 of the Civil Code [a practice in German law to determine whether a crime has been committed] is in no way justified since, based on the facts available, there is no evidence that endangerment to other persons occurred. For this reason, no prosecuting attorney would go along with such an investigation. At the location of the

offense and in the immediate area there were at this point in time no other people except Frau Lehmann and the two police officers in the squad car.

As a result, the *Stasi* had to invent or find a person who would incriminate Elke. They located a couple named Schuller, who had been charged with the theft of three bottles of wine from a wine shop and who at their judicial proceeding asked, "whether one could file charges with the traffic police regarding other drivers who failed to comply with the traffic ordinances." When this was affirmed, Herr Schuller alleged that he was driving down the street keeping a safe distance between him and the other drivers when Elke "crowded into the interval between my car and the cars in front of us," and this forced him to "jam on the brakes." In turn, his children in the back seat "were thrown into the front seat and badly shaken up."

Elke firmly disputed these allegations, insisting that she had seen no car, either in front or in back of her. How could she have seen them when the whole story was a fabrication? For those involved, the made-up story was quite profitable. [From a *Stasi* slush fund] Major Kahl and Captain Kraus of the criminal police each received 500 marks for their complicity, and the Schuller couple received 1000 marks. The rationale, as found in the *Stasi* documents, was:

> The determined investigative efforts and cleverly executed interrogations of both the defendant and the witnesses by the above-named comrades of the criminal police elicited sufficient incriminating evidence that the wife of Pastor Dr. Theo LEHMANN, Elke Lehmann, was in violation of Paragraph 200 (1) of the Civil Code, and this would enable the institution of court proceedings.
>
> The testimony of Comrade Schuller specifically confirmed the violation of Paragraph 200 and this assured the imposition of the prescribed penalty.
>
> Following the conclusion of the main proceedings, the behavior of Frau Lehmann will be utilized to produce an even greater breakdown in her interpersonal contacts as previously outlined in the document *OV "Spinne,"* Reg.-Nr. XIV 374/77.

The receipts were found in Elke's file, together with one for the amount of 110 marks given to an *IM "Klaus"* "for the maintenance of the conspiracy and cooperation with the *MfS*," and another for 300 marks paid to informant *"Anette."* The latter was cited for "demonstrating a high degree of commitment, courage, and personal engagement in the attainment of a complicated and operationally significant objective. By maintaining a careful awareness of the overall conspiratorial plan of action, it was possible to bring about a satisfactory conclusion." Unfortunately, I have never been able to determine who these two *IM*'s were and what role they played.

In August her case went to trial. Herr Schuller recited on the witness stand the statement he had memorized in such a ridiculously mechanical way that even the prosecuting attorney was troubled. With regard to the punishment that was to be meted out, Major Lattermann from *Stasi* Department IX wrote to his superior Major General Gehlert on July 26, 1984, some two weeks before the trial:

> We have the following in mind in the case against Frau Lehmann: The trial will take place by August 13, 1984, at the district court in Karl-Marx Stadt/Mitte Nord. A suspended sentence of one year and six months will be imposed, under penalty of six months in jail if she violates her probation. In addition, a fine of 800 to 1,000 marks will be imposed and her driver's license will be withheld for a period of 2 ½ to 3 years.

The court pronounced judgment, "In the name of the people," and decided upon the highest amount, 1,000 marks for the fine and the loss of driving privileges for three years. On top of these were the court costs and the bill presented by the defense attorney who did not do anything at all.

The trial shattered Elke. From this point on, a change in personality was obvious. She was now a person with a criminal record. She simply couldn't get over the fact that she could not drive for three years. The car, a red VW Beetle that had belonged to my father's second wife and which she gave to Elke, was the only significant thing that she had ever owned. She loved this car and it was absolutely necessary to enable her to maintain contacts with her friends. She never drove again. She withdrew into her own little shell at our home and her whole being changed. During the trial I could only observe her from behind, and I struggled with my own tears the entire time.

My Elke, accused, a defendant! I had to marvel at the way she handled herself, like a well-behaved school girl, and how she answered the questions, without exploding and screaming at the whole system of lies as she was accustomed to doing. What strength must it have cost her to allow this whole "theater," this humiliation, to pass over her—one who always fanatically stood up for truth and justice. She was, apart from the trumped up charge of driving under the influence, not guilty for two other reasons: She had not endangered anyone's life, and she would never have even been charged with reckless driving if she had not been my wife.

NOBODY WANTS TO BE CALLED A SWINE

At the next youth worship service following the trial, I began my sermon from Acts 9 with the words: "The enemies of Christians have never been squeamish about the methods they use. Their oldest method is to make use of false witnesses." In this way I delivered my messages to the *Stasi*, which I often wrapped in the form of a story or a joke. The joke was, so to speak, the mildest form of my communication about a matter. I don't deny that I sometimes had the most fun making use of such jokes.

I also have to admit that I often intentionally pulled the lion by the tail, albeit in naïve ignorance of the dangerous nature of what I was doing. For example, sometimes at the beginning of a worship service I would greet the *Stasi* members in attendance; at other times I would comment upon their absence. One of those times was in 1981 when West German Chancellor Helmut Schmidt met with the GDR Head of State, Erich Honecker, in the Schorfheide, north of Berlin. In my greeting I said, "I notice a few faces are missing that I normally see here. They are probably busy in Güstrow [a city where the two leaders were conferring]. My only consolation is that they aren't missing anything. They had to go to church there too because Schmidt requested it." Then I mocked their meeting in a hunting song in the spirit of the nineteenth century writer Theodor Fontane who hailed from the Schorfheide area:

> The General Secretary
> and the Chancellor
> they met each other,
> neither on the Rhine nor Spree
> but at the Werbellinsee,
> way out in Schorfheide.
> *Tralali. Tralala.*
>
> All that's new and concrete,
> except the wasted money,
> we'll know in a week or two.

Blues Music and Gospel Proclamation

> Oh, yeah! The *main* thing
> we learned from Werbellinsee:
> They spoke to one another.
> *Tralali. Tralala.*

In a letter written anonymously by two pastors at the behest of the *Stasi*, I was warned of the Judgment of God because I "had made that which is holy into something ludicrous" and had "dragged it into the mud." The letter was signed: "A group of brothers and sisters in the faith who can no longer keep silent." In the next worship service I preached a sermon entitled, "False Prophets," and used as my text Jeremiah 23:16 ff. I said: "The people who printed this letter which was intended as internal communication within the church call themselves 'a group of brothers and sisters in the faith,' but I call them false prophets.... A brother who is too cowardly to give his name is a deceiver. And I only hope that at least one of these has his informers sitting here and tells this riff-raff, afraid of the light and with whom he associates, that I would like to know the name found on the bottles from whose necks the stench of anonymous letters pours forth." That was more than plain, but it was, as far as I can remember, the only time I ever dealt with an anonymous action in such a fashion. I never did so again even as their methods became harsher until the bomb threat in the church.

My last youth worship service

After reading the information in my *Stasi* files, I considered how I was going to deal with the *Stasi* people who were still around. A discussion with the main *Stasi* leaders, of course, was not possible, given the fact that these gentlemen had all disappeared or had risen as bosses into higher levels of the business world. I didn't want to have anything to do with the "little fish" from the *Junge Gemeinde,* or other church youth groups, who delivered reports on my sermons to their masters. To be sure, the only person who ever apologized to me came from this group.

That's When Freedom Will Really Be Ours

I directed my attention solely to the informers who were church colleagues and who remained in the service of the church. They were all pastors whose code names the Gauck Commission helped me to decipher. All of them received the following letter from me, and I addressed each of them with their *IM* code names:

> Dear *IM*——
>
> After having studied my *Stasi* files, I would like to advise you to: "Ask God and your acquaintances for forgiveness before you go to Hell."

I never received an answer from any of them. One person, who in the GDR times had published a shameless article attacking me in the Saxon church newspaper without having bothered to speak me beforehand, turned not to me but to the bishop. He was reverting to his old *Stasi* manner of behavior. He got himself all worked up about nothing, namely, the manner of speech in my letter. Incidentally, he was one of those shadowy figures who was given the responsibility of watching over the *Stasi* documents during the time of the *Wende*. That is, he was precisely in the place where he could easily make documents disappear. To other pastors, superintendents, etc. I sent a photocopy of the documents with their statements against me requesting an explanation. Their reaction was silence or flowery, meaningless words. Some claimed they couldn't remember anything. Bottom line: No one apologized.

Unfortunately, I never discovered whether any of the *Stasi* people, who belonged to my most attentive listeners and readers, ever turned to Christ. I did, however, learn that the *Stasi* officer who was assigned the task of listening to the private telephone conversations of pastors was converted after the *Wende*. He told me later that he recognized my voice and, especially, Elke's quite well.

To conclude this section, I would like to add two evaluations made about me but stemming from two quite different perspectives. However, both are very accurate. The Karl-Marx-Stadt District Council made the following statement in 1986, "Regarding Lehmann, he is a very clever, calculating, and shrewd enemy of our socialist state." Later, Jörg Swoboda wrote of me: "In a climate of coldness, mendacity, and fear, in the face of the often demeaning silence of the majority, Theo's open mouth became, for many, a ray of hope regarding human dignity. He looked right through the East German rulers and saw that they covered up their own lack of real power through ostentation. He exposes what is depressing others. He emerges from the protective cover into the full light of day and makes himself the mouthpiece of those who cannot speak."

Back in the GDR days, February 1989 to be exact, I wrote the song, "Then There Will Be Freedom," set to the tune of a Negro spiritual. During the *Wende* it became almost a hymn in Saxony, just like the song "And Yet We Are Standing Again." Upon hearing both songs, thousands stood, unbidden, and sang as they were on their feet.

> Then there will be freedom, and glorious it will be,
> Then there will be freedom when Jesus comes again.
> No sorrow and no Wall, no pain and no sadness,
> Then there will be freedom when Jesus comes again.
>
> We are on a journey to God's new world.
> We suffer here under much we cannot bear.
> There is still war, torture, injustice,
> but no tears in the presence of God's glory.
>
> We have a home in God's new world.
> God's promised it, and since he keeps his Word,
> We keep on keeping on during these days,
> but already we yearn for God's eternity.
>
> We are placing our hope in God's new world,
> where none uses rockets for defense.
> We long for freedom and security.
> And it will be ours, in God's new era.

10

A God for All Situations

I NOT ONLY ATTRACTED the attention of the *Stasi* but also that of the regional church youth pastor, Volker Kress, later to become the Bishop of Saxony. The news about the pastor in Karl-Marx-Stadt who was preaching to thousands of young people every month eventually reached him in Dresden. One day he appeared and asked me if I would be willing to give up my job as pastor of the church, get behind the wheel of a *Trabi* [*Trabant*, the East German people's car], and travel throughout Saxony as a youth evangelist.

I was a dyed-in-the-wool hometown guy who clung to my congregation and family, and I had never considered being a traveling evangelist. The thought of constant separation from Elke was a horrific idea. On the other hand, I was excited by the possibility of being a preacher solely for young people. My answer to Kress was, "If I were a monk, I would immediately agree. But I am not a monk. I am married and have three children. I have to discuss this with the family." We did just that, for a half a year. Elke was at first appalled. She was even more of a homebody than I. She couldn't warm up to this idea of being married to a traveling salesman. I, of course, would never accept the position without her agreement.

Elke could see where my heart lay in the matter and was afraid I would not be happy if she refused to go along with it. She gave her "yes" and let me go ahead with the plan. But she was not at all happy about it. The decisive argument was that when she got married, she had pledged, "Wherever you go, there I will go also." And so she set her mind to follow this path. Now, one could argue that, as a pastor one shouldn't place so much importance on a matter such as this. After all, there are large numbers of other jobs where the husband is separated from his family for weeks at a time, from truck drivers to politicians, from medical doctors to musicians. That's true. But it is also true that such marriages are especially endangered, quite simply because it isn't normal to be constantly apart.

Later, when I tried to recruit younger colleagues for this path of service, I frequently got nowhere because they, too, wanted to remain with their wives. That is justified, and I cannot really criticize them for responding this way. However—if everyone had the same opinion, then no one would leave home. Someone must break loose and bring the message to young people.

Still, such will not work without the agreement of the spouse. An evangelist whose wife isn't standing behind him is not a happy person even if it isn't quite so catastrophic as John Wesley's marriage turned out. It was said of his wife, whom people called "the little ferret," that she pulled "her noble husband" by the hair through the room. "To this day," Wesley noted in his diary, "I don't know why she left me, never to return. I didn't leave her; I didn't send her away. I won't chase after her to get her back." No marriage of an evangelist should end this way. Frankly, I'm not even certain this marriage would have been any different if Wesley were to have stayed home. He simply had the wrong wife, with or without his constant traveling. I had the right one and that was my good fortune.

However, I won't deny that constant absence from home is basically an irresolvable problem for a married couple. And that holds true for all stages of a marriage. If small children are at home, the father and one of the teachers is missing. If the children are not at home, the wife sits there by herself. In our case the children were already independent, and each year another one left the nest. Elke was suddenly completely alone.

Our children departed at the age of 16. The reason was that they—in spite of receiving the top grades—had to discontinue attending school after receiving the tenth grade graduation certificate because they had the wrong father. They had learned this many years earlier. I have always marveled that they nevertheless stuck with their schooling. In any event, their path to the higher secondary school and then to the university was blocked. And the chances for securing an apprenticeship were nil for persons who had not taken part in the communist Youth Dedication Ceremony.

For daughters of pastors in the GDR there existed only two vocational possibilities and that was because the church had its own teaching institutions for them: nurse and children's worker (deaconess). So, two of our daughters became children's deaconesses and the third, a nurse. They are still engaged in these professions and very satisfied with their work because they did not view the situation as their fate but rather as a calling. That was also the way I felt when I had the visit from Volker Kress—it was a calling. After gaining Elke's assent, I happily entered into my traveling service as a youth evangelist in the fall of 1976.

AND YOU ARE NOW AN EVANGELIST

The first thing I did was to ask the local youth administrator and later youth evangelist, Werner Morgenstern, to allow me to accompany him as his "little mouse." I simply wanted to see how the master did it. But that idea went down the tube because my mentor passed on to me several tasks right away. This, together with the on-the-job training I already had, was really the best kind of learning. I needed this because I had no experience in holding mass evangelistic campaigns. As a young man, I had taken part in one in Halle with Wilhelm Busch, but as a student I had never heard anything about it. When I was writing my doctoral thesis, I ran into the phenomenon in American church history.

Also I acquired a German translation of C. H. Spurgeon's book *The Soul-Winner* at the urging of Helmut Thielicke, who had published a book that included some contributions by Spurgeon. They turned out to be quite a revelation to me. One day when I was a scientific assistant in Halle, I was supervising some students. As this meant I had some "time to kill," I took a look at the Spurgeon book. Professor Urner walked past me. Since he was interested in what the up-and-coming generation of theologians was reading, he picked up my book and looked at the title. Then he shut the book and in a patronizing tone of voice said, "I thought we were long past that kind of thing," and went on to his next lecture on Practical Theology. I thought to myself: If only we in the church were involved, even in the very least way, with the things that Spurgeon advises! I have never ceased to recommend to beginners in the ministry that they read this book.

This was all I ever received as far as "training in evangelization" was concerned. Thus equipped—with my experience as pastor of the youth worship service along with a burning heart—I had held my first evangelistic service one year earlier. That was in Görlitz in 1975. Dieter Heise had invited Jörg Swoboda and me to come, and we met beforehand for an evening of preparation. Jörg picked me up at the train station, and on the way to the meeting hall I asked him how we were actually going to carry this off: "How shall we do this? You, one evening, I, the next? Or will we switch off? Or, how about I will do three evenings and you do three? How do you want it?" Jörg said, "You preach, I sing."

And that's the way it has remained to this day. Since that time we have gone throughout Germany as a duo and function as a kind of an interdenominational path breaker. Jörg is a Baptist, and I am a Lutheran. As regards infant baptism, we represent the positions that our churches hold, which are quite different. But our appearances together are a sign of our cooperation and that we do not call upon our hearers to turn to this or that church congregation, but rather to Jesus. And the congregation to which each new convert turns is his/her own decision.

In our very first service, another fundamental decision had to be made, and this characterizes our services until today. The group that had invited us said they were of one opinion that we should "ask inquirers to come to the front" after the sermon. Being a Lutheran I knew nothing of this practice, except in the somewhat ritualized form of confirmation where each candidate, after two years of preparation and a rehearsal, in the presence of all the grandmas and aunts comes forward to the altar to be confirmed. The difference between this and an evangelistic campaign is that in the latter one makes a spontaneous confession of faith in Jesus. As a Baptist, Jörg was accustomed to this procedure and had had some unpleasant experiences involving external pressure. Both of us shrank back from the idea; Jörg from his prior experience and I from lack of it. But then, following prayer and counsel, we both agreed to have an invitation, and we have continued to this day to do so.

The manner in which the call to decision is carried out (the altar call, the counseling time immediately after the conclusion of the service, the raising of hands, etc.) belongs to the most sensitive area of the evangelization event. Every evangelist must determine for himself what the correct way is for him. It is very important that one stands one hundred percent behind whatever is done. For in the moment of the call to decision, one not only is struggling against all kinds of second thoughts, doubts, fears, and reservations, but also against the opposition of God's adversaries, the satanic forces and spirits in the air.

At this point there must not be any doubts or uncertainties; every evangelist must find the method he feels most certain is God's way for him. At the beginning I discussed my practice with my colleagues and acted according to the majority vote. But that was only then. Now I no

A God for All Situations

longer make it a matter for negotiation. I tell the inviting group what my customary practice. If they are in agreement, fine; if not I tell them to find another evangelist.

After working out these basic issues, I learned a great number of practical things from Dieter Heise and a week of training with Werner Morgenstern. Now it was time for me to get started and to go it alone.

COMPLETE AS A PAIR

Someone had placed a sickly green *Trabi* at my disposal, one that several previous youth administrators had driven. Whoever has even the faintest idea of the driving style of a Saxon youth administrator can only imagine what the condition of this "winner" of a car was. It broke down on my first trip to an evangelistic campaign. And so, for my "inaugural event," I arrived in front of the parsonage at the end of a tow line pulled by a farmer's tractor. The singer who accompanied me was Ralf Marschner, the banjo player from the band at the Schlosskirche, my later son-in law, and now an associate at the Aussaat publishing house who added all of the brilliantly worded subtitles for each of the chapters in the German edition of this book.

In the meantime, Jörg had taken over responsibility for all the Baptist youth work in the GDR, including representing it on an international level, and he could not be full-time with me. Our cooperation was limited to a few weeks throughout the year. I was, therefore, as far as the musical portion of our services was concerned, dependent on local bands and choirs and often experienced difficulties along the way. The problem was not so much the lack of musical quality of the bands, but rather the repertoire. Several bands wanted simply to provide musical entertainment, a concert, and could, or would, not play music for the "sing-along" portion of the service. Others didn't know the songs we needed or played songs that had nothing to do with my themes. The worst case scenario was when a group performed something that was opposite to what I was preaching. So it turned out that most of the evenings did not form a unified whole. Rather, they were two independent segments that diverged from one another: music from the band and preaching from me. The biggest problem was that they often did not play an invitation number.

Of course, I couldn't really blame anyone for the situation. These bands did provide an indescribably important service in youth work. It was not their fault that they didn't know that evangelistic work is something quite different and it required a different approach from that of regular concerts and similar occasions. I became acquainted with many good bands and singers whom I value highly. But not all of them were suitable as musical collaborators in an evangelistic campaign, regardless of how good their musical repertoires were. I have worked with many an excellent singer in my regular youth worship services but whom I could not use in an evangelistic campaign. Something else was needed there.

In the first place, such events require a different selection of songs than those normally sung in youth groups. Not every good song is automatically an evangelistic one. Precisely what I needed were texts with a simple, clear summary of the biblical message, combined with an evangelical thrust that speaks to the heart and conscience. I find it difficult to express exactly what I mean here.

Secondly, the singer must, in any event, not only have the goal of appealing to the audience, but even more that people come to Jesus, that is, become converted. All other artistic considerations must be subordinated to this main goal, and this requires a certain degree of humility on the part of the singer. To put it another way, the vocalist must not only be a good musician but also just like the preacher: an evangelist.

Over and above this, individuals on the music team must not merely be theologically correct but also able to get along well with the other team members. As an evangelistic duo, two people live day and night with one another. Each one's life must be in order. I had longed for just such a partner from the beginning. I found him, not only in Jörg Swoboda but also in Wolfgang Tost. Working together with these two musicians characterized my service and was my hallmark. I exist as an evangelist only in a "double-pack." This has lots of advantages. One is never alone on the road but always has a brother by his side. Even more important is that the two parts of the service, the music and preaching, do not appear as two separate presentations, next to one another but unconnected. Instead, they form a unity which the listeners will experience as beneficial.

This unity of music and proclamation is our strength. We take pains to design each presentation following the principle that everything must fit together; the songs lead to the message and support it. The impression that everything is done to create a harmonious whole is reinforced by the manner in which song and sermon, in the truest sense of the word, speak the same language. This is why we write songs together, often for a particular sermon, whose thoughts and formulations we use and re-shape in our song. This decades-long cooperation with Jörg and Wolfgang has to be among the greatest gifts and richest experiences of my life.

I was now 42 years old. At a time when others say "good bye" to youth work, I jumped into it full time. And then at 44 I suffered a heart attack. This probably had a number of causes, ranging from heredity (my mother had heart disease), to years of smoking, on down to the constant confrontations with the church and state that caused so much wear and tear on my body. The tensions arising from the issue of where we would be able to live must have contributed as well.

HEART ACHE

As a pastor I lived in an apartment provided by the church. Now that I had left the parish ministry, I would have to vacate it. But, where could I go? In matters like this the church was responsible for its employees. I didn't need to apply at the state-run housing office. I had to wait until space somewhere in Saxony became available. Of course, finding an apartment for a family of five was nearly impossible. And even if one became available, what congregation would want a traveling pastor from whom they got nothing? The churches needed such housing as a means of attracting a new pastor, music director, or laborer in the church cemetery.

Nothing satisfactory seemed to be in sight. The few offers that did come my way were, simply put, impossible. Some were nothing less than outrageous! For example, a place was available in a town on the Czech border. Apart from the factors of time and finances, if I as a "traveling man" were to live at the most distant corner of Saxony and had to travel 40 miles on back roads just to get to an Autobahn, then this was unadvisable from a family standpoint. Werner Morgenstern warned me, based on his experience, that I must reject this for the sake of our marriage. To be stuck in a dump in a little village located in the middle of the forest on the border with no through traffic would be like banishment. In addition, Elke would be alone the entire week while I was gone, and no one was likely to come by to visit her. To this day I am very glad I listened to him.

But no one understood why we rejected the place, and the congregation's pressure to get rid of me became increasingly greater. A successor had already been chosen, but he could not move into the apartment while we were still there and after two years he threw in the towel. Anger ruled on all sides. I went faithfully about the work that the regional church had called me to do and which also was responsible for providing me with a place to live. I simply couldn't do anything in this stupid situation, nor could I personally change it. I saw that I would have to eventually vacate the place because they expected me to do so. When I became unable to work because of the heart attack, another half year went by and nothing at all happened. Then we waited two more years until we could relocate. Four and a half years of this pressure was even a greater burden on Elke than it was on me. It was a real liberation when we finally moved into a house owned by the Saxon church in a suburban village. I still live here today.

The heart attack struck on Mardi Gras Tuesday while I was engaged in my daily chore of carrying coal from the cellar to our third floor apartment. We had five stoves to keep fired up. Earlier in the day, I was driving the car and had a strange feeling of tension in my right arm. But just because of a little pain, a 44-year-old doesn't run to the nearest hospital. But then, as I was filling the buckets with coal briquettes, I was not able to lift them. I was completely helpless, but I didn't understand what was happening. Even after the ambulance took me to the hospital, I still failed to grasp the problem. I simply thought about the "Open Evening" scheduled for the next day in nearby Annaberg and an evangelistic campaign I was to have in Thuringia. So I, the idiot, asked the doctor how long I would be here and when I would get out. Only when he said to me, "Herr Lehmann, listen to me. You are here in the ICU. And right now you can forget everything that lies outside this hospital," did it dawn on me what had happened.

It was a matter of life and death. At night, following an emergency operation, attached to medical cords and tubes, I understood. I was alive! I was alive! And I began to preach a sermon in my head. It was first class! I was all but dead but now have received new life. From this point on I would lead a new life. There were a lot of adjustments: medications, midday naps, exercise. But the most important thing for me was, besides my gratitude, the recognition of how quickly life can come to an end. This episode demonstrated to me again my complete dependence upon God. In turn, I must be independent of people, considerations, and plans. It made me freer and more courageous.

After a lengthy time of recovery from the heart attack I returned to my work by traveling with Jörg to the coastal city of Rostock to prepare for an evangelistic campaign there. When the session was over, the inviting pastor bid us farewell, but he was surprised when we asked him to show us to our quarters. To what quarters? It turned out he had hadn't made any provisions for us at all. Here was one of those academic illiterates who couldn't read letters, one of those Christians who simply didn't stop to think what the two guests he had invited would do at 10:00 p.m., hundreds of miles away from home. Hospitality? Brotherly love? Responsibility? Or even simply, thinking? All were unknown concepts to him.

Our dear fellow clergyman proceeded to stick us in the *Junge Gemeinde* meeting room, and we spent the night on a hard, narrow wooden bench. There were a few dirty cushions which reeked from the flatulence of generations of teenagers. These were offered to us as pillows! And not even a pillowcase! It was revolting. I tried to lay my face on my handkerchief. Of course, there was no sheet or anything like it. This was my first night away after the heart attack, hospital care, and recuperation at a spa. It was also my first extended trip by car and my first assignment. The church had me again! It was astonishing that I didn't have another heart flare-up with such treatment. And even more astonishing was that the colleagues who had invited us to lead a service dared to treat us like dirt.

GARBAGE IDYLL

Could this be possible? Our quarters! My father once recommended to me that I should entitle my autobiography, *I Slept in a Thousand Beds*. If only they had all been beds! Sometimes it was a camping cot, sometimes a worn-out sofa whose wire springs poked into my body so that after a restless night on a smelly piece of furniture in a cold attic I woke up and felt absolutely beat. The soothing, apologetic comment given by the host usually went something like this: "Brother Lehmann, we aren't a luxury hotel here, but for one night (or even one week) this should be OK." The good man didn't realize that half of the year consisted of such nights and weeks.

Preparing my sermon

I have never put much emphasis on luxury in my life. But when a person is on the road for a week and has worked hard, he really does need a place where he can feel at home, at least a little bit. That was hardly possible between the worn-out, cast off furniture from grandma's time or the first years of marriage. But also, apart from the aesthetics of it, I also needed a table at which I could work and where I could lay my manuscripts, Bibles, books, notes, etc. How often have I had no usable table or wardrobe for my clothes and had to live from my suitcase lying on the floor. Since I most frequently shared the room with the singer, one can just imagine what the place looked like. In addition to my things, there were the guitars, notes, and the suitcase of my partner lying around. "That should be OK for just this one week...." Yeah, but how! And above all: Why isn't it possible to do better? To be sure, I did make a distinction between the hosts who simply did not have anything better, and those who were shamelessly inhospitable.

In the GDR period it was understood that we would be put up in private quarters—at the home of the pastor, youth administrator, or some church members. During these years I was lodged in a hotel only one single time. That was in Löbau (in eastern Saxony) and the reason was that the church staff simply didn't have enough rooms to take us in. It was a very salutary occasion because we (Wolfgang and I) stayed with the band under the same roof and had ready contact with them. Such never occurred elsewhere. The norm was staying either in a private residence or an available room at the church.

On our very first evangelistic trip—Jörg, another colleague, and I—slept on mattresses lying on the floor in the cellar of a church fellowship hall. There was neither a bath, shower, or even warm water. We had to make do with a cold water spigot for eight days. One time I camped out with Jörg for a week in a little garden house. We washed with water from a garden hose. In another place the wash basin was in a men's toilet that could not be locked.

Noteworthy was the room Wolfgang and I shared in Freital near Dresden. A young man had given up his own room for us and moved in with others for the week. We knew that this truly was an act of Christian love. This young man, like so many of our helpers, simply gave everything that he had. That was the most important factor, even though his "everything" was rather modest. But here existed a problem with washing. There was a wash basin and above it a cold water spigot which surprisingly worked. The difficulty was that under the basin was no wastewater pipe. The "City Council" had not yet gotten around to granting permission to have this fixed. If anyone ran water into it, a bucket had to be placed beneath the drain.

The best situation was when we stayed with a youth administrator. It was of inestimable value to stay where I was immersed in the life of a family and its world, with the conversation and sense of community. I had a difficult time, though, with a retired pastor. In the evening, after we had preached, sung, and talked for hours, he offered the singer and me a single bottle of apple juice with a pitcher of water to dilute it. For breakfast each of us had one bread roll—no more. Neither he nor any of the three pastors from the town invited us over for a meal or even a cup of coffee. The result was that I wound up with the singer every afternoon in the local cafe where we made our preparations for the evening service.

Inside the quarters for the evangelists

After the *Wende* I enjoyed being put up in a hotel, pension, or a really nice villa whenever that occurred. Such treatment really did us good! In the West I got to know some rather wealthy Christians who placed their homes at our disposal out of a true spirit of generosity. A little footnote here—it is now over 15 years since the *Wende*. The difference between a pastor's house in the West and one in the East is enormous. I have learned like the Apostle Paul to be able to do both—to be poor and to be rich and to stay in modest as well in elegant quarters. I recall only one instance when we were preaching in the West that we were housed in quarters considerably below a person's dignity. This I could not understand.

It was a one-week evangelization campaign and Wolfgang Tost, Michael Gundlach, and I were lodged in a garden house made of wood. All day long the local children romped and played around outside. This one room mini-house had hardly enough space for us to set up our suitcases. We slept on small bunks under the roof, which required great acrobatic agility to reach. One had to climb up a ladder—even I as an older, retired man—and then scramble onto the camp beds. It was impossible to sit upright because of a lack of room. This may be lots of fun for teens on vacation, but for us it was an unreasonable demand. In addition, the warm water in the shower only lasted five minutes, then the next one of us had to wait a half an hour for it to warm up again. Getting any rest during the noon break was out of the question because of the noisy children running around the place. I finally made a "pilgrimage" to the pastor's house where I could use a sofa.

Another thing that disturbed us was when they told us that some years earlier our good friends from West Germany, Manfred Siebald and Johannes Hansen, were in town for a campaign, and they held their discussions with coworkers in their hotel. Imagine that—in their *hotel*. They didn't have to stay in the garden shed, which was good enough for us *Ossis,* formerly citizens of the GDR. It was a special treat for us to imagine how Hansen and Siebald, both truly noble spirits, would have climbed the ladder and crawled into their sacks. These men would never have done it, and no one would have dared to ask them to do so. But when it came to *Ossis* it was a different matter, and for us this was a bitter pill to swallow.

Outside the quarters for the evangelists

But here's what took the cake. The church member who owned the little hut where we were staying went out to the place after we had left for the services and turned off the heat. When we came back "home" at night, weary after our spiritual struggles in the meeting, and were looking forward to eating our supper, we found the place to be quite cold. It's often difficult not to despair with certain brothers.

Probably the absolute low point of Jörg's and my experience in this regard was the time a married couple, both teachers, took us in. I myself was given a room, but poor Jörg had a bed in an upstairs corridor that essentially was a thoroughfare. His space was enclosed merely by curtains. From six o'clock in the morning on, the two daughters, alternately, started traipsing to the bathroom, in and out, out and in. Each time they made noise as they walked past the curtains behind which Jörg was lying. It was an unacceptable, impossible situation. Sleep was totally out of the question once the girls had awakened. When I appeared at the breakfast table, Jörg had already stowed his luggage in the car and greeted me with the news that we were moving out. We departed after leaving a goodbye letter. That was the only time that we actually rejected the quarters offered to us. A bed behind curtains, with two girls constantly running by, was simply too much!

One last example from my travel diary: "Stopped at 10 p.m. after a 300 mile trip. The apartment seemed to be furnished with junk from the 1950s. The room for Wolfgang and myself was an unreasonable place, to say the least. It was so small that Wolfgang's feet touched the top of my head. We had difficulties trying to bathe. Children and grandchildren ran through the house. At breakfast we heard the whining of the kids who then parked themselves in front of the television set. Everything was unpleasant; neither of us slept well...."

All the more thankful we were when we sensed that some hosts were doing their best to see that we felt at home during our time with them. Now I'll admit that I'm an aesthete, and I am quite disturbed whenever I have to camp out in a room full of the discarded furniture, ugliness, and tastelessness of bygone eras. To be sure, I have nothing against old things. Quite the contrary, I love them. And in my desire for beauty and culture I enjoy staying with host families who have fixed up their homes tastefully. *Kitsch* makes me sick, above all when it is religious *kitsch*—for example, a plastic copy of Dürer's *Praying Hands*.

More and more I look forward after a week on the road to returning to my beloved apartment with its pictures, beautiful objects and antiques, and numerous brass candle holders with red candles in whose light the icons with their gold background shimmer. It is a place where I can have a relaxing glass of wine, not seated on the edge of my bed and drinking from the wash basin glass but rather from a beautiful, old, fancy glass. Add to this the sound from one of my favorite swing or blues CD's. This is what I call "coming home, being home." Finally comes the high point, sleeping in my own bed. I have slept in a thousand beds....

Blues Music and Gospel Proclamation

MEETING NICE COLLEAGUES

Even more interesting than these bed stories were my many encounters with fellow preachers. One time Wolfgang and I were invited to hold a youth evangelistic campaign. On the morning of the first day, we were busily setting up our equipment in the church. A man appeared dressed in an outfit like that of the British comedian Mr. Bean, and with unkempt hair shooting out in all directions with a few pieces of wood shavings mixed in. His hair resembled that of the children's cartoon character, Pumuckl, and I thought for certain that he had just cleaned out a rabbit hutch. At once I thought to myself, "That's the pastor!" He didn't say a word, not even "good day," "a hearty welcome," "God's blessing on the youth week," or anything of that sort. He merely said if I were Herr Lehmann I was wanted on the telephone. Then he asked me to follow him to the phone.

Moaning to himself, he shuffled along ahead of me. He mumbled something like "they would have to run another line for us," and led me into the office. Now, I figured he was either a worker in the church cemetery or an office employee. Later, he wandered back into the church just as Wolfgang was looking for an electrical outlet. He asked the man if he could help us and if he were the pastor. "No," he said, he wasn't the pastor and he didn't know anything about wall plugs.

It got to be midday. We were told we would have lunch with the superintendent. So, at 12 noon we went to his place and rang the doorbell. His wife led us into the kitchen without passing through either the living or dining room. We were fed in the kitchen, as is the custom with "guest workers," with emphasis on "workers." Then the door opened and who came in? My Pumuckl! And now we understood that he was the superintendent. Although he came to eat with us every day, he managed to say not one single word to us about the services.

I have encountered many pastoral colleagues who could not, and did not want to, conduct an evangelistic campaign. To disarm their prejudices and gain their support and cooperation for a campaign I offered to meet with them—in addition to the time on the evening of preparation—regularly during the week for a conversation. The offer was seldom accepted. Often we couldn't even determine a time when we could meet, or if we did, not even one of the pastors in the district showed up. In one instance, only the Baptist pastor and his wife appeared. In another, the superintendent had "forgotten" to send out the invitations. Although the youth administrator went ahead and did so, not one pastor showed up. To our astonishment, the room where the conversation was to take place had a beautifully decorated coffee table all set up. Unfortunately, as we soon found out, this was for someone else, not us.

I have dealt with pastors who avoided us for days and would not greet us with "good day" or even shake our hands. Many times I had the feeling I was a leper or someone who brings the plague into town. Often I had to express to Jörg my shame for the uncouthness of my Lutheran colleagues, because I had never encountered such nasty behavior and rejection when I was with Baptists. In contrast, with them I experienced something that I simply had never known in my own church.

The congregation to which I belong (my house stands only 35 feet behind the church building) and which I attend regularly when I am not traveling has never asked me where I had spent the last week in an evangelistic campaign, or where I would be going in the coming week. Nor have they ever mentioned that they had prayed for the traveling evangelist while he was on the road. There is simply no interest there; I feel as though they have hung me out to dry.

The Baptists are so different. During a period when I was often with Jörg in Berlin, I went to his church. It was a given that people there asked us, "Well, Brother, where are you going this week?" And when we named the place, they always replied, "May God be with you. The Lord bless you." On such occasions I felt much more at home in this Baptist congregation in Berlin than in my own in Chemnitz. It also could be like this when we arrived in the town to which we had been invited. Often we were tired, feeling a little uncertain and awkward amidst a lot of unfamiliar faces. And then someone would come up to us and say, "Welcome, it's nice that you are here. God bless you!" That does a person good. That encourages a person. It is edifying.

In Riesa, north of Dresden, a pastor stood in front of the church and loudly protested in the hearing of non-Christians against my policy of asking people to come forward to make a decision for Christ. On the next evening this continued. A large group of non-Christians wanted to speak with me about God—the dream of every pastor—but not this one. He pushed us out of the church, locked the door, and relegated us to sitting on the front lawn in order to talk.

Other pastors disgustingly disturbed our prayer time before the meetings through their loud gabbing instead of taking part in it. It is my custom on the last evening of a campaign, after everything has been taken down and cleaned up, to gather all those who worked with us in a semicircle around the altar. We thanked God for everything, most of all for the new converts. One time as we were standing around the altar, the pastor loudly talked with the district catechist at the back of the church. I noted in my diary, "We tried to silence them with loud singing—to no avail. Of course, there was no 'Good bye.'"

My entry regarding a week of meetings in the notorious chemical city of Bitterfeld in 1985 is interesting: "Here we have no quarrels with the pastors because there aren't any." We were in a very large church building. The pastors had left the city. Only the preacher of a Free Church congregation and the Baptist pastor remained. There hadn't been a church youth group for years. A Baptist woman tried to start a youth ministry at the church. The region was extremely polluted and had been destroyed by industry. Because of the smell, I abandoned my morning jogging routine. Everything seemed apocalyptic; the people were as run down as the environment. Broken marriages were more frequent than new marriages. The superintendent had given a sermon entitled "Until death do us part." He got a divorce the very next week. In this miserable atmosphere, God gave us many souls.

In another town, where there were also many decisions for Christ (and a collection of 13,000 marks), the pastor never even shook my hand the entire week. During the final prayer of the campaign, he, two other pastors, and a cleaning lady not only did not take part but also they disturbed our prayers with the loud noise they made while cleaning up the church.

We were reproached in strange ways by some of our colleagues. At a pastors' convention in Greifswald in which we were involved, one person condemned Jörg for "exerting pressure" because he had said the evening before that "Christians prayed in the sacristy for the evangelization meetings." In Plauen, some Methodists accused me of standing in the place of Christ and behaving like the pope. The reason they gave was that I had quoted II Corinthians 5:20: "So we are ambassadors for Christ, since God is making his appeal through us; we entreat you on behalf of Christ, be reconciled to God." I said to one colleague, "When you pronounce the forgiveness of sins during confession, you, too, have to say in the stead of and in the name of Jesus." He answered: "No, I think the same as the others that Christ has already forgiven us of our sins." A pastor who doesn't feel he can pronounce the forgiveness of sins in the name of Jesus denies the office of reconciliation, one of the absolutely distinctive features of our pastoral duties.

Equally catastrophic was the statement made by another of my pastoral brethren who didn't know how to pronounce the blessing upon a person. For decades, I have had someone bless the musician and me right before the service begins. We pray together, then we kneel, and the brother blesses us by the laying on of hands. A pastor whom I had requested to perform this service turned to me and, in a rather embarrassed manner, admitted, "I've never done that." A pastor who had never blessed a person! What kind of shepherds are they? Or people?

On the other hand, I can praise God that He gave me other brothers who did not study theology for years at a university nor prattled about the campus of a preachers' seminary. They are so-called laypeople, untrained Christians who know their Bibles and have an intimate relationship with their Lord Jesus. How many times have I been blessed by such great God-empowered individuals. It is men such as these that I consider to be "mature" Christians. Such a person is not the type of church convention windbag who waves with his violet scarf to the Dalai Lama but a believing Christian. He can pronounce the blessing with his own mouth in one of the many biblical wordings or in a free formulation of his own. I prefer to work with such mature Christians than with the "professionals" who can't even offer a word of blessing.

I also had little understanding for a pastor who swiped my Bible. When I came back into the sacristy after being in the altar area, I discovered it had disappeared from the desk. At least the culprit had left my sermon manuscript there, much to my relief. There was a great deal of excitement and searching around by our co-workers: "Who's seen Theo's Bible?" A few minutes before the beginning of the evening meeting, the pastor appeared and handed it to me. He "had just borrowed it."

In one church, just before the closing prayer of the evening meeting, a pastor jumped all over me saying: "I don't mind if you still want to pray, but not until you have cleared out the people who were standing in front of the altar." The person then went on to make racket in the back of the church, but we thanked God anyway.

Another pastor used the occasion of the prayer gathering for the workers prior to the evangelistic service to criticize my sermon of the previous evening. First of all, it was not necessary to emphasize that someone is the forerunner who prepares the way to God. This was an attack upon our use of the Bob Dylan song, "Gotta Serve Somebody," which we rewrote as, "You are a forerunner for somebody. It can be, it is the Devil. It can be, it is God." We followed this with a challenge to connect with Jesus. Second, the pastor not only believed but knew for certain that, "Jesus also goes along with the lost into Hell." Third, we were assured that many party comrades would be ahead of Christians in heaven. I am still amazed that God gave me the composure not to stand up and leave the room.

If you think about these examples, then you understand the prayer of a youth administrator "for protection from the evil one, starting with the Devil on up to the pastors." However, not all of the youth leaders were friends of the evangelistic campaigns. At one meeting was a group of bearded individuals, rather dark types who constantly had a smirk on their faces and did not sing along. I suspected all the while that they had come to disrupt the meeting with some sort of action. Afterwards I learned that they were from a convention of youth administrators at a neighboring church.

COMICAL INSECT DISCOVERED

In 1988 I was with Wolfgang Tost for a campaign in the Luther city of Wittenberg. Although constant noise and unrest was apparent in the church, many atheists were converted that evening. I had hoped to have the opportunity to speak with the young ministerial students at the local Preachers' Seminary [they were alternative theological colleges that did not require an *Abitur* for admission] about the topic of evangelization. However, they weren't interested at all in a meeting with a practicing evangelist. We only heard the word "tolerance," which meant not speaking with us but also not doing anything against us.

I saw this tolerance in action that evening when a group of these future pastors entered the church and headed for the balcony, the area where the candidates for confirmation usually sit. Then they proceeded to behave just like them. While Wolfgang and I wrestled with all our strength of body and soul for the souls of the lost young people, these future pastors made a joke of the event, perhaps as a substitute for a missed beer evening. They had brought a long medieval telescope with which they eyed me like some strange extinct insect: "What, he's talking about conversion? Never heard of such."

A God for All Situations

Once, Bishop Klaus Engelhardt, at the time president of the EKD council [after 1990 it was again the umbrella organization for all the German Protestant churches], asked me how I felt in the church and how I would describe my position. I then related to him this story and explained that it was rather typical for me as an evangelist in the church. I had been persecuted by the *Stasi* as a "spider" that had to be squashed, was mocked during an evangelistic campaign in the very heart of Reformation country, and viewed as a curiosity from a bygone world as if I were a long-dead insect, but strangely one that was still alive.

But I was neither a spider nor a mythological animal. I was a fisher of men, who, assisted by a handful of ordinary, unlearned co-workers from the GDR, each of whom had a burning heart for souls, was swimming against the stream. We threw out our nets and were able to rescue many from the Red flood. Given our good fortune to be able to take part in God's rescue action, the belly-aching of pastors and the contemptible actions of the *Stasi* were to us as nothing.

It was like the birth of a child—when the baby arrives, all the pain is forgotten. It had to be among the most beautiful moments of my life when I was permitted to serve as a "midwife" at such a birth and see a new-born child of God. I spoke with many young people, day after day, evening after evening, in agonizing discussions that brought me to the point of physical exhaustion. I struggled with them and prayed for them. Being permitted to experience the return home of a lost son or daughter was more than enough compensation for what mean-spirited colleagues had done to me with their malicious criticism. These poor people, who don't believe there is any such thing as coming to Christ, have no idea what a joy this is. I have often run around praying aloud and thanking God following a conversion. Many times I have thought to myself, "All you doubters go take a flying leap!" Saved! In contrast to this, the bad mouthing of the theological naysayers counts as nothing.

Two things are among the most beautiful sights in my life as an evangelist. The first one is the sight of a young couple that has heeded the call to decision and comes forward hand in hand to kneel before the cross. Such an occasion simply bowls me over. The second is when after the conclusion of a meeting, the workers counsel with those who have made a decision for Christ. They sit together in pairs on the pews with an open Bible in their hands. I watch how these young co-workers with seriousness and zeal explain the plan of salvation to the seekers and show them how to take their first steps in the faith. Often at the end they put their heads together and pray. For me, these are among the loveliest scenes I can think of. I can do nothing but thank God for the young people and ask Him to bless them. Such experiences are far more important to me than the worst forms of opposition that sadly I have also encountered.

THE LEIPZIG RUBBISH

Jörg and I were invited to conduct a youth evangelization in Leipzig in 1979. One could write a book about that week! In fact, he has an entire chapter on it in one of his books. There were problems right from the start. Doctrinal matters deeply divided the co-workers on the team, resulting in constant arguments which continued right up until we celebrated the Lord's Supper before the opening meeting. I stayed with Burkhardt Zimmermann, the person responsible for youth evangelism in Leipzig and who had invited us. Three of us slept on mattresses on the floor in one room. Gunther Pohlert, the banjo man of the Schlosskirche band, who provided the preliminary music, watched over the equipment in the church as a sentry and slept on a hard pew.

Finally, we all were sick with colds. One evening the band simply stopped playing and my cold almost caused my voice to give out. Another night the friction among the workers at the Lord's Supper was so bad that Jörg, with a firm hand, held me down in my chair because I wanted to walk out. Several times during the week I was ready to cancel the whole thing because I felt that when a team was so splintered, God could not bless the endeavor. But it turned out to be a time of some of the richest blessings I have ever experienced. It was certainly was a miracle that the attendees did not realize what was happening behind the scenes. Never again did problems at an evangelistic meeting put me under so much strain as at this one. Still, many were converted, including a theology student.

The evangelization took place in the downtown Nikolaikirche, a building rich in tradition. From this church the students of the Leipzig Mission had been commissioned, including my father. Elke and I often attended the worship service here when I was a student. It wasn't possible to post notices about events on or in front of the church, not even a small card. Permission to print posters was hard to come by. Normally, invitation leaflets were handmade. So, youthful Christians spent many evenings making leaflets advertising the meetings, accompanied by prayer and giggling. This limitation on our advertising, which gave us cause for grief, actually had a great advantage—it required involvement. The one who put so much effort into writing out the text was not about to just simply throw it into any old mailbox, but took great care that the valuable leaflet was placed directly into someone's hand and was read. It was clear that young Christians who had invested so much effort in the production of these advertisements made the campaign their own.

It was very difficult to affix posters in public places, but sometimes owners of private businesses (of which there were a few) were willing to hang up a poster in their store or shop window. Most of the advertising was by word of mouth. In fact, we owed the schools, *FDJ*, and *SED* a debt of gratitude for providing us with the very best advertising. Agitating against the evangelistic campaign or forbidding participation in it was the best possible thing that could happen. Remember the famous sentence by writer Wolf Biermann, "For whatever is forbidden, that is something we have got to have or to do." In Leipzig 2000 came on the

1979 evangelistic campaign at the Leipzig Nikolaikirche

first evening and 4000 the last one, while on some nights the church doors had to be closed because the building was overfilled. Hundreds remained after the services, and everywhere in the church conversations and discussions took place. We were always in the center of these.

One evening, approximately 15 young people cornered me. I took fire from every side. I could see from their manner of argumentation that they were living, breathing atheists who were rejecting my message. Then Millo, a theology student whom I knew, came by and told me: "They are all theology students." They had gone so far in their disgraceful hypocrisy to claim they were atheists during pastoral conversations with our young personal workers in order to test their faith. We countered the nasty deviousness of our future pastoral colleagues with the suggestion that we hold a public debate at their Theological Faculty. This was the same place where I had begun my studies.

This took place on the fourth day of our week in Leipzig. We entered the lions' den, a tense, hostile atmosphere. The first question was addressed to me: "Are you a prophet?" My answer was: "Yes, and in the sense that I defined it yesterday when I was speaking about Elijah. Prophets are speakers for God who direct the message so that it strikes the heart. I pray every time before I proclaim the gospel for this gift of prophecy." That was harmless enough and, at least, it was a theological topic. We stuck with this topic for a while and the air was filled with accusations and wild claims such as a God of love would not carry out a Last Judgment. Jörg tried to answer the emotionally charged assertions ("I can't even imagine a God, but . . .") with biblical passages. But that didn't work with people for whom the Bible is not the Word of God and the final authority.

The atmosphere got more and more electric, tense, and non-objective. We were accused of creating "mass hysteria." What a grotesque charge! There were thousands of young people in the church; they sang together, listened to my thirty minute sermon quietly, and a few made decisions for Christ, although none on the first evening. Afterwards, many of them discussed various things with us for hours. Where was the hysteria? It was only on the side of our critics who reacted to our message excessively, even hysterically. Now, the furor really got out of hand. They said we were like the Nazis. Someone compared me to Goebbels. That went much too far. I told the one who made this accusation that I was no longer willing to talk with him. I wondered the whole time about how calmly I heard myself talking and the kind of composure God had given me in this caustic discussion.

Then came the high point. A student named Christian Mendt (whom I won't honor by giving the rest of his biography except to note he is still a pastor in the Saxon church) shouted out in the overcrowded lecture hall where all this was taking place, "After all, because of your manner of preaching, you drove a young man to commit suicide." At this point I exploded. As though I had been bitten by a tarantula, I interrupted him and demanded the name and address of the alleged dead person. Mendt hemmed and hawed. Again I insisted that he give me the name. He had publicly incriminated me; therefore, he must give me the opportunity to defend myself. Since I wouldn't let go of him and would not continue the discussion unless he revealed the name, he finally coughed up the name: Eberhard Fuchs.

I always carry a little notebook with me. It is my custom when I engage in such a conversation to make some notes. I held it up high and said, "This is a gift from Eberhard Fuchs. In fact, I just talked with him this

A God for All Situations

week by telephone. He is alive and well." That was the first but unfortunately not the last time that Christians, or should I say church co-workers, publicly accused me of driving someone to commit suicide. Before this confrontation I had never thought it possible that church colleagues, because of their hatred, would go this far and be capable of such lies.

The laughing third party in the whole affair was of course the *Stasi*. A Berlin vicar who claimed to be a church colleague experienced the whole incident. After the meetings were over, he caught a ride back to Berlin with Jörg and me. Actually, he was a police informant and was able to report "Johnny-on-the-spot" how roughly my "brothers" treated me.

Moreover, the evangelization week was accompanied by an anonymous postal card campaign. The word "Judas" appeared, like the one I had already found on the hood of my Wartburg. There were a variety of different texts. One card began with the sentence, "We don't want any Judas in Leipzig." Another was even sent to the address of our Leipzig quarters. So I evangelized in Leipzig in the face of a massive barrage from both church and state.

This turbulent campaign week had both a special postlude and a special consequence. The postlude was that a group of theologians led by Dr. Jürgen Ziemer and Dr. Christoph Kähler (the later bishop of Thuringia) made an extensive analysis of my sermons and sent them to two members of the Regional Church Administrative Office in Dresden: Senior Church Counselor Mendt (father of the above-mentioned theology student, Christian M.) and Dr. Schwintek. Presumably the objective was to lay the groundwork for proceedings against me. It called into question my "manner of preaching the gospel." My methodology, theological foundation, image of God (it is "demonic"), and statements about sin, conversion, sexuality, and abortion were dissected and criticized. They labeled the sentence, "You are a sinner," as a loveless "accusation." They called the challenge, "Be converted and decide for Jesus," a repulsive "demand for obedience," and concluded that "Not much joy remains here."

I was happy that I didn't have to deal with this document. Jörg, however, prepared an extensive rebuttal to it. I never heard a word from the *LKA* regarding the whole matter. Apparently the long list of charges against me failed to convince even those who did not particularly care for me that they should discipline me.

Some years later, after the *Wende, MDR* (Middle German Radio) made a film about me and my life as an evangelist. I was asked whether I also had critics and opponents. I named the co-author of the Leipzig report, Dr. Kähler, as one of my sharpest theological opponents. So the camera team went to him and questioned him. The utterly ridiculous things that he said in front of the camera I will not repeat here. Very interesting was his comment that he had never met anyone who had been converted through my ministry.

He did not realize that the joke was on him. The voice of the speaker for this film was just such a one. The man had been staggering around in Dresden one evening. He saw the lights in the Annenkirche were on and went in. I was preaching on the text from Matthew 6 ("Do not worry about your life..."). From hearing the message he recognized that "Truth and freedom is with you [i.e., our team]." Wolfgang counseled him at the end of the service and he came to Christ. On the following morning he began doing some evangelistic work at *MDR* by playing songs on the air from the CD that Wolfgang had given him.

And now I turn to a distinctive result of the evangelization in Leipzig. A few years later I met a man who told me that he had been one of the team members. Following the week of meetings, the leaders met and discussed how the thing should continue. They did not want this effort just to come to an end but rather to have some sort of an ongoing impact on the city. From this was born the idea of the "prayers for peace" that became a weekly event in the Nikolaikirche. The repercussions of these times of prayer are well-known. If the report of this man is correct—and I have no reason to doubt him—then an evangelistic campaign stood at the very beginning of the peaceful "revolution of the candles" that brought an end to communist rule. "Give our God the glory!"

Two months after Leipzig, I passed out. It occurred during the regular January gathering of Saxon youth workers. I had completed my customary jogging exercise before breakfast and was standing at the table as the blessing was being pronounced. Suddenly my eyes saw only black, and in full view of all the youth workers, I collapsed like a wet sack. After readjusting my medications and taking a short break, I was able to return to the circuit. I was now more and more frequently conducting campaigns outside Saxony—in Saxony-Anhalt, Thuringia, Brandenburg, and Mecklenburg. There I faced a real scandal in 1987.

A God for All Situations

NO DESIRE IN LUDWIGSLUST

Jörg and I went to Ludwigslust, a county seat in southwestern Mecklenburg. The meetings would take place in a church located on the campus of the Bethlehemstift, a deaconess and medical facility. One could hardly imagine a godlier place than this. But the Devil was hard at work here, and there was friction from the outset. Some colleagues of one pastor were grousing behind the scenes without actually saying what made them unhappy. The explosion came on the third evening. I had spoken about Nicodemus and the necessity for a conversion experience. Following this, Jörg gave the call to repentance and two girls, around 13 years in age, came forward. Just at the moment when he was to say the prayer of surrender with the girls, a man stepped to the altar, stopped the prayer, and began speaking. Jörg would not allow him to continue. I thought this person who interrupted the service was just some guy off the street and I said to him, "You can't speak here now." He replied: "Oh, but I can!"

Then I heard someone shout, "That's the pastor." How was I to know? He was so uncouth that that he had not even greeted us or introduced us as guests at his church even though we had been here three days. After all, we weren't clairvoyants who could determine that this stranger who blathered his way into our prayer was in fact the pastor here. But, since it was he, we couldn't forbid him to speak in his own church and had to listen to his tirade. In brief, he said: Rebirth takes place at baptism and isn't the same as conversion. Since the children were baptized (not so, one had not been), he felt compelled to stand as a protection between us and them and thus prevent the prayer of repentance.

Here was the usual false understanding of the doctrine of baptismal regeneration, which lies like a shroud over so many churches and suffocates all efforts to bring about conversion. The embarrassing thing is that the individuals who hide behind this doctrine claim to be Lutherans. In actuality, they cannot base their belief on Luther himself, the Lutheran confessions, or the Lutheran dogmatic theologians. It is exactly the reverse. Infant baptism makes conversion not superfluous but rather necessary. A church that baptizes children is compelled to evangelize.

After his speech, everything fell apart. Those seated in the sanctuary were appalled. The two girls were flabbergasted. They didn't understand what was going on and they held each others' hands. I did not know what to do. Jörg whispered to me that I should close the service with the benediction. I resorted to the liturgical form, but felt uncomfortable in doing so.

Following this, the discussion raged on in the church, first in small groups and then over the microphone. The pastor's fans, who constantly interrupted each speaker and would not allow persons to have their say, clapped loudly. Then the pastor took some fire. A girl asked him how he knew what was in a person's heart. He cannot judge whether someone wants to become a Christian. Finally, after things calmed down, she gave her heart to Jesus.

Next, the girl who had come to Christ the day before spoke, along with a young woman who had been converted at eight years of age and was thankful that it had occurred so early in her life and that it remained so up to now. After her, a former alcoholic declared: "My family was a mess, my health was ruined. I was without hope and in the gutter. That is how bad my situation had become. Then I met some Christians, and finally, Christ himself. He helped me and forgave me my sin. My life became new. Jesus even healed my shattered marriage."

While the debate was still raging, I went into the sacristy. There sat the two girls, weeping bitterly. A young woman who gave religious instruction to children tried to comfort them. I asked the girls if they still would like to give their life to Christ and pray the prayer of faith. Through the sniffling came a clear "yes," and so I prayed with them. After repeating it after me, they left, with the woman alongside them, as newborn children of God.

The heated conversations continued. Both chaplain-pastors of the Bethlehemstift (the ones who had invited us) distanced themselves from the church pastor's behavior and diatribe and stood solidly behind us. I jumped back into the fray. The pastor made the arrogant comment about Jörg that he ought to inform himself better about the meaning of the cross in the Greek New Testament. He said this before a packed church and acted as if he were speaking of an unlearned young school boy. I would not let this pass without a sharp challenge, since at this time Jörg was serving as a Greek teacher at the East German Baptists' seminary. Just that morning we had read together from the text of Romans in the original. The pastor's personal defamation made the theological contrast between him and us all the more clear.

In the course of the public discussion, it was mentioned that the night before someone had torn down the announcements of the youth evangelization that were posted on the grounds of the deaconess institution. In two places new posters were affixed, one being on the church door itself, which read: "Jesus Christ is dead. Theo crucified him. Theo lives." One would have expected a general outrage over such an atrocious act, particularly the one on the church door. No, the argumentation went the other way around: We had put the people under so much pressure that they were compelled to commit such aggressive acts. We wouldn't take them seriously, but simply ignored the matter and swept it under the table. They operated, so to speak, on the principle that the victim is responsible for the crime. We knew nothing about the poster fiasco and fortunately, our co-workers didn't blame us for the matter.

Then we were informed that the Bible is not God's Word but merely contains the collected experiences of our forebears. The pastor even asserted that Paul had regretted his conversion later on in life. I demanded the biblical proof for this, and he responded with Galatians Chapter 1, which really contains not a word of regret from Paul about his conversion. Moreover, the pastor, who claimed he had acted as he did out of a feeling of "pastoral responsibility," did not visit the families of the children on the following day, but made a telephone appointment for the day after next. Soon after this he called the people concerned, canceled the scheduled visit completely, and left for a clergy retreat. So much for "pastoral responsibility."

When the pastor said, "Good night," to me, I answered: "I wish you from the bottom of my heart a very uneasy night," because he had to answer to God for his actions. He had tried to prevent two girls from coming to God. I accused him of having disturbed a worship service and doing that in front of unbelievers. One colleague said that the only one who had been served by his "stage performance" was the Devil. The pastor: "That's what I thought; now I am being condemned as Satan's helper."

Until two in the morning Jörg and I sat in bed, dazed but talking and praying together. It was well that we were there for one another!

On the next day I spoke with the mother of one of the girls. She could not understand why the pastor had tried to prevent the conversion of her daughter. The religious instructor called on the other girl's grandmother, who didn't belong to the church. The granny said, "Better to go to church than the disco."

In the afternoon we had an hour-long session chaired by the superior of the deaconesses, which is somewhat like an order of Protestant nuns.

We were accused of putting so much pressure on the people that they couldn't do anything else but convert. (Until then, except for the two children in question only two other girls had come to Christ.) They claimed we created such an intensely emotional situation that the people were simply "swept along." We proposed to our conversation partners that we agree upon a common strategy, since the terms "pressure" and "intensely emotional" were contradictory.

In the evening a distraught team gathered for the preparation meeting. I was in charge of the Lord's Supper. How could I get these discouraged people back on their feet? With the Scriptures! Only with the Scriptures! I chose my favorite verse from the Bible, Romans 8:28: "We know that all things work together for good for those who love God." I began my devotional thus: "We have encountered hatred. We shouldn't be astonished. Jesus told us we should expect this. And the words that are on this shocking poster are true." Startled, several of the heads hanging down popped up and stared at me in amazement. I continued, "Yes, that is the truth. I killed Jesus. He died because of my sins. And because He died, I live."

Then I quoted the Passion hymn by Paul Gerhardt from the hymnbook:

> I, I and my sins,
> which are like the grains
> of sand by the sea,
> they have aroused
> the misery that pains you
> and the grieving army of martyrs.

At this point we were at the heart of the biblical message of justification. The team members listened up, breathed a sigh of relief, and sat upright. A laugh was heard, indicating an easing of tensions. I quoted Genesis 50:20: "Even though you intended to do harm to me, God intended it for good." Strengthened in spirit and with the blessing of Pastor Schwechten, a supportive Ludwigslust pastor, we went forward into the evening.

A superintendent from the Mecklenburg regional church entered the church that was now filled to overflowing. Behind him in single file marched a line of pastors. The group went past us without even acknowledging our presence. They positioned themselves in the balcony and turned a tape recorder on. Again and again we heard whispering and small talk from their area. Jörg sang his heart out. Although I was nervous, I preached uncompromisingly about turning to Christ. At the end, the "board of inspectors" departed and once again walked past us without a greeting of any kind. There was no conversation at all.

But, shortly thereafter, I had a brief conversation with the one in charge of preventing conversions, the pastor. He tried to justify his actions of the night before, explaining to me that Doreen (one of the girls who had come forward) suffered from asthma. Given the current weather conditions and a packed church, it was really dangerous for her. For this reason he had stood in front of her to protect her. I went after him and told him he could spare us his crocodile tears about the girl's illness. He ought rather to consider how much damage he had done to my health. I accused him of having acted in the way he did because he was fundamentally opposed to evangelistic campaigns. (I had heard that he had also caused a lot of trouble during one of Peter Fischer's meetings.) He told me that he had slept quite well. He took that as a sign that he wasn't acting under the Devil's influence and that God was standing at his side. And with the sentence, "I won't let you take that from me," he left the church without a further word.

Next morning I was sitting in the institution's office because I wanted to call Elke. A man sauntered through the room, shook the hand of the deaconess on duty and did the same to me, but without saying a word. Later I heard another deaconess address him as Herr Blank. I shot out of my seat in the corner of the room, ran after him, and asked "Aren't you the regional church superintendent?" "Yes," he said.

I snapped at him that we were appalled at his behavior for walking past us without a word or sign of recognition. And now he again sneaked by me. In addition, to tape record the meeting without asking our permission was ignorant, shameful, unchristian, and inhospitable. Then he roared that my comments about baptism were outrageous. This will be investigated and there will be consequences. The consequence was that I, in effect, was placed under a gag order and forbidden to preach there. A congregation that had booked me for a future campaign canceled its invitation. I never again was invited to hold meetings in the territory of the Mecklenburg regional church. Since Ludwigslust, it has remained closed to me.

One of the doctors at the Bethlehemstift hospital wanted to make things a bit worse for me. He said loudly in the church that I should be "locked up in an institution." One positive thing that resulted from all this was that never before had there been so much discussion about conversion to Jesus at Ludwigslust. The same held true for the various hospital wards and the nurses' training school.

On the final evening, on which four young people came forward, the whole pathetic scene took place again. We could not believe our eyes. After the concluding song, once again a man, unknown to us, appeared next to the altar, and without introducing himself began to speak. It was a higher official, Provost Günter, who had been contacted by phone to come to the church. He criticized the idea of conversion, even though the four young people who had given their hearts to Christ were standing right in front of him. He played the hypocritical card of baptismal theology once again: "I am baptized; that means I am born again. . . . My conversion is absolutely not necessary for me today."

As before, a tumultuous situation resulted. A man cried out: "In the name of Jesus, I must say something here!" Frau Pastor Finger shouted: "In the name of Jesus, I forbid you to speak!" He yelled all the louder, "The provost is a heretic! He is teaching false doctrine that conversion isn't necessary and that infant baptism is the same as conversion. My daughter is among those who was converted this evening and I thank God for it. Herr Provost, you are a heretic."

The wife of the "heretic" jumped into the fray with quite a different argument: "If you allow minors to convert without the agreement of their parents who may be atheists, you drive a wedge between parents and children. What you are doing is, in the end, endangering the security of the state. For where families find no peace, that nation cannot enjoy peace." The lady seemed unaware of Matthew 10:34–39.

After that evening I was completely wiped out. Outside the support of our colleagues and the encouragement from many others, what strengthened us most of all during the week were the Bible verses from the *Moravian Daily Texts*. The topic of the reading for the second evening was "Do not be afraid." "Do not fear, O soul; be glad and rejoice, for the Lord has done great things!" (Joel 2:21). "The God of peace will shortly crush Satan under your feet. The grace of our Lord Jesus Christ be with you" (Rom 16:20). On the third evening, when the battle began, the text was: "He will clear his threshing floor, and will gather his wheat into the granary; but the chaff he will burn with unquenchable fire" (Matt 3:12).

A God for All Situations

On the evening before the final night, they were: "The fear of others brings a snare; but one who trusts in the Lord is secure" (Prov 29:25). "Only live your life in a manner worthy of the gospel of Christ, so that ... you are standing firm in one spirit, striving side by side with one mind for the faith of the gospel. And [you] are in no way intimidated by your opponents" (Phil 1:27–28). The last evening's text was: "The crowds were astonished at his teaching, for he taught them as one having authority, and not as their scribes" (Matt 7:28–29). And on Sunday when we left Ludwigslust to return home, it was: "I have been with you wherever you went" (2 Sam 7:9).

The thunderclap at Ludwigslust had a marvelous sequel. A few years later I was at the annual Evangelical Alliance Conference in Bad Blankenburg. A young girl came up to me and asked if I recognized her. I had no clue who she was. Then she told me that she was one of the two girls from that turbulent night with whom I had prayed the prayer of surrender in the sacristy. A child's conversion that had "taken"! She is still walking with Jesus. Marvelous! A few more years went by and I learned that she was now a missionary in Thailand. She is working for Jesus. Marvelous!

A month after the evangelization in Ludwigslust, I wrote a letter to the workers there: "Of course, I still have a lot of struggling to do before I can get over the situations we faced in your city. After all, we aren't stones. How must Jesus have suffered when he came to rescue mankind and to call God's beloved people to repentance! On the other hand, how can we even think of comparing these little pin pricks with Jesus' sufferings! Our time in Ludwigslust helps me to have a much greater understanding of the Passion of Christ. I now will let myself be hacked to pieces to show there is only one way to come to God and that is through faith in Jesus Christ. That and that alone is what we have preached."

Hardly had I come to terms with the Ludwigslust experience when, at my next campaign in March 1987, new waves of hatred crashed about us.

THE POTSDAM POST COACH DRIVER

This time they weren't citizens of Mecklenburg dressed up as Lutherans, but rather Prussians claiming to be humanistic rationalists who descended on us. For them such a thing as conversion was something not worth talking about. But what they did attack was everything else of eternal significance: sin, lostness, hell, etc. In their opinion, these had no place in a Christian sermon. In contrast, they sang boldly the old song "The Good in Mankind" and looked for the truth in other religions.

It was my good fortune to have Wolfgang Tost as my companion and singer. Naturally, I had told him rather energetically everything about the meetings in Ludwigslust. But this decent young man, who had grown up in a conservative church situation and had become a church worker, simply couldn't comprehend what I told him. And although I had warned him in advance, he was totally bowled over as he encountered for the first time in his life intense hatred from church people. Up until now, he had naively believed that Christians wouldn't tear one another apart like wolves and certainly not in public. Potsdam, however, taught him something worse.

A front page article in the *Potsdamer Kirchenzeitung* produced a hostile mood against me even before I arrived in town. The headline read "Deceptive Labeling." I had seen all this before. That had been the argument of the pastor at Ludwigslust, who compared us to deceptive horse traders who persuade a customer to buy a half-blind work horse. The article's author, a school pastor named Hans-Ulrich Schulz, was upset about the motto for the evangelistic effort "A God for All Situations." He maintained that: "There is no such thing as a God for all situations." Therefore, the sentence in my leaflet, "He always knows a way out," was deceptive labeling.

Because I am firmly confident that "He always knows a way out," I drove to Potsdam with forebodings. I had "butterflies in my stomach." Compared to the things that my "brother Christians" were about to put me through, the usual squabbles with the state authorities (such as the refusal to permit our banner on the Potsdam Nikolaikirche "A God for all Situations" to be illuminated at night) seemed like a trifle.

On the opening night, the church was filled to capacity, including the upstairs galleries, and the atmosphere was good. But right after the preaching portion of the service the discussions began. In Potsdam lived about 1,500 church workers, mainly employed at various educational institutions around the area. These trainees with their teachers immediately jumped on us and told us we were doing everything wrong. But we were glad that on the very first evening four young people came forward. On the second evening no one came forward, but some found Christ during the conversations afterwards. On the third evening, during a question and answer period regarding homosexuality there was an uproar, but approximately twelve gave their lives to Christ.

On the fourth evening, everything went well until the invitation, when several responded. Then things exploded and events ran a similar course to that in Ludwigslust. As I began to pray with those who had come forward, a pastor's daughter, "a real wild one," wanted to speak over the microphone. Our host, Pastor Hering, refused to let her do so. Wolfgang tried to save the situation by starting to sing a song. The pastor's little daughter ran from one mike to another and spoke into each of them in turn, until a non-Christian came up and attempted to pull her away from them. While I was praying the prayer of commitment, another girl came up and tried to speak into my microphone.

I had to ask for quiet during the prayer. But the prayer and blessing were drowned out by talking and shouting. A student from the local church seminary stood on a church pew with his backside towards me and dropped his pants. Wolfgang launched into the the final hymn, "Peace Be with You," and we sang at the top of our lungs as the tumult raged before us. Some girls screamed that I had no right to preach and that there was no Devil. All of this was accompanied by loud whistling and shouts of agreement.

A soldier of the National People's Army in uniform took an enormous risk by confessing his newfound faith in Christ in front of this raging mob. There was general chaos. An angry crowd surrounded me and everyone demanded the mike. We stood our ground and I would not allow this. They accused us of behaving like those at a communist party meeting where no one could give his own opinion. Then, to top it off, someone said "We live by the freedom of a Christian man." I asked, "Have you read this short book by Luther?" "No."

And so, on this student *niveau* the raucous brawling continued. Pastor Hering suggested that the group besetting me on every side move into another room to continue the conversation. A few came hesitantly, but right after the first question, they all left and plunged into the general disorder in the church. They really didn't want to have a serious discussion, but simply were bent on keeping things stirred up. In yet another room we finally were able to get a discussion going on homosexuality. At midnight we left the church, exhausted.

We spent the following morning from 9 until 12 in a conversation with the church workers who had become so angry with us. They had already used up all their powder and had nothing left. The encounter was harmless.

On the fifth day, the district youth pastor, who lived in the apartment above our quarters, extended his hand to me for the first time. Once again it was midnight when a man said, "Hello, my name is Schwochow," and walked on past us. I called out to him "Then you are probably the regional youth pastor." It was he indeed. (The parallels to Ludwigslust were unavoidable—uncultured louts with horrendous behavior both here and there). He expressed his concern about matters and said the church would now need months to correct the false image of God among the young people who had seen our slogan, "A God for All Situations."

Co-workers assumed that the photos distributed during the meeting that evening had been produced in the youth pastor's office. Under a photo of me preaching from a pulpit was the caption, "Caution: Theo-L-ogy of Death." Handwritten on the edge was: "Theo—a scaremonger for all situations," and Matthew 7:5: "You, hypocrite, first take the log out of your own eye."

I follow the practice of paying particular attention to the Bible words and topics that are emphasized at the Lord's Supper before our services and in the prayer sessions. I have had some really astonishing experiences whenever, out of countless verses in the Bible, precisely that one finds its way into my sermon. I need only to look at Wolfgang and we know: We are on the right path. I always take this as a confirming sign from God.

On the evening in Potsdam when the racket started, my topic was "Busy." The Bible verse I had selected had to do with the fact that Jesus came "to destroy the works of the Devil" (I John 3:8). On the night before it was precisely this key word that was also used in the Lord's Supper. And now on our last evening, Pastor Hering said, "Heaven and earth will pass away, but my words will not pass away" (Mark 13:31), and that was the first sentence of my sermon. A co-worker gave as "God's Word for our discussion," the passage "I am standing at the door, knocking" (Rev 3:20), that proved to be the text for both the altar call and the hymn used during it.

We didn't need any more signs of confirmation. We went calmly into the meeting. No one responded during the invitation, but immediately at the end of the closing song, four boys came forward to receive Christ. Once again we left the church at midnight, worn out, happy, and thankful. We have a God for all situations.

A God for All Situations

I wrote the following song with Peter Krause.

A God for all situations knows what's best all the time,
He's never embarrassed when it comes to tough matters.

Call on the God of all situations.
In any event, you simply must try it
so your case will be heard
at the highest level.

A God for all situations sees the end of the tunnel;
he'll be your light if you're fully burned out.

A God for all situations hears your cries at all times.
He'll help you to your feet,
but you must walk on your own.

A God for all situations keeps his word at all times.
He won't lead you astray,
so cast your doubts overboard.

11

There Is a Word

I AND MY SINGER Peter Krause were invited in November 1985 to hold an evangelization in Mittweida, about 20 miles northeast of my home. People told me that there were only two truly devout members in the church—the deacon, and the custodian/boiler operator. The huge church was indeed warm, and the boiler man, Gerhard, a true "father in Christ," laid hands on us with a blessing every evening before the meeting.

In the musical portion prior to the actual service, the group that played was "The Mustard Seed Band," with Ralf Gotter as director. When the band began at 6:30, the church was still empty. There was only an older lady sitting alone in the very last row. The band gave her a special concert. There aren't many bands prepared to demonstrate this type of humility, only those who desire to proclaim Jesus, and not to lift themselves up. And that was the goal of the "Mustard Seeds." For this reason I have held countless meetings with this group, the longest serving band in Saxony.

Nevertheless, during the entire week, the church was completely full. In the background there were the usual skirmishes with the state authorities. One evening my program was entitled, "Concert in Prison," as I planned to speak on Paul and Silas in prison. The authorities did not permit this title, and so we changed it to "Concert at Midnight" and pasted the new title over the old one on the public posters. Somewhere along the line this change of title had been overlooked. The Dresden District Council called the *LKA* and telephone calls bounced back and forth until things were smoothed over. Apart from this, everything was calm and normal until the fourth evening when another storm broke loose.

As is my custom, I had a box where people could drop in written questions to which I would respond. Someone asked about AIDS, a phenomenon which was just coming to public awareness at the time. I replied: "Normally, apart from a few exceptions, this sickness is transmitted by sexual intercourse," primarily through extramarital and same-sex relations, both of which I felt were "strictly forbidden in the Bible." I then mentioned an article from the latest number of the health magazine *Gesundheit* on the topic, "Homosexuality." It stated that homosexuality "had contradicted the views of the church." I went on to say "it not only had contradicted the views of the church, it still contradicts the views of the church. The Bible rejects homosexuality and extramarital intercourse. And those who live according to the Bible have the greatest protection against contracting this disease. My friends, the good old Bible is the best book, even regarding our sex life."

KÖRNER, THE BABBLER

When I had finished my last pastoral conversation with inquirers at about 10 o'clock, Pastor Körner was waiting for me at the altar area. He ran toward me and was shouting. He hadn't been there on that evening, but someone had told him what I had said. He ranted that he couldn't leave my comments unchallenged. He said he would report me to the *LKA*. He was yelling so loudly that the other conversations going on around us ceased. Soon we were surrounded by a cluster of curious people. Then came the hammer blow: I would drive homosexuals to commit suicide.

The discussion in the altar area centered on the expression "the doctrine of the church" and the understanding of the scripture. He instructed me, in the hearing of everyone present, that it is not simply a matter of taking the Bible as it is, as I usually do, but theology is also necessary. Being a Doctor of Theology, this wasn't totally unknown to me.

On the next morning, he telephoned and informed me, as he had already said the night before, that he was going to prepare a statement regarding my sermon that he would give to the congregation. I advised him first to listen to the tape recording of the sermon that had been made but he would not do that. He did accept my proposal that I read the text and dictate to him what I had said. He grew very quiet as I did so since the term "doctrine of the church" did not appear at all.

I informed the superintendent, Dr. Ihmels. He agreed with each of my statements and asked Körner, for the sake of unbelievers, not to carry out his intention. The entire team also implored him to avoid this sad spectacle. He refused to listen and said that the matter had been agreed upon at the highest level. To the director of evangelism, Willi Gotter, he added that he had prayed about this. Gotter replied: "The only question is, to whom?" Körner's face turned all different colors. We decided, regardless of what the pastor said, we would not say a word about it. In sadistic fashion, I was assigned the task of introducing Körner that evening. He said three things:

1. One can't say homosexuality contradicts church views.

2. It is to this day a controversial issue among theologians, whether one should consider this statement of the Apostle Paul as a revelation from God or as a contemporary human view which no longer accords with today's humanistic-scientific knowledge.

3. He would agree with me if I were to say, "I, Theo Lehmann, based on my understanding of the Bible, believe that homosexuality is incompatible with my experience as a Christian."

He ended by pronouncing a blessing upon the youth week. It was embarrassing.

Of course, I was itching to express my opinion. It bothered me that he always referred to himself as pastor, but simply called me Theo Lehmann. He was trying to shove me into a private corner. But I am not a free-floating preacher, rather an ordained pastor and an evangelist appointed by the Lutheran Regional Church of Saxony. We had, however, decided to remain silent, regardless of what he might say. Also, he had not fulfilled his promise to give me a copy of his remarks.

Unfortunately, a Baptist co-worker did not hold to this commitment and read the first chapter of Romans that included the controversial passage commonly regarded as criticizing homosexual activity. It really didn't make any difference. I don't know what I would have done if I had had to preach right after this turn of events. I noted in my diary, "It was satanic!"

Peter sang a few more songs. I regained my composure, preached, and gave the altar call. I couldn't believe my eyes when seven young boys come forward. My diary read: "As usual, the evening that Satan disrupted in a big way (in the church itself was constant loud laughing and talking), turned out to be the most blessed one of all."

The collection of the evening amounted to 666.66 marks. The co-workers insisted that they didn't doctor the figures. I took it as a sign that the Antichrist, who I believe will come out of the church, was present that evening. Of course, someone dropped in the question box: "Homosexuality—is it a natural predisposition?"

I answered: "Homosexuality is not inherited but is acquired in the course of the body's development. It is not a physical but an emotional problem in the sense that a faulty emotional development occurred in one's childhood and prevented one from gaining a normal sexual identity as a man or a woman. It is, therefore, a molding of character for which the person in question has seldom personally decided. But the predisposition does not relieve one from his or her responsibility.

"The Bible speaks not about homosexual predisposition but only homosexual actions. In every reference to homosexuality in the Bible it is not condoned, e.g., I Corinthians 6: 9–11 where it is listed among the category of sins which excludes a person from the kingdom of God." But before reading this verse, I immediately went to a second question, which the same person had written on the slip of paper: "Why do you only read from a text in Luther's German, which is very difficult to understand, when there are modern, more understandable versions." I said I would gladly do him the favor of reading the passage from *Die gute Nachricht* [the German equivalent to the *Good News Bible* in North America]:

> Do you not know that the wicked will not inherit the kingdom of God? Do not be deceived: Neither the sexually immoral nor idolaters nor adulterers nor male prostitutes nor homosexual offenders nor thieves nor the greedy nor drunkards nor slanderers nor swindlers will inherit the kingdom of God. And that is what some of you were. But you were washed, you were sanctified, you were justified in the name of the Lord Jesus Christ and by the Spirit of our God [NIV; its wording is very close to the German Good News version]

This Bible verse, I continued, "is the great hope of homosexuals for it shows that God loves all homosexuals, that God forgives them, that there were homosexuals in the church from the very beginning, and that people who previously had practiced such a lifestyle now no longer will do so since they have taken Jesus into their lives."

All of what happened in Mittweida was only the prelude to the tragedy that now unfolded. Since there were so many reports and inquiries, Regional Church Bishop Hempel found himself compelled to invite Körner and me to a conversation in his office. Since I wanted to know before this took place who had given permission to Pastor Körner to publicly accuse me—a unique occurrence in our regional church—I sent a formal request to the *LKA*: "Can you tell me who authorized this, or tell me to whom I may turn to find out? Brother Bretschneider knows who it was but isn't permitted to tell me. With whom can I speak about the matter? I find this 'hide and seek' game to be contemptible. At this point, it looks as though the one who allowed it has changed his mind." In the letter I got back was a casually handwritten comment at the bottom: "P.S. Brother Fritz will write you—It was he. . . ."

After several months the coward finally contacted me. He wrote that Körner had telephoned him, "briefly" reported about my statements, and talked about "consequences that raised great concerns among the parties involved." He knew about the acute danger of suicides among homosexuals, and spoke of people "who, due to your statements, felt driven to despair." To counter this danger, he wanted us to allow him to make a corrective statement.

In my answer, I accused Senior Church Councilor Fritz of failing to contact me about the serious charges that were being leveled against me. I asked him if Körner had even read to him what I had said and what he felt was wrong about it. Above all, I protested against this gossip about suicide and rejected Körner's statements as character assassination since he had not produced any proof to back them up. Also, I wanted to know from him, "whether I will be able to carry out my responsibilities as a preacher in the Saxon church unhindered. Or, must I reckon with the fact that I will be attacked publicly by church officials in the course of performing my official duties because of my understanding of the scriptures, as long as these individuals had cleared their actions with the *LKA* by a telephone call."

THE SWEET MUSH IN THE BISHOP'S CHANCELLERY

Before the "Fritz case" escalated, my meeting with the bishop took place. Körner was there as well and he flew into a rage in front of the bishop about my comments regarding the 666.66 marks collection. He asked, "What kind of spirit lies behind this?" I replied: "We are engaged in a conflict of the spirits."

At the outset, Bishop Hempel said he would not have acted as Körner had done and that Fritz "had run into a trap and had made an error." He then proposed five theses, of which this is the most important: "I take the apostolic exhortation seriously, but not literally, regarding the position of male/female and sexuality." He pointed out that the Saxon Regional Church had, for the first time, stepped back from a literal interpretation of the apostolic exhortation when it permitted the ordination of women. If I insist upon the literal meaning of the every word in the Bible then I would logically have to reject the ordination of women also. He made big, wide eyes when I replied that it was precisely this issue that was the breach in the dike. I asked him to look through my file. While I was still a theology student, I had signed a declaration against the ordination of women because I believed it was contrary to scripture.

Then the bishop asked me which Bible verse I had used in my proclamation on the topic of "Homosexuality." I said: "Shall I read it to you?" "Yes, please." So, I opened up my Bible and read I Corinthians 6 to the bishop and Senior Church Councilor Schnerrer, who was seated with him. It was like reading in a school classroom.

The next thing he wanted to know was how I justify that extramarital sexual intercourse was forbidden. I pointed to the entire sweep of the scriptures, from the creation of the world to the book of Revelation. I also referred to the image of the church as the bride of Christ and to individual verses such as the ones I had read. He commented that he did not like my term "strictly forbidden." One can't say "the church says" or "the Bible says." I responded: "This book here is the Bible. I have just read what it says. I'll stick with this. I won't let anyone talk me out of 'The Bible says.'" Then I said to Körner that my understanding of the scriptures is that the Bible is the Word of God and has the highest authority. He, on the other hand, places ever newer knowledge from the humanistic sciences ahead of the scriptures and judges them by the former. That is the main difference between us.

The bishop came back at me by saying that I, too, from time to time would not take a text literally. For example, in my Christmas sermon I said about the birth of Jesus that instead of fanfare there was the sound of cows, instead of flags, there were diapers.

As the *niveau* of our theological conversation reached the low point of this ridiculous argument, Schnerrer suddenly brought the conversation around to the topic of suicide. I exploded, saying this was unacceptable, and demanded that Körner, in front of the bishop, give the name and address of the one whom he alleged I had driven to commit suicide. He replied that before our week of youth evangelism, the preaching of Baptists "who also joined with us in our youth week" had driven a young man to attempt suicide. However, the individual in question had not set foot in the church during the time of the campaign (and, I heard later, that his attempt to take his own life had nothing at all to do with homosexuality). I thought to myself, "I'm going insane!" I blew my top. What does what some Baptists did before our meetings have to do with me? Where are my suicides now? Körner mumbled something about two persons with suicidal tendencies (no names, though) that I had driven "in this direction." In other words: All lies!

With this lie Körner publicly committed defamation of character, admitted he had secured the permission of Fritz to appear during the worship service as a witness against me, and besmirched my name in the presence of the bishop. I could not believe what was happening. Even worse, I could not grasp why the bishop remained silent. He simply sat there and said nothing. He should have implemented proceedings against this pastor who had spread such lies about another pastor—a formal reprimand, removal from his duties, some kind of rebuke for this flagrant violation of the Commandment, "Thou shalt not bear false witness." The least he could have demanded of the hypocrite was that he apologize to me on the spot. Nothing. Was I still in a world of reality? Am I in the bishop's office? Am I in the church?

After Körner's outrageous untruthfulness and unbelievable impudence and conduct unbecoming a Christian brother was brought to light, the babbling conversation continued as if nothing had happened. I tried once again to get back to the point and referred to the Judgment of God before whom all three of us would have to give an account. I told Körner that at that time I would not call upon any humanistic knowledge I might have gained. To the bishop I said I would not appeal to any of his statements, but rather to the words of the Bible. Nothing else would count when we stand before the Judgment of God. And as for the charge of legalism that people were constantly leveling against me, I categorically rejected it. There is a difference between obligation and legalism. One who proclaims and lives God's Word in an authoritative way, isn't legalistic in the negative sense as the word is often used. In conclusion, I said to Hempel, that he as a Lutheran bishop was so fearful of being accused of legalism that he no longer had the courage to make authoritative statements.

There Is a Word

The bishop sat silently and wrung his hands. He could not understand why Körner and I, both of whom in his mind were competent, good people, were unable to get along with each other. How could I have anything in common with a liar? At the end of the discussion, the bishop asked me if I had an explanation as to why two such capable people as we could not bear one another. I don't recall whether I actually said the words or simply thought it in my head: "Because I am in the service of God. I don't know in whose service this man is."

After the *Wende* I learned some details about those whom Körner served. He worked under the supervision of the *Stasi* with the codename Operative "*Bühne*" ("Stage"). Here are some of the rewards he received for his service, as listed by Pastor Dr. Edmund Käbisch in his book about the subversion of the church by the *Stasi*: Körner ranked among the honored guests at the District Council's commemoration of the 40th anniversary of the liberation from fascism (1985). He was invited by the First Secretary of the District *SED* Administration to the festivities celebrating the founding of the GDR in 1987. He, his wife, and children were allowed to use the vacation homes of the Minister for Church Matters—the "House of Good Fortune" at Tabarz in the Thuringian mountains, and the "House of Peace" at Juliusruh on the Baltic coast—for fourteen days at a time, without any charge.

To cover a winter vacation in Tabarz, the District Council's Section on Church Matters gave him 1,053 marks for which a receipt exists. In May of 1988 he received a coveted decoration, the Medal of Honor from the National Council of the National Front. In addition, as president of the Church Brotherhood of Saxony, he received a bonus of 300 marks, and so on and so forth. The reports of his conversations about the youth services with the official responsible for church affairs in Hainichen County, where Mittweida is located, have been preserved.

In 1995 I wrote Körner: "After studying my *Stasi* documents it is with great satisfaction that I can report to you that none of the actions against me and my service in the Saxon Regional Church proclaiming the Gospel was successful. Included in this were those in which your name appeared. Further, I would stress that the lie that you used against me at the office of the regional church and the bishop and at the *LKA* has not hindered my preaching work." The letter was never answered.

THE BRUSH-OFF BY FRITZ

On the other hand, following the conversation with the bishop I received a letter from Senior Church Councilor Fritz, but unfortunately it did not reply to my question about what was wrong with my statements. When I asked him again for an answer, he invited me to a conversation at the *LKA* in April 1986. At once I raised that question and again received no answer. We both got rather sharp with one another. Fritz mentioned twice that the call from Körner had been at the end of the workday when he was quite tired. I told him that I personally could not transmit an argument like that to my co-workers, since all of the church lay workers do their work after hours. He then stood up and yelled at me that I had no idea how hard people work in the *LKA*. I was simply taking up his valuable time. I ought to just give this matter up. After all I had already stolen time from the bishop and Church Councilors Rau and Auerbach as well. When he sat down again, he apologized for his outburst.

What was new to me was that Körner had said on the phone that my statements were a matter for the criminal police. I asked Fritz whether he had by now distanced himself from the suicide charges after it became clear when we were with the bishop that Körner had lied. Fritz countered that I was making a serious charge. He was not ready to apologize to me or to my co-workers. When I demanded that the charge regarding suicide be expunged from my personnel file, he began to rant once more. He jumped up and was about to run out of the room and get a lawyer. When he finally calmed down, the conversation turned to homosexuality. He accused me of not speaking in the spirit of love in the comments I made at Mittweida. I asked him if he knew what I had said there, or read it, or heard it on a tape. Answer: "No!" The man hadn't even made an effort to find out what I had actually said. I offered to read it aloud to him. He: "Even if I were to hear it—I'm not your judge." I: "But you have judged me this whole time without even having heard my statements."

My impression—this poor man, this poor church! The biblical foundations are being abandoned step by step. Should I not abandon this church as well?

I have often pondered this question. One of my friends took this step and went over to the Lutheran Free Church [German initials, *SELKD*]. He repeatedly told me that if I remained in the Regional Church, I would, for all practical intents and purposes, be agreeing with the false doctrines which they permit. He, on the other hand, did not want to be found in a church where the pure doctrine was being chipped away when Jesus returned. I sympathized with what he was saying, but I just had to reply, "When Jesus returns, I don't want to be caught in a church which, to be sure, keeps close watch over 'pure doctrine' but doesn't evangelize."

Only two times have I been invited by an *SELKD* congregation to conduct an evangelistic campaign, although this is the church where I feel most at home, not only theologically but also regarding my own family's church relationships. My father served one of its congregations when we were in Halle. I was a member of this church and was married in it, and my children were baptized there. On occasions when other churches, for theological reasons, were out of the question for me, I had sufficient opportunity to become familiar with some free churches in depth. Then I soon discovered that these other ones, in many ways, were experiencing things very similar to our church.

And so I have stayed with the Saxon church. True, there are many things here I can't bear, but as long as our church stands officially upon the Lutheran Confessions, I will appeal to this foundation. In fact, to find out to what extent the Regional Church holds to this foundation, I asked the *LKA* to institute canon law proceedings against me and conduct a church investigation into my theological correctness with respect to the doctrines of the Lutheran Church.

At an official training session for workers in our church a lecturer had said, "Everyone who dies here (*da*) enters into the Kingdom of God." Apart from his pompous manner of speech, with this superfluous word *da* thrown in (which disturbs my language sensibility and arouses my suspicion that he is a hypocrite), this open propagation of universal salvation was too much for me. That is why I turned myself in at the *LKA* and said that I—and many other pastors and youth workers—had been teaching exactly the opposite until now, and we will continue to do so. Only the person who believes in Jesus comes into the Kingdom of God. And, I would please like to know right now, what does our church teach on this point?

Now the usual procedure was set in motion. First, a formal conversation was scheduled. This took place at the highest level at the *LKA*. And the final result—no decision—showed me that this conversation stunt didn't serve to clarify things but rather to gum things up. At first, I was assured that our church, of course, rejects the doctrine of universal salvation, but before I could get settled comfortably in my chair again, I was asked in a pastoral tone of voice about what I would say if a good friend or relative had died and I had to preach the funeral. This person did not believe in Jesus but still was a very decent man. In other words, universalism was made socially acceptable, brought in through the back door in the disguise of so-called pastoral action. The discussion among the theologians ended as another theologian—probably Karl Barth—had once said, "Whoever officially preaches the doctrine of universal salvation is an ass, and whoever doesn't believe it is an even greater ass."

Since then I have had less and less desire to take part in such meaningless conversations. Instead I have concentrated on performing my service as a preacher to the best of my knowledge and conscience, based on the foundations of the Bible and the Confessions.

There is a Word in this world.
There is a Word in this world,
That carries more weight than all others,
There is a Word in this world.

And this Word, it comes from God.
And this Word, it comes from God.
It is the name, Jesus Christ,
And this Word, it comes from God.

There are many great words,
And they don't sound bad.
But there's only one in this world
Upon which I can rely.

There are many empty words
that offer us no help.
There is only one in this world
that can forgive my sin.

There are many small words
that can cause great harm.
There is but one on this earth
that consoles me in death.

There Is a Word

And this Word, it comes from God.
And this Word, it comes from God.
It is the name, Jesus Christ.
And this Word, it comes from God.

Jesus Christ has the final Word!
Jesus Christ has the final Word!
Even our death is not final.
Jesus Christ has the final Word!

12

God Wants Everyone

I DON'T REMEMBER WHEN I stopped applying for permission to travel to the West. All attempts in this direction—such as to participate in congresses of the International Society for Hymnology, of which I was a member, were in vain. A trip to West Germany wasn't much of a consideration for me anyway because I always was afraid that what happened to Wolf Biermann could happen to me. As I pointed out earlier, the authorities granted him permission to leave the country but then would not allow him to return.

But then the invitation came to attend the Congress on World Evangelization in Pattaya, Thailand. In this case, I could lay aside my Biermann complex since, as a member of a delegation from the Evangelists' Conference, I would fly out of and return to East Berlin. Accordingly, there was no surface border at which I could have been refused reentry. So in 1981, I was off to Thailand!

A TASTE OF THE WORLD WITH COGNAC

My first airplane flight, the first encounter with Muslims, the first time in a foreign country! And all of this happened in a fairy-tale world of palm trees, the sea, a swanky hotel, and meeting Christians from around the world who were at the congress. It was like a dream to me. The brothers accompanying me soon went to sleep in our three-bed room following the exhausting trip. I, on the other hand, thought I would explode from the combination of amazement, good luck, and excitement. I, an *Ossi,* in these incredible environs!

I felt that in this historical situation it was simply pointless to turn in so early. I needed to celebrate! This was the first mistake I made. I marched into one of the hotel restaurants and ordered a cognac. I was unaware that drinking alcohol isn't customary among most evangelicals. But even if I had known that, in my euphoria it wouldn't have made any difference. I simply had to celebrate, come what may. And it did, very soon!

I relaxed in my bamboo armchair and tried to comprehend that "little old Theo" from the East had landed in a fairy-tale world. Then, a brother came up to my table. He was the one who had paid for our flights and had given us a modest amount of spending money. We had been turned loose into the capitalistic world without so much as a penny in our pockets. While this noble donor asked about my well-being, conspicuously sitting on the table in front of me was a huge cognac glass, ten times larger than the little puddle of alcohol swishing at the bottom. I nearly died of shame. I thought to myself, what must the man be thinking: "So this poor little mouse from the East that I sponsored has nothing better to do than to get a little high on alcohol from the money I gave him."

How should I explain to such a worldly-wise person what it meant to this 46-year-old man to be in a foreign land for the very first time? How could I make him understand the kinds of feelings raging in me and that with this one cognac I was trying to calm the turmoil in my soul and at the same time give some dignity to this historic moment. I decided just to say nothing. Being as embarrassed as I was, I just retreated into the shell of my *Ossi* complex. Some years later, as we were sitting together enjoying a simple bockwurst, I related to him my pangs of conscience during that moment in Pattaya. His friendly response revealed that he had either not been aware of my predicament or had simply forgotten it.

A particular handicap was my limited knowledge of English. My relationship to it was like that with my wife: I loved her, but I didn't have mastery over her. I had had virtually no formal instruction in it. Most of the English that I knew came from the jazz programs I had listened to on the radio and from reading. I never had opportunity to practice speaking it. I was thankful that the speeches in the plenary sessions were simultaneously translated. But in the small-group seminars there were no translators, and my situation was even worse in the meetings of the Lausanne Committee on World Evangelism, of which I was a member. There it was, every man for himself, so to speak.

The Americans rattled on unrestrainedly, and I often had difficulty simply figuring out what topic was being discussed. It then got "dangerous" for me when, after the discussion of each agenda item ended, Billy Graham asked one of us to offer a prayer. Since I often missed what they had been talking about and I found myself hard-pressed to pray for something I didn't know about, I had great anxiety over the possibility of being called upon to pray. It was as though I had experienced time travel back to my school days. It was my custom to hide behind the student in front of me due to my fear of being asked a question by the teacher. Just like that schoolboy, I ducked down behind the back of the brother sitting in front of me. I had only one prayer, that is, not to have to pray.

This prayer was heard, but it exemplified the difficulties we *Ossis* faced when we moved in international circles. Before I, the greenhorn, had understood how such a huge conference as this functioned, and what tricks one could use to get more out of it (e.g., reading the texts and documents), the meeting had already ended. Strongly motivated and enriched by so many new contacts, I flew back into my GDR cage. Nevertheless, I had escaped it for three weeks and had breathed the air of the great wide world.

This happened once again in 1986 when I was allowed to travel to the Conference on Itinerant Evangelists in Amsterdam—but only after I had to endure more harassment. As I went to pick up my passport on the day of departure, the official was unable to find it. All the other GDR delegates left without me and I sat mournfully like Konrad in the children's book *Struwwelpeter*:

> Konrad, said his dear, sweet mother,
> I'm going out and you'll stay here.
> Be right decent and please behave
> Until I come back home again.

One day later, they did allow me to leave. That was the last time I was permitted a trip to a foreign country until I went to the Manila Congress on Evangelism in 1989. (The costs for these trips always had to be covered by the hosts; the GDR would not authorize us to receive any foreign exchange from the State Bank to attend religious meetings abroad.)

GREATER THAN MEGALOMANIA

Even more difficult than obtaining permission for foreign travel was to be allowed to go to the Federal Republic of Germany. However, I was successful in doing so in 1988 when I was invited to participate in a large youth rally known as the *Christival*, which would take place in Nuremberg. The

God Wants Everyone

festival slogan was "God Wants Everyone." Full of faith and confidence that he could pull this off, Ulrich Parzany, head of the YMCA and a prominent evangelical, invited me to preach at the concluding mass meeting and to have Wolfgang Tost and Jörg Swoboda with me.

Jörg and I wrote the *Christival* theme song, "Strong Roots, Good Fruit." Actually, we had composed it the summer before, although at the time we did not even know about the planned *Christival*. At the beginning of 1988 Parzany and some others from the West met with us in East Berlin to make preparations for the rally. In the course of the discussion we learned that there was, as yet, no *Christival* theme song, so we told them about our new song. We squeezed into my Wartburg which had a tape deck and I inserted a cassette that contained the song and a segment of one of our worship services. I played it for the Western brothers, and as we climbed out of the car, our piece was declared the song for the event.

In action

We and ten additional workers were granted permission to travel to Nuremberg. Even this didn't happen without harassment. We had Giselher Hickel, a submissive henchman of the *SED* state, to thank for the fact that we had to report the evening before in East Berlin. We spent the night in an office room of an association for young men on Sophienstrasse. Our passports were only issued the next morning, right before our scheduled departure. This was their way of preventing us from leaving earlier so we could get off the train and spend an entertaining evening in West Berlin. The situation was the same on the way back. Just as soon as the meeting ended, we were required to return to our socialist fatherland. But we were able to enjoy the intervening days free from harassment by the "comrades."

Only once did our "*Ossi*-ness" play a trick on us. One day we had a morning free of responsibilities, and Jörg and I decided to go downtown. To our great surprise, the Nuremberg subway had hardly any passengers, no one was standing around in the stations, and the shops were closed. Then it dawned on us *Ossis*: It was June 17, a holiday in the West. [The anniversary of the East German workers' uprising in 1953, it commemorated the longing for German unity.] All along I was plagued with a deep sense of unease about whether Western young people would accept me, an *Ossi,* as a preacher. Jörg reassured me by saying, "They asked you to come here precisely because of your manner of preaching."

The other mornings I stood with Jörg on the stage of a hall that seated 8,000 people. I led the Bible studies and he sang. It was our normal manner of working. After a while Jörg whispered to me in the pause between two songs, "Everything is just as it is at home." There were the same reactions, the same enthusiastic singing. Our initial misgivings went away. We no longer felt like strangers but as family members. We were among friends.

That didn't change things when I came to the concluding service; I had greater anxiety than at any other time I had preached before. Again and again I read through the sermon, even at night in bed. Once again, Jörg came to the rescue: "Don't drive yourself crazy about this! Enjoy a peaceful sleep."

On the day before, I had to go to a rehearsal since the West German TV network *ZDF* was going to going to broadcast the service. It would take place on the Zeppelinwiese, a vast open field where Adolf Hitler hosted the annual Nazi Party congress in the 1930s. Although most of the structures had been torn down after the war, the long rows of elevated stone risers at the far end of the parade ground were still there as well as the speakers' platform in the middle. Here the Nazi big shots were seated as they watched the marching troops and military exercises.. During a break I climbed up to the place where Hitler had stood behind his microphone and shouted out his satanic speeches. As I was standing there alone, the grounds were empty and silent. Only the sound of the wind was audible. No Hitler was there. It was an eerie moment, a bizarre situation.

On the following morning, 30,000 young people sat on the field and gave God the glory. It was an overwhelming, joyful situation. As I climbed the steps to the stage on the grassy field and set my foot upon the platform, I thought my knees were caving in. Never before had I preached to so many people. A great help for me was that I could carry out this service with my brothers Wolfgang and Jörg, Ulrich Parzany, Jürgen Werth, Manfred Siebald and many others with whom I had been associated for so many years.

Finally, the moment came when I had to move from my seat to the podium at the edge of the stage. Even when the fears (Can I do it?) and the doubts (Am I here at the right place? And, why me, of all people?)

tormented me, and I felt as though I should crawl into the nearest mouse hole—at that moment, when I begin to speak the message of God, then all of this flew away, simply away.

The most important experience of the *Christival* for me was when Jörg sang our song just before my sermon, "Whoever Follows God Risks His Dreams." We had written this during the darkest hours of the GDR to encourage and strengthen the young Christians living under communist rule. One stanza goes:

> "The mighty come and go
> And every monument is bound to fall.
> Only he remains who stands on God's Word.
> The safest place on earth."

At the line "The mighty come and go" Jörg took his hand away from his guitar for a few seconds and pointed with outstretched finger to the spot where Adolf Hitler had stood. His place was empty. He who once had been the most powerful man in the world, before whom millions trembled, was no longer there. The milieu of the Nazi Party Congress Parade Ground and Jörg's short gesture became for us all an overwhelming confirmation of the words which we had just sung. It gave me courage to preach the Word of God.

Unfortunately, what I had to say about the Last Judgment was cut from the *ZDF* broadcast by the church TV representative. Even in this regard, I felt as though I were at home. This type of censorship and pruning of the biblical message was well-known to me in the GDR. That it also happened in the free democratic West was new to me. Since then I have learned a lot more about what can happen there.

FRUIT AND LITTLE FRUITS

I had to learn here, too, how to deal with bitter opposition. In 1997 in Duisburg-Rheinhausen I experienced one of the dreariest and emptiest weeks of my career. On the posters the name of the musician was misspelled, while the song sheets were a catastrophe. The pastor wasn't present at the preparation evening and we were suspicious of him from the beginning. He carried on his regular church program for the entire week. On the first evening we had to wait with our co-workers outside the church hall until 6:00 because he was holding his "children's afternoon program." In the hectic rush to set up the hall and the electronic equipment we didn't have time to celebrate the preparatory Lord's Supper with all the workers. The pastor admonished the musicians to play softly because he had a meeting in the next room. The sounds of the regular choir rehearsal disturbed the sermon.

Not until the third evening did the pastor even enter the hall, but he sat in the last row and then disappeared a few minutes after I began speaking. He had removed the poster from the church display case and the front of the church hall—nowhere was there a hint that right now an evangelistic meeting was in progress. Wolfgang and I both came down with sore throats and a nagging cough. No questions, very few conversations, and for the first time ever an entire week without any decisions for Christ.

The only glimmer of light during the week was our landlady, a 76-year-old widow. Her late husband had built a bar in the cellar which was stocked with an unbelievable amount of whiskey. We consoled ourselves here every evening. Wolfgang stood behind the counter as bartender and the lady and I sat on stools in front of it. We made a desperate attempt to escape the sabotage actions of the pastor who came up with something new every day, as well as the inertia of an unresponsive audience. We went back home like whipped puppy dogs. We had fished the entire week and caught nothing.

However, as far as fruit is concerned, it is easy to be deceived by appearances. In 1984, I was invited to Ballenstedt in the Harz Mountains for a youth week and there were difficulties at that location as well. I had such a bad cold that I lost my voice during the sermon and Wolfgang saved the situation by jumping in with a song. Moreover, my father had died and was buried that week. I had to attend the funeral in Halle and then return to speak in the evening on the topic of death (2 Cor 5:8). It is amazing that I had sufficient strength to carry on. I had some intense discussions with theology students regarding the doctrine of universal salvation. One young man came forward and afterwards a few others were converted. But otherwise the week dragged on and we left feeling rather discouraged.

Almost ten years later, I met the deacon who reminded me that we had left with the impression that nothing really had happened there. Perhaps so, but he pointed out that much did, in fact, happen afterwards. Seven of those who had received Christ were now active church workers, and prayer circles had been formed. Experiences like this have caused me to give up the habit of judging a given week as "successful" or "unsuccessful." I know that we as Christians ought not to use such terms as "success" or "failure." But it must be soberly recognized that both we and the sponsors record and evaluate the results of our meetings.

In the end, we constantly prayed for conversions. After all, that is the reason we put in so much time and effort, money and involvement into an evangelization week. So we are happy when many are converted and sad when this does not happen. Sometimes I retreat into a corner of the sacristy after I have delivered a sermon in which I have given everything I can and no one comes to faith in Christ, and ask myself, how can I explain the gospel better? How can I make it more penetrating? Why doesn't anything happen? Why doesn't God do something? I tell Jesus that I simply don't understand it. But I also tell him that I accept his decision.

I have determined that it doesn't make any sense to try to puzzle over why God has done or not done this or that. It is, of course, strange. Often I use the same sermons, the same singer, and the same songs. In one town no one responds to the message, while in another one a few weeks later, many do. We do basically the same thing every time, and yet something different occurs. It is clear that we are not the ones who do the converting, but God. I consider myself to be the one who calls and I go as far as I possibly can. But when I make the call to commitment at the end, my job is really over. Then it is up to God. Just to know this clear differentiation of our roles takes a great burden from my shoulders. Of course, each evening I have my feelings and impressions about how things have gone. That is true, but I have become accustomed to not drawing conclusions about the lasting effect of the meeting on those present.

In the 1990s

TREMBLING IN ZITTAU

In the same year in which I had my most depressing week, 1997, I also had the noisiest one. It was in Zittau. We were in the massive Johanneskirche once again, a religious temple that is quite inimical to distinct communication. Although 260 people were present, it seemed poorly attended. We

Blues Music and Gospel Proclamation

Bible study in a vineyard

had a good start. Approximately 10 young people came forward on the first evening. And then the storm broke around us. The second evening was the most difficult and enervating meeting I had ever had until then. In the church the noise was so loud that I had to shout the sermon. Most of it was lost in the raging noise and the constant milling around. I lost my train of thought several times and said things that weren't written in my text.

But what I couldn't fight against was the extremely loud noise level. I simply couldn't be heard in the church. The greatest commotion was caused by the son of Dankmar Fischer, the former head of the Salvation Army in Hamburg. As is so often the case, children of Christian workers frequently go so far astray that they cause more trouble than all the others. Then there was a Neo-Nazi group that brought the whole circus to its low point of absurdity. Their leader came to me two evenings later for a long conversation.

During the customary question and answer period I had called Hitler one of the greatest mass murderers of history. In his drunken state the Neo-Nazi had not fully understood what I had said. Now, somewhat more sober and with his bald head, boots, and military pants, he approached me to ask why I had slandered "the grand cause." Then he proceeded to explain "the grand cause" complete with his faith in Wotan. The god allegedly gave him as much strength as Jesus. What did not set very well with me was his claim that his Germanic religion allowed him to cut off my head or that of anyone else who attacks him. After all, there isn't any Final Judgment. The hatred that this man exuded literally got to me physically, and I felt very threatened.

All the more did I rejoice when I heard later that he had been converted following the youth week—just as Christian Fischer, the main cause of the disturbance, had also turned to Christ. The former Wotan worshiper confessed to the co-workers that he had in a frenzy under the influence of voodoo beaten people so badly that blood flowed. And now he became one who says that he will no longer hit back. The youth administrator of Zittau wrote me, "I have never before seen such a radical change in a person!"

I marveled at her and her colleagues. They put up with the noise every evening and interacted with these rowdies for hours after the services. (They had hauled in a few old sofas, placed them in front of the church, and just sat there.) In spite of all the provocations, they dealt with them in love. In short, we experienced a miracle. Nearly all of the youths kept coming until the end and listened intently. Absolute silence prevailed during the sermon.

Some years earlier when I was in Zittau for a youth evangelism week I had also had problems, not from shouting Hitler fans but from my own co-workers. Pastor Pilz (later, superintendent, but then dismissed because of his *Stasi* contacts) had compared me to Hitler. During a monthly pastoral meeting where Superintendent Mendt was present, Youth Administrator Andreas Guder demanded that Pilz make a public apology. Not only did he refuse to apologize, but also he announced a one-day bicycle outing for the *Junge Gemeinde* members during the time of our youth evangelism campaign in his own church. Incidentally, it had to be cancelled due to rain.

The second problem was the female singer in the preliminary program. On the third day, I learned that she was living together with a married man. The matter was supposed to have been cleared up before the youth week began, but M. was not available for conversations with the band members or with a pastor. She insisted upon the rightness of her life style. And now here she was in the preliminary program standing on the stage singing Christian music. I hadn't really been aware of her because she hadn't come to our preparatory Lord's Supper meeting. And immediately following her performance, before the evangelization portion of the meeting started, she left the church. The Bible reading of the previous day, I Corinthians 10:1–13, and passages such as I Corinthians 5:6 ff. made it clear to us we would have to insist that she not perform again for the sake of the evangelistic campaign, for the sake of the truth, and also for her own sake. We would do so even if the entire band walked out.

Jörg and I discussed the matter with the youth administrator and the band leader. Shortly before the beginning of the preliminary program when M. appeared, I took her and the band into the sacristy. I told M. she would have to decide either to end her adulterous relationship or not to sing again in front of the young people. She refused to discuss the matter. She made her position clear, and consequently we would not allow her to perform. Although one girl cried, the band was relieved that finally a decision had been made. I admired the band for continuing to stay with us.

On this evening the first ten young people came forward. Next morning, Superintendent Mendt called us in our quarters from his office and accused us of legalism and non-evangelical behavior. He asked whether any of us were sinners and whether we had ever heard the verse, "Let him who is without sin cast the first stone." Yes, we had. But we had never heard that someone who, in spite of discussions on the matter, refuses to give up an adulterous relationship should still remain as a co-worker proclaiming the Gospel of Christ. Even if, in the meantime, people in the church have come to think and act differently than before, I am sticking with the biblical standards. That all of this hit us very hard is clear, I'm sure. But I suffered personally even more when I had a musician in the Schlosskirche band whom I liked very much who also was having an extra-marital affair and refused to call it off. But for the sake of our credibility and his salvation, I had to part company with him. This decisive break in our working relationship and our friendship cost both of us bitter tears.

In the GDR it was no great problem to get people to come to church. Following the *Wende*, it did become one. The magnitude of the problem finally hit me after Wolfgang and I had preached in a poorly-attended church in a West German city. On the day after we stood in a pedestrian zone in front of the building and watched the masses of young people going past us in both directions. We thought, "These are the ones to whom we ought to be preaching. But if they won't come to us in the church, then we will have to go to them." Street preaching? We had absolutely no experience in such.

God Wants Everyone

REEPERBAHN, INC.

After I got to know Dankmar Fischer, then the head of the Salvation Army in Hamburg, I asked him if I could come to his place and learn about the work there. I really wanted to know how this whole street preaching business functioned. The year was 1991. He agreed to take me to the Reeperbahn. This boulevard, which runs through Hamburg's St. Pauli quarter (the harbor area on the Elbe River), is the center of the most notorious "entertainment" district in Europe. Bars, bordellos, cafes, theaters, and gambling dens line the Reeperbahn and its connecting side streets. Legal prostitution and illegal drug dealing are a way of life here.

Late in the afternoon we drove—Fischer, his wife, a co-worker of theirs, and I—from their quarters to the Reeperbahn. The conversation in the car ceased as we reached the brightly lit area. From this point on, we only prayed and sang ("Come, Lord, bless us...."). This manner of entering their field of labor impressed me greatly. After a Bible study in which I spoke, the people were divided into teams that would go into action on the streets. My group, which included Mrs. Fischer, another woman, and a young Polish fellow, was posted to the Hafenstrasse, the principal street leading down to the harbor. Everything proceeded in a calm fashion, without much ado—one might say, in a rather dignified manner. Nothing was done: There were no attempts to convert the passers-by. The Salvation Army was simply present. Mostly friendly greetings were exchanged, but some just went around us as we four stood in a circle on the sidewalk in front of a hashish bar and prayed. During our walk I learned a great deal about the Hafenstrasse, and what Salvation Army workers do from day to day, for example, visiting the dying.

After a while we reassembled and walked back up the street. Ahead of us marched Dankmar Fischer, a giant of a fellow with a huge Bible under his arm. This man didn't just walk, he strode. From head to toe he exuded authority—God's steamroller. Then came a flag bearer, a person carrying a cross, and a guitarist (in her daily life she was an AIDS doctor). The rest lined up two abreast. Except for me and Uve Simon, the evangelist who marched beside me, everyone was in uniform. The oldest co-worker bounced around the whole procession. He was proud of the fact that he had been in all the bars of Hamburg. A very short, friendly, gnomelike little man, he held out the collection box to the onlookers on all sides of the group. We had received small song books, something that we could look into because I didn't dare to lift up my eyes. I thought the entire time what a sight that must be: Theo in this parade! But nobody took a picture. No one knows me in Hamburg.

While I stared intensely into my songbook and sang along, I spotted out of the corner of my eye, standing at the edge of the street among a number of passers-by, my wife Elke with her friend Rita. Elke was visiting with her at this time and asked to have a look at the Reeperbahn. I looked straight ahead and thought that in so doing I'd somehow be invisible. But I already sensed that Elke wouldn't let this historic moment pass without taking action. She broke loose from the crowd of onlookers, crossed the street, and ran toward the Salvation Army procession. When she reached the spot where I was, she hugged me, planted a loud kiss on my cheek, and quickly returned to the spectators. All of this took place so fast, in a matter of seconds. I marched bravely on, but I had the feeling I ought to explain to my partner. I told him, "That was my wife. I don't let just anyone kiss me." He ignored my comment, mumbled something like, "On the Reeperbahn everything is possible," and kept on singing. I had the suspicion that he didn't take my explanation very seriously.

In this manner, emotionally in turmoil, I moved along with the group, singing all the time, in the direction of the entrance to a closed off area through which no women went except the Salvation Army workers. There the prostitutes waited for their customers. We felt a few splashes of beer coming out of a window. A madam reached out of another window and dropped a coin in the collection box. From yet another, a prostitute yelled out about the loud noise, "We have to work here." Fischer said something into the mike, and suddenly without any warning, he pressed it into my hand and I had to preach. It was a sneak attack, but pedagogically well done. Otherwise I would never have dared to open my mouth here.

Since we were standing in front of the locked doors of the prostitution houses, I preached from the words of Jesus, "I stand before the door and knock." As we slowly made our trek back to the main street, Dankmar repeated this pedagogical procedure several times. From this I gained my first impression of street preaching. But I didn't see that this could be my way. I am a manuscript person. I need time to develop the biblical text. I simply have a different approach to preaching. J. H. Wichern, the nineteenth century Christian social reformer from Hamburg, was right when he stated that Germany needed more street preachers. But it was clear that I am not particularly suited to it. Remorsefully, I returned to my lectern and notes.

Prior to this I set foot in a prison for the first time in my life. I was supposed to preach at the Hamburg-Fuhlsbüttel penitentiary, where terrorists and murderers are incarcerated. Uve Simon accompanied me. As I entered the chapel where I was to speak, I was quite astonished as I looked at the altar. On the left and right sides were the words of the Ten Commandments in large letters. The prisoners had to look at these whenever they went to a worship service here. I had never seen anything like this before. That suited me just fine since I was planning to preach about them (Matthew 19, the rich young man). And that I did.

The atmosphere here was stiff and cool. I was nervous, inhibited. But that wasn't the problem. The worst thing was the faces of the Protestant and Catholic chaplains and a female assistant. They sat among the small number of prisoners. Their petrified faces didn't betray anything good. While the prisoners reacted positively to the sermon, the clerics crawled all over me as though I spent the half hour preaching obscenities rather the Word of God. They charged me with being self-righteous. The woman was downright bitter as she said Jesus also died in Auschwitz. I: "What does Auschwitz have to do with my sermon?" No answer. Next accusation: I am intolerant. I asked them, where I did I wrongly interpret the text? The Catholic colleague explained to me that I can't simply say, "Jesus is the main thing." I quoted the verse, "Whoever has the Son has life. . . ." He: "What does that mean? What does it mean that Jesus produces a new creation?"

I reminded him that Uve Simon had described in a conversation three examples of conversions, including one of a double murderer, and then proceeded to give his name and address. The priest rolled his eyes, obviously bored. On the basis of his drivel, I asked him if he knew he was truly following Jesus and is saved from his sin. He couldn't say! I: "Then you are lacking the fundamental requirement for being a preacher and priest." He was out of there! That left the Protestant colleague. He bombarded me for another half hour. He claimed that one can't simply quote the Ten Commandments as I had done. One can't simply uproot them and plunk them down into our era and make use of them at will. And that was that!

My point: It is no problem to preach to prostitutes, terrorists, and murderers. But preaching to pastors of this sort—that is the hardest thing. It is depressing.

Later, some Christian believers condemned me because I had preached at the *Kirchentag*, the well-attended biennial church convention. They said my presence justified the godless "Dalai Lama Show" that also took place there. I always answered such critics: When I preached in the red light district of St. Pauli, I didn't cover up prostitution by so doing. My conclusion was always the exact opposite:

If I could preach in a bordello then I can preach at the *Kirchentag*. For this reason I penned these lines with Wolfgang Tost:

> None is too good or bad for God.
> Whoever comes to him, that's whom he wants.
> God wants everyone.
>
> Rockers who display their rats,
> Pastors who are true to their office,
> The aging homeless sitting in their shelters,
> Waiters who scurry for their guests.
>
> The weak who always seem to fail,
> The strong who can take the heat,
> The old who tremble at death,
> The sick whom sorrow doesn't embitter.
>
> Women who sell themselves for money,
> Men who drink away theirs,
> Parents who beat their children,
> Children who build castles in the air.
>
> Speakers who throw sand in our eyes,
> Sinners who admit their guilt,
> Ladies who wear chic clothes,
> Seekers who ask about truth.
>
> Tramps who live under bridges,
> Playboys who race through the streets,
> Girls who abort their babies,
> Mothers who dearly love theirs.
>
> Rockers who live for their crowd,
> Christians who give glory to God,
> The rich who think only of pleasure,
> The poor who'd give you the shirt off their backs.

13

Thank You, Jesus, Thank You

Having God with you while traveling is to experience both his miracles and the attacks of his archenemy. I always keep with me a little holder in which I carry cards with Bible verses on them. At the end of a conversation I often let my speaking partner draw a card—as a memento. After I had finished preaching one evening, a young man who was fighting back tears came up to me. I explained to him his spiritual situation, and he prayed the sinner's prayer and gave his life to Christ. Then I let him draw a card. He tugged on one, pushed it back, and then pulled out another one. We read it together: "I have heard your prayer and seen your tears." (2 Kgs 20:5).

During one evangelistic meeting, I was housed at a church-run group home for mentally handicapped women and girls. One morning, the director of the home found in an ash bucket a singed, unaddressed, sealed envelope. She opened it and determined from the handwriting on the card inside, one that lacked a salutation or signature, that a young woman in the home had written it. When the person came to the facility ten years earlier she could not speak, and it took some years before even a simple greeting or answer to a question would come from her lips. The director handed me the singed piece of paper and I read, "I live in isolation, and, although there are a lot of people around me, I have thoughts of suicide. I cannot do it because I am afraid of what happens after death. I am afraid to talk with anyone. And I often think that Jesus can't help me because of my fear. How can I get out of this situation?"

I spoke to the girl and asked her to whom she had written the letter. To me, she said. She wanted to bring it to my room in the evening, but the door was already closed. So she threw it in the ash bucket. I told her, "There you have the proof of God's care for you. You couldn't get the letter to me and nevertheless it reached me. God always finds a way, even if it is the way of the ash bucket." Then she heartily laughed about the matter, which for her was quite unusual.

BRIGHT NIGHTS FOR SINISTER POWERS

I was in no laughing mood when a young man came forward at a meeting and just at the moment when I started to pray with him, a loud car alarm went off outside the hall. It stopped at the very moment I concluded. At a workers' prayer meeting afterwards the consensus was that something demonic had happened. The church leader who was leading the prayer group, a solid, experienced Christian, testified that at the time the alarm went off, he and some others were standing near the car and nothing or no one had touched the vehicle. Its owner, a pastor, who ran outside when the horn sounded, confirmed this.

Some years earlier I had had a run-in with this same man regarding the occult. He denied that there was any such force at work in his congregation. He attacked Jörg and me because we had spoken about the subject. The grotesque thing about this conversation was that a woman sitting on the sofa next to him in his office was an admitted fortune teller. Who knows what kinds of connections existed? Interestingly, the Moravian devotional book verse for the day following the auto alarm incident was: "Your adversary, the Devil, goes about like a roaring lion" (1 Pet 5:8).

In a meeting in Lichtenstein near Chemnitz, two boys who called themselves Christians accused me on the very first evening of preaching too harsh a sermon. Two days later I spoke with them again, and one of them confessed that he was a Nazi. He collected Nazi literature and defended the Second World War and the gassing of the Jews. He knew that this didn't fit with his being a Christian. But it simply must be "his thing" and he felt driven to do it.

I told him he was obviously possessed by a Nazi demon and that he must deny the Devil and accept Jesus as Lord. I spoke hard and direct. Step by step he approached the point where he admitted that this must come to an end. We kneeled at the altar and he prayed the prayer of renunciation of his old life and surrender to Christ. I blessed him and hugged him. After this struggle, I was torn by inner turmoil, overwhelmed and beaten, but happy. On the next day he glowingly reported to me that he and his mother had cleaned all of the fascist junk out of his room and thrown it into the trash. Three months later, I learned that he radiantly testified about his conversion in a youth worship service.

Even when the encounter with the forces of darkness isn't always so direct, one always has to deal with the most varied of forms of evil. When Wolfgang Tost and I were on the way to a preliminary meeting with some pastors, I told him he should look at the faces and determine who is against us. In our little circle I spotted three "unredeemed mugs" as the Chemnitz youth administrator, Kurt Stroer, liked to say. They were people who clearly needed Christ. And it was precisely these three who turned out to be our foes. Right after the meeting that evening, they attacked us verbally. Moreover, the Lord's Supper as preparation for the service took place in a tense, joyless atmosphere under the theme of "Anxiety," a strange start for an evangelistic campaign.

In 1991 a preacher in Naumburg, south of Halle, invited Wolfgang and me to hold meetings in his town. He belonged to the very evangelical group of "Fellowship" (*Gemeinschaft*) congregations within the Regional Churches in Germany. The local pastors' association was dead-set against the idea and denied us entry into all the town's churches. The infuriated pastor retorted, "Then Brother Lehmann will preach on the street. I will ask the mayor for permission." At this point the superintendent stepped in and consented to making a building available for the meetings but the church disclaimed all "responsibility" for the campaign. Just before this, the Baptists jumped ship since they didn't have any kind of a youth group. Practically speaking, the sole supporting body we had was the Fellowship Movement. Only a retired pastor directly worked with us—for twenty years he had longed for such an evangelistic campaign.

The church was unheated and, without our bright lights, it would have been totally dark. The older people were unfamiliar with the texts on the song sheets and they essentially made up the entire audience. On the advertising posters the words "young people" were missing, and they depicted only older and handicapped people. No one could possibly imagine that this evangelistic week was intended for young people.

We had no opportunity during the entire week to take a shower. True, there was a heating unit for the bath, but it did not function. So, cold baths! Wolfgang camped out in a tiny, unheated attic room with only enough room for his suitcase on the floor. The highpoint was the noon meal that we were supposed to have two times at the home of a pastor's widow. The nice old lady was very devout and the meal was very good.

Unfortunately, everything was covered with black dog hairs which came from the two little dogs that lived with her--the table cloth, plates, napkins, the food, even the lady herself. Somehow we choked the food down, but it came close to reversing its direction. And we had to return the next day!

It was a miracle that we didn't get sick during the cold and rainy week accompanied by nightly frost. And, an even greater miracle was that during this effort, which included one morning preaching in a prison, people did come to Christ. Yet, not a single pastor greeted us, spoke to us, or invited us for a cup of coffee. We felt like lepers although we, in fact, were the King's messengers.

FROM SPIRIT-FILLED TO SPIRIT-LESS

Quite different were the problems I encountered with many of the charismatics who were working with us. The leader of the prayer group in Aue in 1993 pointed to the evil faces looking down upon us in the hall where we were meeting. But I could not see any such apparition. He also lectured me that I needed to re-examine my evangelization techniques since signs and wonders were lacking. I rejected his request to celebrate a second Lord's Supper with just his prayer group. He arrived late with his people at the regular Lord's Supper and did not utter a single word of greeting to the workers. We had the impression that this group, whether within or outside the entire corps of workers, intended to do its own thing.

After the meeting one evening at which approximately 20 young people and an older alcoholic turned to Christ, this fellow sneaked around with a dark demeanor and said he wanted to talk with me, but only after he had spoken with another worker. I waited a long time for him, which I spent in prayer seeking above all the gift of the discernment of spirits (1 Cor 12:10). After he had spoken with that individual, he said he no longer wished to speak to me. Since I wanted to know what had happened, I inquired of my colleague and learned the following: In the prayer circle, he declared God had shown that there was sin among the team of workers and it was blocking the effectiveness of the evangelistic effort. It was made clear to this group that the sin in question was adultery, and the guilty party was this co-worker. Then the prayer leader looked him in the eye and said: "You are living in adultery."

Since this absolutely was not the case, I informed the superintendent about the matter. Then I ordered the prayer group leader to come to me and I told him point blank:

1. You are a false prophet.
2. You have transgressed against the Second Commandment because you ascribed to God thoughts that were really your own.
3. You must repent
4. You must apologize to the co-workers.
5. You may no longer participate in this evangelistic effort.

From then on, the entire prayer circle did not participate in the Lord's Supper and the co-worker consultations. Apart from this group, which, in a grotesque turn of events, had prayed the most for peace and unity, the evangelistic campaign proceeded harmoniously.

A few months later I was with Wolfgang at a church in Berlin. The preparation for the meeting was deficient. As a result, a bad mood was established even before we began. Juice rather than wine had been set out for the Lord's Supper. The church was dark, few were in attendance, and no one made a decision for Christ. On the second evening, communion was canceled for no reason at all. Instead, one of the female co-workers said, with tear-filled eyes, that God had showed her that we must all march around the church building seven times that night. Was she thinking of Joshua and Jericho?

Precisely the same thing I had already heard in Aue. It seemed as though it was becoming the thing to do. We, the team of evangelists, said we were not going to do that, and we told the co-workers that we would all go to our quarters, and drink our evangelization beer, and then get eight hours of sleep. Furthermore, we explained to them that it had been their task last year to train the Christians so that each one would bring a non-Christian. The lady who had been in tears had never gotten the message. I said that no one should take the blame for the slip-ups in the preparation for this youth week and the Holy Spirit will quickly iron out things. He will bring the people into the church that the others had neglected to invite.

Another "communication" from the Holy Spirit was made known very soon after this incident. The co-workers must sanctify themselves. I replied that this is precisely the reason why we normally begin each evening with the Lord's Supper. But the group had discontinued the practice. So it was the same old game—instead of drawing upon the resources that God offers to us (the Lord's Supper), these are simply tossed out and unauthorized substitutes (like marching around the church building) introduced. Human failures are then attributed to the demons, and the Holy Spirit has to do what the co-workers failed to do. Strangely, these enthusiasts who were so moved by the Spirit did not trust the Holy Spirit to lead people to the altar to be converted. They wanted to let one of their own come forward to the altar like a draft horse, in the hope that this would induce others to follow. This type of tactic we have always rejected. Four people came forward that evening.

The next day could have been my last. I was alone in my quarters (a smelly *Pension* behind a pub; we had to go past the bar just to get to our room), and while eating a grapefruit I swallowed a portion of it and it went down the wrong way. I began gasping for breath and terrifying seconds passed without getting any air. I believed I would die of asphyxiation. My only prayer was "Jesus!" Anyhow, I finally got my breath back and collapsed onto the bed. That evening, we celebrated the Lord's Supper, but again it was omitted on the next one.

The annoyance caused by unpunctuality, improperly-placed loud speakers, etc. faded when a young man showed up who had been converted 20 years before at a meeting that Jörg and I had held in Oranienburg, just outside Berlin. He was an alcoholic but had been dry since. Then I had a conversation with a young woman who had come forward and was happy to be starting "a new life." She read me the Bible verse she pulled from my little stack of cards: "Everything old has passed away; see, everything has become new" (2 Cor 5:17). She was a bit upset, assuming that it was the only verse on all of my cards. I pacified her by showing her all the other Bible verses in my packet.

That evening a drunk tried to disrupt the meeting. He yelled and ran toward the podium twice as the program was beginning. Then he fell on the floor, still hollering at the top of his voice, and flipped over on his back like a June bug with his arms uncontrollably thrashing about. Workers tried to calm him but to no avail. The pastor standing over him commanded the demonic powers to leave him since it appeared that he was demon-possessed. The chaotic scene burdened me the entire evening.

Adding to the "spirit-inspired" mess of the week was the sad business of the offering. The special collection of 400 marks that was designated for a future evangelization effort had, after four months, not been conveyed to the intended recipient. I called on the telephone about it and was told that the money had been stolen. I demanded the money be turned over to me at once, but I saw about as much of it as I did an explanation, excuse, or expression of regret.

NO SACRILEGE, JUST A WAR OF NERVES

In spite of the vanished collection, the projected evangelistic campaign in Ortmannsdorf near Zwickau did take place. However, upon arrival we learned that the church wasn't heated, even though it was February. There was no podium, no box for questions, no name tags for workers, no printed copies of the prayer of surrender. On the advertising flyers the topics were mixed up. And yet the church was full, with

The preacher

more than 550 young people in attendance. The oldest participant was a 94-year-old lady who let Wolfgang tune her guitar on the next day. On several evenings so many inquirers gathered at the front that the workers were simply overwhelmed. On the last evening there was a huge collection of 1,100 marks.

One week I was holding a tent meeting, and I had a rather strange experience. I had included a section in my sermon dealing with sexuality, and when I saw almost exclusively older people seated in the audience, I decided to drop it out. However, during the sermon I changed my mind and went on with it anyway. Afterwards, an 84-year-old devout woman from East Prussia appeared for counseling. She said that she had never been married but was being pursued by a 60-year-old married man, and she believed I could help her.

Often I have experienced a situation whereby I say something that wasn't in my hand-written manuscript and someone approaches me following the meeting because this had touched upon a real need. Just as carefully as I prepare my sermon, so I do to my place of labor. Since I prefer not to speak from the elevated pulpit found in most churches, I normally utilize a portable lectern. I set it up at just the right height, the appropriate angle, and distance from my eyes.

One evening, after we had completed setting up the altar area with the lectern, microphones, and technical equipment, we went into the sacristy for the prayer meeting. A *Kantor* walked up who was scheduled to appear in the preliminary program. He hadn't thought about a music stand but then he saw my simple lectern standing there. So he helped himself to it, and arranged things as he saw fit without bothering to ask whether he might use it. When I came back from the prayer time, I went to the altar area first. Right away I saw that my pulpit was gone. Finally, during the few remaining minutes between the preliminary program and the beginning of the meeting, I was able to locate it, fumble around, and re-arrange things according to my needs. But there was an unforeseen problem. With my rheumatic hands I couldn't twist the three screws that I needed to tighten. Then I had problems and uncertainties with the sermon during the entire evening because the adjustment of the lectern was out of kilter.

Earlier I used to have the same problems with my microphone. Everyone who used it without asking adjusted its position as he/she wished. Then at the beginning of the sermon I had to get the microphone back into the right position. Since I need to give full concentration to my opening sentences, this distraction with technical things often threw me off track and hindered me the rest of the evening. Now that I wear my mike on my lapel, I am free of this problem. The struggle for control of the lectern, however, remains my constant companion.

At the beginning of one evening service, as the church bells were ringing and everyone had taken their seats and were quietly meditating, someone stepped forward to photograph the altar that was several hundred years old. My lectern obscured his view so he picked it up and was about to take it away. I hurried to the altar area and told him to put it down. Then he started talking with me and said he found me "curious."

Thank You, Jesus, Thank You

In another city we had a huge stage with sufficient room for a band, our keyboard, Wolfgang's music stand and microphone, even a hundred-voice choir. The only problem was that there was no place for my lectern. It had fallen victim to the covetousness of the choir director who adjusted it to a level that suited him.

The absolute pinnacle of lectern tales was that of a young man seated in the front row who was unhappy about not being able to see the preliminaries from his particular location. He thereupon marched up to the stage and moved Wolfgang's music stand to another location, thus enabling a better viewing angle. Wolfgang had his notes, a harmonica, and a plectrum (plastic guitar pick) lying on it. At the same time, the youth loosened the screws and lowered the stand somewhat. Now he could see fine. Singer Wolfgang just had to make the best of a very bad situation when he came out to perform.

I really got upset over the incident of a *Kantor* who directed his church choir in a number before I rose to speak. Upon finishing his arm waving act, he had the gall to casually fold up my lectern and move it out of the way. What I had taken great care and effort to adjust—this is, after all, my work space—was in seconds destroyed right before my eyes. My astonishment regarding his stupidity and my anger over the shameless way that some fellow Christians deal with other people's things did not put me in a very good mindset to deliver the evening sermon. I always need some time to pull myself together after such incidents.

What I find most intolerable is when someone walks up to me while I am seated in my front row place gathering my thoughts for the sermon and starts talking to me about something of no great importance. One time, a pastor asked me during these last minutes of concentration and getting myself focused if I could be the main speaker at his congregation's centenary celebration. The man has had one hundred years to find a preacher, and he comes blathering to me at such a critical time! Quite apart from the fact that I wasn't sitting there with my appointment calendar in hand, this was the absolute worst time to talk to me about a future engagement. Since the colleague was unrelenting, I grabbed Wolfgang by the arm and we fled to the sacristy. However, even there one does not always find sanctuary.

I always return to the sacristy after each service or at least go into another room or a corner behind the stage. If possible, I lie down on my back or squat in the so-called coachman's position and do a few breathing exercises. In this way I relax and calm myself down. After such an evening, I am completely drained and my heart is racing. Somehow, I have to get my body back to its normal state and that requires a few minutes. In addition, I need some time for prayer. After these moments I am ready to go again and can engage in conversations with seekers for several hours. This break is necessary for my survival, and it involves keeping out of sight for five minutes or so.

For some people this is too long. They just have to speak with the evangelist immediately and will storm into the sacristy without so much as a knock on the door. Then they get downright grouchy when I plead with them to allow me a few minutes alone.

Perhaps the most inconsiderate person I ever encountered was a fellow who pounced on me after I had spoken at a tent meeting on a torrid summer night. The heat in the tent was so unbearable (the spotlights made it even worse) that I was bathed in sweat by the end of my sermon. My clothes were so wet that I could have wrung them out. Retreating to a tiny dressing room behind the stage, I removed my wet shirt and laid on my back, bare-chested, panting and gasping for breath. And then this oaf burst in to my space, totally devoid of compassion for a half-naked evangelist who was struggling for breath. I couldn't come up with any grand explanation for my situation, since it seemed to me to be rather obvious. So in my customary manner I begged for understanding and said I would be available for him in about five minutes. But then he vanished and I never did find out what he wanted. Maybe it was a preaching engagement at a 100-year anniversary....

Of course, the little room in the tent behind the stage was easily accessible. There are no doors, just flaps. This openness, in fact, the entire tent atmosphere, is something I like very much (except the situation just described). People who would probably never set foot in a church or a public meeting hall do come here.

A dog was running around among the benches. His mistress, who was looking for him, appeared dressed in a smock and house slippers, and she decided to sit down. On the grassy area in front of the tent, a group of young men were drinking. When I walked past them, they shouted, "Hey, Jesus!" In the evening they sat with their unclothed, tattooed upper bodies in the first row, beer bottles in hand. They beat it out of there before I began to speak, but four of their girls remained behind. After the meeting, I spoke with them. They had never before heard the message about Jesus nor did they know what we had to say about abortion. While we were talking, some boys crawled under the side of the tent and stole the cold cuts and drinks from the cooler that we had prepared for the workers.

We had a special worker along just to deal with guys like these drinking buddies. An alcoholic, he had come to Christ five years before and had not touched a drop since. Unfortunately, the years of alcohol abuse had scarred him terribly. He was almost blind because while he was in jail he drank a bottle of shaving lotion to satiate his craving. But now his face, although it showed the signs of his former lifestyle, radiated his transformation by Jesus. He was a walking testimony of the new man, a person of whom no one any longer needs to be afraid.

The sort of individuals who do arouse fear were seated in the tent that evening, because someone had written "Satan" in large letters across one of our advertising brochures. The leader of a local satanist group, who was wearing a black cape, squatted grimly and motionless there. He had picked the right time to come—the topic was superstition. On the same evening, we were told to expect another visitor, a 70-year-old man who was an adherent of some Odin cult. He was preparing for a discussion with me. He also sat among the attendees, but he did not appear to be as sure of a victory. He really looked old. He did stay until the end, but then simply disappeared. The people around there called him the "Sorcerer." For him as well it was the right time to be there. At the end, a former prostitute received Christ.

On the next evening, a young woman was breast-feeding her infant in the second row. The alcoholics and the smokers were hanging around the tent entrance and listened to everything that was said. Even the dog was back again. As always, someone ran out because his cell phone rang. Then the book table got turned over. Most of the time I have a good idea of how to comment about such occurrences.

Before I began to preach, I asked a man to give a testimony about his life. When Jörg and I were in this same city 19 years before, someone had dragged him along to the meetings at the church. There he heard the story of the Prodigal Son who returned from the pig sty to the home of his father. As a result he became a Christian and gave up drinking. He has lived free from alcohol for 19 years.

Blues Music and Gospel Proclamation

Thank you, Jesus, thank you. Thank you, Jesus, thank you.
Thank you, Jesus, you make us free.
Yes, you are the Truth, Yes, you are the Truth
Thank you, Jesus, you make us free.

Thank you, Jesus, thank you. Thank you, Jesus, thank you.
Thank you, Jesus, you've overcome death.
You've risen from the dead. You give new life.
Jesus, you are stronger than death.

Thank you, Jesus, thank you. Thank you, Jesus, thank you.
Thank you, Jesus, you've defeated fear.
You've risen from the dead. You give firm hope.
Jesus, you are stronger than our fear.

Thank you, Jesus, thank you. Thank you, Jesus, thank you.
Thank you, Jesus, you overcome our compulsions.
You've risen from the dead. You lead us into freedom.
Jesus, you're stronger than our compulsions.

14

Dr. Blues

I AM REASONABLY SATISFIED with my life but there are two things that I deeply regret and would do differently if I had it to do all over again. They have to do with Elke's father and mine. No one helped me along in life as much as my father did. There is no person to whom I owe more thanks than him. For never really telling him this, never really thanking him, I have no excuse.

I never knew Elke's father, about as little as Elke herself knew him. She was an illegitimate child. The official family version is there was a huge row between her mother and father and that was the reason why they never concluded a formal marriage. But it could be that this was only a statement to cover the family, namely, that Elke's father did not marry her mother because of his love and concern for her and thereby saved Elke's life. His name was Zuckmantel and he was a Jew. This made Elke, in the Nazi jargon, a half-Jew. I knew of several examples from the literature whereby such individuals—father, mother, and child—were condemned and sent to their deaths in Nazi concentration camps for allegedly violating the National Socialist racial laws banning miscegenation. They called it "racial-shame," the interbreeding of "Aryan" and "non-Aryan" persons. That could well have been her fate if her father had been listed on her birth certificate as a Jew. Of course, these are simply my own speculations.

The fact is, Herr Zuckmantel disappeared from the radar screen but he did survive the Nazi period. Where? How? And that is the second thing I have deeply regretted—I never undertook measures to try to locate him. For Elke, it was a taboo topic. She had tried as a 16-year-old to contact her father, but when she came to his house door, she lost courage, turned around, and never tried to get in touch with him again. Yet, after her death, I found among her telephone notes some slips of paper with numbers of the personal registration authorities of the town where he had last lived.

She wanted to attempt to establish contact with him shortly before her death. I then tried as well but to no avail.

The matter of her possible Jewish paternity thus remains a mystery, but at least it explains Elke's great love for Israel. During the GDR time an elderly Jewish lady gave us a Star of David. Elke always wore it. And after the *Wende,* she traveled several times to Israel and would like to have remained there. Of course, I knew that according to the Israeli law of return, only a person having a Jewish mother was considered a Jew and thus would be eligible to immigrate there. In any event, I was always proud to have a Jewish wife.

The Nazi practice of *Sippenhaft,* holding all members of a family liable for the crimes of one, resurfaced in the GDR, but in a much weakened form. As I mentioned earlier, our three daughters, Constantia, Mirjam, and Camilla, were, in spite of their excellent grades, excluded from further educational opportunities after the tenth grade solely because they were our children. All three of them found their own way and are very satisfied with it. They and their husbands all belong to Jesus. I have them to thank for a crew of eight grandchildren.

ALWAYS THE SAME TOUR

Once during the GDR era I was standing in line in front of a delicatessen with one of my grandchildren. It was one of those hot August afternoons when I would rather be sitting in the shade or lying around at the public swimming pool, enjoying my vacation, and dozing off. Instead we stood there in the red hot sun and waited patiently until our turn came. I don't remember any longer what we wanted. Maybe it was a pound of cherries or tomatoes, but whatever it was, I had to drop everything else and get in line.

As I stood there, with my grandson's hand in mine, I thought about the time when I was as old as he. And what did I do at that time? Instead of lying in the shade or tanning myself at the outdoor pool or enjoying my vacation and dozing off, I stood in line in front of some grocery store and waited patiently until it was my turn. I don't remember any longer what I wanted. Maybe it was a pound of cherries or tomatoes, and if that was the case, one had to simply let everything drop and get into line. And so, just as the Nazis spoiled our vacations, so did the communists with my grandchildren.

Dr. Blues

And I understood: Decades had passed, but I hadn't progressed one step farther. It was still a matter of filling our bellies. I still stood in line, and my grandchildren were still spending a beautiful August afternoon exactly as their grandfather had then. It was a shattering realization. In addition, there came the usual—for an *Ossi*—envious thoughts about my West German friends, who did not have to squander their time with such wasteful waiting. I often thought when I spent hours hunting down a typewriter ribbon, a spare part for something, letter envelopes, or merely toilet paper, how in that amount of time a *Wessi* could have written another essay.

In addition to this daily struggle for survival, I spent time complaining about these circumstances. I wrote grievance letters to the *Volkskammer* (the East German Parliament), the minister for the post office, First Party Secretary Walter Ulbricht, the customs authorities, editors, you name it. To be sure, I was successful only in the rarest of cases. But this had to be done, even in cases where the chance of success was virtually nil, so that the GDR authorities understood that the population was not pleased with everything that was going on.

Such official letters had to be very diplomatic, but clearly and directly written. It was different when it came to personal communications expressing personal opinions because of the *Stasi* surveillance of private correspondence. In such cases one had to be careful to say things in a roundabout way. Here is what I wrote to a friend after the construction of the Berlin Wall:

> Concerning the development of the pop music industry, I would like to say that the longer a Pigalle hit-parade tune stays on the charts the more revolting it becomes. For a long time now, people have seen through the tendentiousness of this hit-parade music industry. One can only wonder with each new record to what heights the decadence these con men will reach, who document their cultural barbarism by hyping a *castrata* as a top star. However, a good hit tune can't be put together with loud noises alone. Rather, it is qualified production personnel who are *die conditio* which help it to maintain popularity among the listeners. Where dilettantes attempt to conceal their helplessness by means of bombastic percussion solos, the commercial side of the business becomes obvious and gives the lie to the content which is filled to overflowing with love for one's homeland. I think, my dear Ronald, that we are in agreement as to the worthlessness of this kind of hit tunes.

What sounds like a commentary on the hit-parade industry was actually an evaluation of the political situation after the building of the Berlin Wall. "Hit-parade industry" stood for the "politics of the GDR," "*castrata*" referred to the tinny, falsetto-sounding voice of party boss Walter Ulbricht, "percussion solos" represented the use of force by the army, and "love of one's homeland" stood for the assertion that the building of the Berlin Wall was for the protection of the populace while, in reality, it was erected to protect the GDR rulers ("commercialization"). At that time, a big hit tune was "Pigalle, Pigalle, that's the big mousetrap (*Mausefalle*) in the middle of Paris." It was my code word for the Wall.

The *Stasi* either did not understand this letter or else never got their hands on it. But things were different when I sent out my New Year's greeting card for 1984. This year was also the title of a well-known book by George Orwell portraying a dictatorship utopia that sounded like Stalin's Russia. If the police found this book in someone's possession, it definitely was no laughing matter. Therefore I wrote to my friends, "May this New Year be better than its literary reputation." And I did that on an open post card. The copy I sent to Helmut Matthies of the West German evangelical news magazine, *idea*, turned up in my *Stasi* documents. In spite of the seriousness of our situation, we had to have some fun. It was one of the special "pleasures" of the GDR everyday experience to be able to communicate with like-minded friends in this way.

FINALLY, FREEDOM

In the final days of the GDR I had a similar experience to the one with my grandson that I just described. It was during one of the Monday demonstrations. When I heard the loud shouts, "Freedom, Freedom," I remembered that I had shouted these same words decades before on June 17, 1953. I spent that entire day in Leipzig yelling until I was hoarse, "We demand free elections and the resignation of the government." Then, I was an unmarried student, now, a grandfather. Freedom did not happen, but the longing for it remained. I was still, or was it once again, shouting on the streets for freedom. And as I realized that here, too, I hadn't come one step farther; I continued to shout, as if out of contrariness, while the tears were streaming down my face. Then, things had gone sour. The tanks rolled in. That must not happen again. It *must* work this time!

Dr. Blues

In our city a rumor was going around that a demonstration would take place at 6:00 P.M. and the assembly place was the Luxor cinema. I did just as other drivers were doing and hung a notice in my car window announcing the demonstration. I had already attached a sign to the rear window that read "No Violence!" I parked the car in a side street and walked to the Luxor. There was a large number of people milling around in the street rather aimlessly. No one knew whether the person next to him was a *Stasi* officer or a demonstrator. The atmosphere was tense and an uncertain and expectant silence prevailed. No one knew what was coming, how one ought to act, or even how a "demo" gets started. While we were standing there with no idea of what we should do, suddenly, within a matter of seconds, the first row of demonstrators formed. Some people were obviously providing a measure of leadership.

Bestowing the Saxon Medal of Honor

Immediately, others joined them, and a procession of people began moving in the direction of the "*Nischel*," the giant ugly sculpture of the head of Karl Marx that stood in a green area in front of the communist party headquarters. I ran along in the demo, with my collar pulled up concealing my head, scared to death that beatings and shootings could result. I had personally experienced how tanks and gun fire ended the demonstration on June 17, 1953. The young people around me didn't have this perspective and naively pushed forward. They simply couldn't imagine that Germans would shoot at Germans.

I envisioned all of this, but I had no choice. I must go along. The *Volkspolizei* stood at the edge of the street with their legs spread apart, silent and motionless. When I realized that they were doing nothing and were not lifting a finger to stop us, my fear subsided. My head emerged from inside my coat collar, my stride became increasingly bold and confident, my voice louder and louder: "Freedom! Freedom!" And so I marched, after a life under two dictatorships, for the first time into true freedom!

When I later received the Saxon Medal of Honor, "in recognition of special contributions in the liberal, democratic development of the Free State of Saxony," I really did not know at first how I should deal with it. The achievement of freedom was primarily due to the solidarity of hundreds of thousands of demonstrators. Therefore, I felt what the president of the Saxon state parliament said when he conferred the award on me went a little too far: "Through people like you, our peaceful revolution and with it our Free State of Saxony, was made possible." And yet I can agree with the next part of his statement: "Even if the call to conversion, to return to Jesus, is the center point of your entire work to this very day, your sermons were always political statements as well."

Harald Bretschneider, the regional youth pastor at the time of the *Wende*, characterized the Saxon youth ministry as "devout and political." Many times these two wings of the youth work were not in tune with each other. And frequently after the *Wende* I was frustrated when the contributions made by the devout wing received no mention at all. For us, it all was about conversion to Jesus, and from that the necessary consequences would follow. But in the encomium of the president of the state legislature, I felt understood and my contribution to the correct relationship between sermons and politics was appreciated. And that I could contribute my little mite to the development of the Free State of Saxony fills me with great gratitude.

Every time when I am driving on the autobahn in my VW Golf and see the "Free State of Saxony" sign as I cross the state border, I loudly shout, "Saxony!" and thank God to be able to live in a Free State. Wolfgang Tost and I even carry out this ritual together when we are on the road. If others are traveling with, they must wonder what in the world is going on when we approach the border sign and start making a "zah" sound. Then it grows increasing louder until, at the decisive moment we pass the sign, we let loose with our "Saxony!" primal scream. In fact, Wolfgang and I wrote the song "Thank you for Freedom" in which we proclaimed our appreciation to God for this gift.

At the time of the awarding of the medal, I was thinking about something quite different. The formal presentation took place in Dresden in the building where the stairs leading to the Brühl Terrace are located. From the window I could see the Hofkirche, the Semper Opera House, the bridge over the Elbe, and directly beneath the figures of the "Four Times of Day," on which one of my ancestors had worked, as I mentioned earlier. On the square between the Hofkirche and the palace, my mother as a child had made her formal curtsy whenever the royal coach went past. Later, she showed us the coffins in the crypt beneath the Hofkirche as we crouched and looked in the windows at ground level. These and many other memories connect me to this place. And it was here, of all places, where I received this honor and I thought the whole time: If only my dear parents could have experienced this!

"The God-Wants-Everyone-Tour"

In her first diary entry about me, my mother had written: "On the earth it is very nice, even when one suffers sorrow, if one only has 'the one thing that is necessary,' and stands in the true and proper faith to Him and lives in Him. Above all things I wish this for our dear little Theodor: If only he would desire to experience many blessings in life and desire to be a blessing for others! That is what we would say with his name: *Dasan* = [the Tamil word for] servant. May he serve both God and mankind!" This wish of my mother has been fulfilled. I am one who has been truly blessed!

IN THE END ONLY GOD'S NEW WORLD COUNTS

Among the blessings of my life belong, above all, my encounter with the world of music, which has bestowed upon me unending riches. Here belong my relationships with musicians like Jörg Swoboda, Wolfgang Tost, and Lutz Scheufler, my friends, co-workers, and comrades-in-arms over the decades. The "God Wants Everyone Tour" which we make (with pianist Ronny Neumann) annually throughout Germany is for me always the highpoint of the year.

My contribution is to moderate the proceedings and to give a short message. The musicians carry the main weight of these meetings. Working together with these magnificent and very creative individuals and the mutual effort we expend in shaping the concerts with the songs that we have written together is something I enjoy every time afresh.

During another tour, I sat in the back part of the stage, dazzled by the stage lights, and saw the silhouettes of these three men who are the closest to me. I watched as they brought the message of God with their guitars and voices to a hall filled with attentive listeners. At this moment I sensed—the stage, the presentation of this message to people—this is my world. And, as so often it has happened in my life, whenever I was especially happy, I had to think of the fact that this too, someday, will come to an end, that there will be a last time when the curtain finally falls. And as much as I love this life and want to hang on to it, my main objective is to be there "when we walk through the streets of heaven."

That was the last song for which I wrote the lyrics before Elke died. When we (Jörg or Wolfgang along with me) had finished the lyrics and melody of a song, we tore into the kitchen with the text and the guitar looking for Elke. We pulled her into my study, sat her on a chair, and sang it for her. So she was often the first person to hear the new song. And she not only listened but gave her evaluation of it, including some rather harsh and relentless criticism. "Streets of Heaven" was the last song that Wolfgang sang to her:

> When we walk through the streets of heaven,
> the struggle and sorrows are past.
> We've finally arrived at our heavenly home.
> We're saved, with the Lord, we are free.
>
> When we walk through the streets of heaven
> We'll stand before God's Son.
> All our longings for eternal peace
> are not dreams, they're fulfilled, we now know!

Dr. Blues

> When we walk through the streets of heaven,
> All God's promises are fulfilled,
> and the children of the eternal God
> heave a sigh, they've reached the goal, they see clearly.

"Streets of Heaven" is also the title for a CD which Jörg sang, with song texts by me written to melodies of spirituals and blues. The *Sir Gusche Band*—all fellows of my generation, that is, old jazz fanatics—provided a fantastic Dixieland accompaniment. This CD is, for me, a crowning conclusion of my musical passion. In it, the two musical streams which have held my attention most—jazz and song composition—come together and all of it is interpreted by my friend Jörg. There is only one term for this CD: powerful. My whole theology is contained in these simple, clear texts, which characterized the singing of the

70th birthday: "Dr. Blues" hears *Dr. Blues*

youth work in Saxony for decades, from the first to the last song. And then there is a second CD which has very special significance for me: "Dr. Blues." These blues songs were presented to me on my seventieth birthday by my friend and successor, Lutz Scheufler. And one has to be a very, very good friend when one writes such a song. It summarizes my entire life.

> Seventy years the Old Guy is
> And still quite fit at that.
> Gray hair and thin legs,
> yet the pump still works well.
> Without the blues he cannot live
> for he's got blues in his blood.
> When e'er he hears songs of old "blueser,"
> Only red wine fills the bill.
>
> Dr. Blues—is going his own way today.
> Dr. Blues—once more on a narrow path.
> Dr. Blues—is never all on his own.
> Dr. Blues—can be thankful for his life.

Blues Music and Gospel Proclamation

With his Bible in the pulpit
He stood up for the truth.
His words could strike hard.
For that, they struck back at him.
Therefore, he found not only friends,
Many didn't want to hear him.
They laid a lot of stumbling blocks
in order to stop his preaching.

Also at the mighty in the land
he aimed clear words of truth:
"If you fight God and curse him
he'll cast you from your throne."
And that "friends" were enemies,
was something he barely grasped.
Yet he went forward boldly,
strengthened by his faith in God.

"Blues means sickness, woe, and dying,"
he wrote earlier in his book
Blues and trouble were his life.
Never understood it as a curse.
They carried his love to the graveyard.
His sorrow was unutterably deep.
He never said "It was an error
when God called my dearest home."

He wants to follow Jesus,
who understood the blues while dying.
The Old Guy will carry the blues
boldly to the Promised Land.
Christ is waiting for the tears
that the Old Guy inwardly weeps.
And then there'll be no more blues
since only the sun shines there.

Dr. Blues—is going his own way today.
Dr. Blues—once more on a narrow path
Dr. Blues—is never all on his own.
Dr. Blues—can be thankful for his life.

Yes, that I am!

Dr. Blues

"Dr. Blues" goes on his way

Addendum for German-Speaking Readers

CHAPTER TITLES, INCLUDING THE ORIGINAL GERMAN HEADINGS AND SUBTITLES

THIS TRANSLATION PROVIDED ME with a special challenge; the titles and subtitles of the chapters. Theo charged his son-in-law, Ralf Marschner, with creating these as he had done in other books Theo had written. He took this opportunity to make up some very interesting and clever ones. Many of them are plays on words or word rhymes. Some deal with situations that only the individuals involved would readily recognize. I found them fascinating, but at times frustrating.

In spite of many years of teaching German and my numerous personal contacts in the German Democratic Republic, a few of the titles "brought me to my knees," so to speak. I needed help and I went directly to the authors. Why bother? I first planned to include the German titles in parentheses right in the text itself so that a reader who knows German could see the clever word play and perhaps even come up with a better translation. We concluded, however, that it might be a distraction for some readers. Frankly, some of these do not make much sense at all unless the reader has a fairly intimate knowledge of the East German system. Hence, in this addendum I have tried to duplicate the rhyme or play on words where possible, but most of the time it is too difficult or contrived in another language.

First, a word about the title itself. The German title is *Freiheit wird dann sein: Aus meinem Leben* (*Then There Will Be Freedom: From My Life*). It is clear that this would have little drawing power for an American audience. Few people in the US have ever heard of Dr. Lehmann. Secondly, we have freedom, and do not consider ourselves to be under subjection to any totalitarian government. We chose the one we did because it introduces two significant aspects of his life—Theo's most unusual predilection for blues, gospel, and spirituals in a communist country back in the 1960s, hence the nickname "Dr. Blues," while "Courageous Pastor" is a perfect description of this man of God who faced down the atheistic powers that ruled over him.

CHAPTER ONE

The Answer, My Friend (*Die Antwort, mein Freund*)
The Call to India (*Dann ging es Richtung Ganges*)
A Young Boy's Dreams (*Auf Bäumen träumen*)
Traumatic School Experiences (*Mit Graus ins Schulhaus*)
Clever Tricks (*Kühne Künste*)
Through the Stench to the School Bench (*Durch Gestank zur Schulbank*)
Family Ties (*Familienbande*)
In Brief —School Days at Vitzthum (*Kurzum   Vitzthum*)
A Prisoner in a Mass Society (*Massen-Haft*)
> Many times during the "good old days" of the German Democratic Republic my pen pals there would talk, but not *write*, about their trips to other countries in the Soviet bloc. They would refer to such trips as travel from one prison into another.

Night (*Nacht*)
No More Phoenix (*Nix Phönix*)

CHAPTER TWO

Precious Lord, Take My Hand (*Nimm mich, Herr, bei der Hand*)
Ruination by Alcohol (*Zoff bei Zöffel*)
Everything Could Be Used for Smoking (*Alles war zum Rauchen zu gebrauchen*)
Plates for the Trash, Words of Delight (*Teller für die Tonne, Worte voller Wonne*)

CHAPTER THREE

When Christ Returns (*Wenn Christus kommt*)
Moses' Pots of Meat (*Moses' Fleischtöpfe*)
Sheaves of Grain Are Better Than Starving (*Besser Garben als darben*)

Addendum

A Short Word about Kurt (*Kurz für Kurt*)
For One Semester a Horse Tester (*Für ein Semester Pferdetester*)
God's Church Stands Firm (*Gottes Fest steht fest*)

CHAPTER FOUR

Yet We Are Standing Again! (*Doch wir stehen wieder auf!*)
Misery from Frau Perkatz (*Perkatzenjammer*)
No Operas Played in This Upper House (*Im Oberhaus fällt jede Oper aus*)
   The word *Oberhaus* (upper house, a branch of government; Senate in the US) sounds almost like the German word *Opernhaus* (opera house)

The Sorrows of the Young Lehmann (*Die Leiden des jungen L.*)
   Johann Wolfgang von Goethe, Germany's Shakespeare, wrote a play entitled *The Sorrows of Young Werther*.

A Goatee and Glasses Are Not the Will of the People (*Spitzbart und Brille sind nicht des Volkes Wille*)
   The reference here to Walter Ulbricht, former Chairman of the Council of State and First Secretary of the *SED*, is hardly a veiled one. His face was plastered on the walls of all government buildings and in stores and public places during his tenure.

Theo in Theology (*Theo in Theologie*)

CHAPTER FIVE

Blues & Trouble (*Blues & Trouble*)
Sounds Like Swing (*Klingt wie beswingt*)
Clueless Rudi (*Rudi Ratlos*)
Blue from the Blues (*Vom Blues blau*)
The Stage in Buna (*Bühne in Buna*)
Please Help me Blues (*Please Help me Blues*)
Monkey Business by a Lot of Ne'er-do-wells (*Machenschaften von manchen Schuften*)

CHAPTER SIX

No, We're Not Any Better (*Besser sind wir nicht*)

In the Hall on the Saale (*Im Saal an der Saale*)

Black Music on White Pages (*Schwarze Musik auf weissen Seiten*)

Spirituals as a Stroke of Luck (*Spiritual als Glücksfall*)

No Joke—Chemnitz (*Kein Witz—Chemnitz*)

The Attempts of the Tempters (*Die Versuche der Versucher*)

When Anglo-Saxons Go Angling in Saxony (*Wenn Angelsachsen in Sachsen angeln*)

CHAPTER SEVEN

Only One Way (*Nur ein einziger Weg*)

The Smell of Rumors *(Der Geruch der Gerüchte)*

One Man's Sadness Is the *Stasi*'s Joy (*Des Einen Leid ist der Stasi Freud*)

A Shock and No Chocolate (*Ein Schock und keine Schokolade*)

CHAPTER EIGHT

With You Alone (*Nur mit Dir*)

Away with the Powder Barrier (*Sense mit der Puderbremse*)

Even a New Tune Often Makes Many Uneasy (*Auch neuer Klang macht manchen manchmal bang*)

Let's Go with Rumpelstolz and Co. (*Sowieso mit Rumpelstolz und Co.*)
I had considerable difficulty with this subtitle. Although the German name for Rumpelstiltskin does appear in another segment, he had nothing whatsoever to do with this chapter. I eventually contacted both Dr. Marschner as well as Theo in order to get it "straight from the horses' mouths." I had assumed that this name, *similar to*, but *not identical to* this mischievous troublemaker of a Grimm Brothers' fairy tale was somehow the reason for this title. Nothing of the kind! Marschner wrote to me: "The background of this heading is simple, even if I don't know how one can translate it into English." He went on to explain:

Addendum

"In the GDR everything was produced in a very uniform manner. On the labels of most products there were the initials '*VEB*' followed by the name of the factory. The *VEB* stood for the 'People's Own Factory.' As a result I was surprised when I bought a washboard around 1973 which had been produced in the Erzgebirge region of the GDR. The company had a long tradition dating back to a time before the GDR. The firm was obviously rather insignificant and therefore had not been nationalized, i.e., designated as *VEB*. The joke was that the firm was literally named '*Rumpelstolz und Co.*' The verb 'rumpeln' in the Saxon dialect means not only a muffled rolling sound, but it was also used by our band to designate the type of music we made on the washboard. As a result it was possible for us to use the word as a synonym for the *Schlossband*, the Palace Church Band. So that was what lay behind this heading." But the little fairy tale character does make an appearance in another chapter. Here, Theo adds the sentence: "Ambe, who was playing the washboard, jumped up and down like Rumpelstiltskin."

Again and Again New Songs (*Immer wieder neue Lieder*)

No Chattering, No If's, And's or But's (*Kein Gelaber, Kein Wenn und Aber*)

The *Wende* as a Beginning But Not a Conclusion (*Wende am Anfang und nicht als Ende*)

CHAPTER NINE

That's When Freedom Will Really Be Ours (*Freiheit wird dann sein*)

The Monkey Wants to Get on My Back (*Die Krake will mir an den Kragen*)

Brotherly Love and Sideswipes (*Bruderliebe und Seitenhiebe*)

Beautiful Counterfeits in *Stasi* Garb (*Schöne Blüten der Stasitüten*)
  Dr. Marschner suggested this translation to give the essence of the original title.

Just One Refrain—Let Us Be Free! (*Nur ein Schrei—lasst uns frei!*)

Best of All, Get Rid of Him in the West (*Am besten in den Westen*)

Out to Pasture! No Way! (*Von wegen auf Eis legen*)

Good Weather for a Bombing (*Bombenwetter*)

Here There's No Beer, Man. (*Da gibt's kein Bier, Mann*)
   The significance of this is the play on words Beer, Man, and *Bier, Mann*. It works the name Biermann into the subtitle. As mentioned in the text, Rolf Biermann's case received world-wide attention in 1976. Permitted to leave the country to perform a concert in West Germany, his actions so displeased the authorities in East Berlin that he was denied re-entry at the GDR border and thus was stripped of his citizenship.

A Wagner *Festspiel* (*Wagner-Festspiele*)
A Harsh Punishment (*Straffe Strafe*)
Nobody Wants to Be Called a Swine (*Keiner will das Schwein sein*)

CHAPTER TEN

A God for All Situations (*Ein Gott für alle Fälle*)
And You Are Now an Evangelist (*Und du bist Evangelist*)
Complete as a Pair (*Komplett im Duett*)
Heart Ache (*Herzschmerz*)
Garbage Idyll (*Müllidyll*)
Meeting Nice Colleagues (*Netten Kollegen begegnen*)
Comical Insect Discovered (*Komisches Insekt entdeckt*)
The Leipzig Rubbish (*Der Leipziger Unrat*)
No Desire in Ludwigslust (*Unlust in Ludwigslust*)
Potsdam Post Coach Driver (*Potsdamer Postkutscher*)
   This is the first line of a German tongue twister ("*Der Potsdamer Postkutscher putzt den Potsdamer Postkutschkasten*"). It symbolizes the lack of communication among the various parties involved in the disputes during the evangelistic meetings in Potsdam. Each seemed to be speaking in meaningless phrases that went right past their opponents.

CHAPTER ELEVEN

There Is a Word (*Es gibt ein Wort*)
Körner, the Babbler (*Ein Körnerpicker*)
   "*Körnerpicker*" has to do with a Pastor Körner who was Theo's nemesis and tried to throw a monkey wrench into his efforts time after

Addendum

time. He later was unmasked as an unofficial informant for the *Stasi*. The word *Körnerpicker* is translated as a "babbler" in Acts 17:18 of a German Bible translation that is roughly equivalent to the NIV.

The Sweet Mush in the Bishop's Chancellery (*Der süsse Brei in der Bischofskanzlei*)
The Brush-off by Fritz (*Abblitzen bei Fritzen*)

CHAPTER TWELVE

God Wants Everyone (*Gott will alle*)
A Taste of the World with Cognac (*Weltgeschmack mit Cognac*)
Greater Than Megalomania (*Grösser als der Grössenwahn*)
Fruit and Little Fruits (*Frucht und Früchtchen*)
Trembling in Zittau (*In Zittau zittern*)
Reeperbahn, Inc. (*Reeperbahn AG*)

CHAPTER THIRTEEN

Thank You, Jesus, Thank You (*Danke, Jesus, danke*)
Bright Nights for Sinister Powers (*Helle Nächte für dunkle Mächte*)
From Spirit-filled to Spirit-less (*Von geistlich bis geistlos*)
No Sacrilege, Only a War of Nerves (*Kein Sakrileg, nur Nervenkrieg*)

CHAPTER FOURTEEN

Dr. Blues (*Dr. Blues*)
Always the Same Tour (*Immer nur dieselbe Tour*)
Finally, Freedom (*Endlich Freiheit*)
In the End Only God's New World Counts (*Am Ende zählt Gottes neue Welt*)

www.ingramcontent.com/pod-product-compliance
Lightning Source LLC
Chambersburg PA
CBHW050846230426
43667CB00012B/2166